ON WISCONSIN!

A Celebration of Football, Basketball, and Other Badger Sports

Don Kopriva

Jim Mott

SPORTS
PUBLISHING

Sports Publishing books may be purchased in bulk at special discounts for sales promotion, corporate gifts, fund-raising, or educational purposes. Special editions can also be created to specifications. For details, contact the Special Sales Department, Sports Publishing, 307 West 36th Street, 11th Floor, New York, NY 10018 or info@skyhorsepublishing.com.

Sports Publishing® is a registered trademark of Skyhorse Publishing, Inc.®, a Delaware corporation.

All photos in this book were provided by the University of Wisconsin's Sports Information Department.

The indicia included herein are owned and protected by the University of Wisconsin, and may not be reproduced without the express written permission of the University of Wisconsin's Director of Trademark Licensing.

Visit our website at www.skyhorsepublishing.com.

10 9 8 7 6 5 4 3 2 1

Library of Congress Cataloging-in-Publication Data is available on file.

ISBN: 978-1-61321-342-1

Printed in Canada

To all Badger athletes—past, present and future—with great appreciation for their talent, their determination, and their commitment to excellence in athletics and academics that has become emblematic of the Wisconsin ideal.

To Badger coaches—past, present, and future—with heartfelt thanks for their work ethic and their coaching prowess on behalf of Wisconsin's teams.

And to the memory of Jim Mott, a great SID and an even better man.

—Don Kopriva

EDITOR'S NOTE:

This book, which was previously published in 1998, has been updated through the 2012–13 season where applicable. Some text remains as originally written in 2001.

CONTENTS

FOREWORD

It has been nearly 60 years since I first played football for Wisconsin and more than 30 since I had the privilege of being named athletic director.

But in many ways, those days of yesteryear seem like just yesterday, thanks to the good memories that have accumulated and kept my Badger spirit alive over the years.

Many things have changed over the decades but one thing that has stayed constant is a belief in the Wisconsin idea, which from the beginning has recognized that excellence in athletics—as in academics—is critical to the mission of the University.

We've never suffered academically at Wisconsin and have steadily maintained our reputation as one of the nation's premier institutions of higher learning. We have gone through some difficult times athletically, but we have come out the stronger and the better for it. And that in large measure is because of our many loyal fans throughout the state and around the nation who have "kept the faith."

And they've been rewarded, especially in recent years. They've been able to enjoy the sights of the Badgers in the Rose Bowl and in the NCAA basketball and volleyball tournaments and to celebrate recent NCAA championships in hockey, men's and women's cross country and men's soccer.

We are fortunate indeed to have fans such as these—current students, faculty and staff, alumni and friends—who have stuck with the Badgers through thick and thin.

I know that they've always been important to me, as a player and as director of athletics. I know also that their support is critical to the success of all Wisconsin's teams.

This book—which chronicles more than 100 years of Wisconsin sports, athletes, coaches and administrators—is also the story of these dedicated fans without whom the victories never would have been possible.

On, Wisconsin!

Elroy Hirsch

Editor's Note: This foreword was first written for the 1998 publication of *On Wisconsin!*. Elroy Hirsch passed away in 2004.

MESSAGE FROM BARRY ALVAREZ

The University of Wisconsin has a lengthy and proud athletics history and it has been a great pleasure to be a part of it for the past quarter-century. One of the best things about history is that it can be re-lived over and over and that's what the following pages will let readers do.

We all have our favorite memories. Rose Bowls. NCAA and Big Ten championships. Cool, crisp Saturdays at Camp Randall. Unforgettable days and nights at the Field House and the Kohl Center. Great student-athletes and record-breaking performances. Upset victories. It's all here in this wonderful trip down memory lane.

Badger fans are a legendary group of people and their loyalty to our teams is second to none. I'm pleased that this latest edition of *On Wisconsin!* is being made available and that supporters of Wisconsin athletics have a book they can reference again and again to re-visit their favorite moments.

On Wisconsin!

Barry Alvarez
Director of Athletics

A WORLD-CLASS UNIVERSITY

The University of Wisconsin-Madison, one of the nation's leading institutions of higher education, is dedicated to the support of academic freedom.

Founded in 1848, the university enrolled 17 students in its first class on February 5, 1849. Today, it is one of the nation's most productive institutions of higher learning and the student body is one of the most diverse in the country, with students coming from every state and around the world.

Award-winning research spanning the academic disciplines has earned UW-Madison, which has 21 schools, a place among the world's elite institutions. It annually enrolls about 40,000 students and is one of only two doctorate-awarding universities in the 13-school UW system.

Several undergraduate programs at UW-Madison have been ranked among the top 10 in the nation. Among those were sociology, business, German, chemical engineering, geography, ecology, genetics, statistics, molecular biology and biochemistry, French, Spanish, political science, industrial engineering, computer science, chemistry, mathematics and history.

UW-Madison faculty or alumni have been awarded 17 Nobel Prizes and 26 Pulitzer Prizes.

UW-Madison, one of the nation's first land-grant colleges, established a tradition of research in agriculture and the life sciences. The founders of the university developed the "Wisconsin Idea" as making "the beneficent influence of the university available to every home in the state."

The largest and oldest institution in the University of Wisconsin system, UW-Madison has multiple historic landmarks on campus, including the Science Hall and Red Gym.

Schools and Colleges

* College of Agricultural and Life Sciences
* Arts
* Wisconsin School of Business
* Division of Continuing Studies
* School of Education
* College of Engineering
* Nelson Institute for Environmental Studies
* Graduate School
* School of Human Ecology
* Division of International Studies
* School of Journalism and Mass Communication
* Law School
* College of Letters & Science
* School of Library and Information Studies
* School of Medicine and Public Health
* School of Music
* School of Nursing
* School of Pharmacy
* Robert M. La Follette School of Public Affairs
* School of Social Work
* School of Veterinary Medicine

Quick facts

(as of November 2012)

Location   Madison, Wisconsin
Founded   1848 (First class: February 1849)
Campus   936 acres (main campus)
Chancellor   Rebecca M. Blank
Budget $2,830,200,000
Research expenditure ranking (national) 4th (2010–11)
Students earning credits for study abroad 2,159
Degrees awarded (2011–12):
Bachelor's   6,452
Master's   2,104

Schools and colleges   13
Faculty and staff   21,624
Enrollment   42,820
Undergraduate   29,118
Graduate   9,183
Special   1,745
Professional   2,774
Research doctorate   810
Professional/clinical doctorate   709
Living alumni   400,372

THE HISTORY OF UW ATHLETICS

The University of Wisconsin Athletic Association was formed in February 1892, by the union of the baseball, football and tennis associations and the University Boat Club.

Its stated objective was to advance the athletic interests of the University of Wisconsin in all lines. All students of the university could become members of the association upon payment of one dollar.

President of the UW Athletic Association for the first year of its existence was E. H. Ahara, a member of both the football and baseball associations, Harvey Clark and Knox Kinney of the baseball association were vice president and secretary, respectively, and G.L. Hunner was treasurer.

In 1895, the UW Athletic Association was headed by John R. Richards as president and the board of directors included a member of the board of regents, an alumnus, three faculty members and 10 undergraduates.

The Women's Athletic Association was founded in 1907. During this year the society was called the "Girls' Athletic Association." Miss Grace Hobbins was the first president of the organization.

In 1908, the name was changed to the Women's Athletics Association and it was reorganized as a secret honorary association with elective membership. Ten honors could be won, three of which entitled the member to a pin, and five honors to a "W" award.

In 1913, the society was again organized on a new basis and, instead of the secret, exclusive organization of the past, W.A.A. became broader and much more inclusive. Its stated purpose was to promote interest in athletics and sports of all kinds, not only among the girls who were "especially adapted for such work," but also among those who had little experience in athletics before they came to the university.

The record shows that the chairman of the physical education department was also in charge of intercollegiate athletics following the dismissal of the graduate manager set–up in the early 1900s.

Thomas E. Jones, who had come to Wisconsin in 1912 as coach of the school's track and cross country teams, received his professorship in 1916 and upon the resignation of Professor George Wolf Ehler, became acting athletic director, serving until George Little came to Madison from Michigan in 1925.

Wisconsin Athletic Directors

1916–24
Professor Thomas E. Jones

1925–32
George Little

1933–35
Dr. Walter E. Meanwell

1936–50
Harry Stuhldreher

1950–55
Guy Sundt

1955–69
Ivan Williamson

1969–87
Elroy Hirsch

1987–89
A. L. "Ade" Sponberg

1989–2004
Pat Richter

2004–Present
Barry Alvarez

THE BIRTH OF UW WOMEN'S ATHLETICS

Women's athletics at the University of Wisconsin actually dates back to 1889 when Clara Ballard introduced women's physical education to the UW. Other early references to women's athletics include Coach Andrew O'Dea consenting to coach a women's crew in 1895 and the beginning of women's basketball in 1897.

In 1917, Women's Recreation Associations were nationally organized by the UW's Blanche Trilling, and Badger yearbooks from that period show women's teams receiving honor letters and wearing athletic sweaters.

Sponsored by the physical education department, Wisconsin's WRA was run by a coalition of students and faculty. The WRA lasted until the 1960s when the growth of women's sports program required more control and consistency.

It wasn't until 1967, that the UW saw an increased interest and growth in the competitive sports programs for women. Facilities, equipment and office space were made available, limited use of fleet cars and a half-time position for the sports coordinator/WRA advisor were funded and some release time was allocated for sports advisors.

In 1967, Kit Saunders was named the administrator of the women's sports program. A club sports program was organized in 1970 through the Intramural Recreation Board with a budget of $2,000. In 1972–73, this was raised to $8,000 and to $18,000 for 1973–74. During this time, the cost and time commitment of women's athletics was getting to be too much for the physical education department. The passage of Title IX of the Educational Amendments Act of 1972, which applied to discrimination on the basis of sex, became the single most important factor in the gains of women's sports.

In July of 1972, UW Chancellor Edwin Young appointed a committee to study women's athletics. With no progress being made on the issue, on April 3, 1973, a complaint against the UW was filed with the HEW Office of Civil Rights in violation of Title IX.

By April 19, 1973, a new committee had been formed and by May, that committee had made recommendations that women be allowed to use all physical recreation facilities on the UW campus and that the division provide for the administration of women's competitive sports.

During December of that year, a proposal to combine men's and women's athletic programs was put forth. This proposal included appointing a women's athletics director, the hiring of separate coaches, and providing salaries, uniforms, equipment and practice times.

A task force was formed to study this proposal and by May, 1974, the UW Athletic Board voted to add a 12-sport women's intercollegiate athletic program under the Athletic Department. The 12 sports were: badminton, basketball, cross country fencing, field hockey, golf, gymnastics, rowing, swimming and diving, tennis, track and field, and volleyball.

Kit Saunders-Nordeen was named the first Women's Athletics Director as women became an official part of the UW Athletic Department on July 1, 1974.

The Men's and Women's deparments were combined under a single athletics director in 1983.

Wisconsin Women's Athletics Administrators

1974–1983
Kit Saunders-Nordeen

1983–89
Paula Bonner Associate Athletic Director

1989–90
Kit Saunders-Nordeen Associate Athletic Director

1990–2005
Cheryl Marra Associate Athletic Director

2005–Present
Terry Gawlik Associate Athletic Director

ON WISCONSIN!

1870s
UW PRESIDENTS AND CHANCELLORS

John Hiram Lathiop, chancellor (1849–58)

Henry Barnard, president (1859–60)

John W. Sterling,
executive officer (1860–67)

Paul A. Chadbourne, president (1867–70)

John W. Twombly, president (1871–74)

John A. Bascom, president (1874–87)

Thomas C. Chamberlin,
president (1887–92)

Charles K. Adams, president (1892–1901)

Edward A. Birge,
acting president (1901–03)

Charles R. Van Hise, president (1903–18)

Edward A. Birge, president (1918–25)

Glenn Frank, president (1925–37)

George C. Sellery,
acting president (1937)

Clarence A. Dykstra, president (1937–45)

Edwin Broun Fred, president (1945–58)

Conrad A. Elvehjem, president (1958–62)

Fred Harvey Harrington,
president* (1962–70)

Robben Fleming, chancellor (1964–67)

William Sewell, chancellor (1967–68)

Bryant Kearl, acting chancellor (1968)

Edwin Young, chancellor (1968–77)

Glenn S. Pound,
acting chancellor (1977)

Irving Shain, chancellor (1977–86)

Bernard Cohen, acting chancellor (1987)

Donna E. Shalala, chancellor (1988–93)

David Ward, chancellor (1993–2000)

John Duncan Wiley, chancellor (2001–2008)

Carolyn "Biddy" Martin, chancellor
(2008–2011)

David Ward, chancellor (2011–2013)

Rebecca Blank (2013–Present)

*administrative structure changed in 1964

The Big Event

Athletic teams begin to develop at the UW

As the University of Wisconsin approached the 25th anniversary of its founding, fledgling sports teams began to develop on the campus. Baseball and rowing were, according to all reliable records, the first and dominant teams throughout the 1870s.

Baseball seems to have been the first intercollegiate sport at Wisconsin, with its beginnings traced back to the spring of 1870 when some of the diamond enthusiasts on campus banded together to form a club known as the Mendotas.

By the middle of the decade, rowing began to develop and by 1878 rowing had become part of intramural competition. But Wisconsin alumnus C.B. Bradish noted in a 1912 letter that his father told him that "he rowed on the first crew Wisconsin ever had" in 1874.

The first recorded baseball game took place on April 30, 1870, with the Mendotas outscoring the Capital City Club 53–18. Lack of a suitable playing field delayed the organization of the 1871 team but before the school term closed a game was arranged with Albion, which promptly defeated the Mendotas 26–24 to avenge their loss of 1870.

No games were played in 1872 or 1875 but a pair of games was played in both 1873 and 1874. The Mendotas split games in '73, losing to Albion but beating Beloit, while in 1874 Milton College swept them. A single game was played in each of the 1876 and 1877 seasons, with Wisconsin winning the former and losing the latter.

A baseball association was finally formed in 1877, with P.V. Larson elected president. No games were played in 1878 and in 1879 the university club split a series with Beloit.

WISCONSIN TIMELINE

1870: The U.S. Weather Bureau was established.

1873: Representatives of Columbia, Princeton, Rutgers and Yale universities drew up the first rules governing intercollegiate football games.

1875: Aristides won the first Kentucky Derby.

1876: Alexander Graham Bell received a patent for the telephone.

1877: Alexander Graham Bell demonstrated the telephone with a hookup between Boston and Salem, Massachusetts.

1878: The first daily college newspaper, the Yale News, began publication in New Haven, Connecticut.

1880S
WISCONSIN FACULTY REPRESENTATIVES

1896: C.R. Barnes
1896–99: E.A. Birge
1899–1905: C.S. Slichter
1905–06: T.S. Adams
1906–09: CP0. Hutchins
1910–12: G.W. Ehler
1912–31: J. F. A. Pyre
1932–35: A. T. Weaver
1936–47: William F. Lorenz
1947–51: Kenneth Little
1951–54: Kurt F. Wendt
1954–59: George Young
1959–70: Frank Remington
1970–71: George Young
1971–86: Frank Remington
1981–87: Diane Lindstrom
1986–87: David Tarr
1987–89: Jane Voichick
1987–91: Ted Finman
1989–92: Cyrena Pondrum
1991–Present: James Hoyt
1992–94: Jane Robbins
1994–96: Barbara L. Wolfe
1996–99: Robin Douthitt
1999–2003: Gloria Ladson-Billings
2000–2003: Robert Haveman
2003–2007: Bruce Jones
2007–2011: Walter Dickey
2009: Sheila McGuirk
2011: Dale Bjorling

The Big Event

Sports teams grow, become better organized

Sports continued to flourish at Wisconsin in the 1880s, although lack of coaches, lack of rules and lack of suitable playing sites often contributed to controversy.

Football debuted in 1889, but baseball and crew were the dominant athletic activities on campus. No baseball games were played in 1880 but Chicago, Racine and Northwestern jointly formed the Western Intercollegiate Baseball League, which prodded Wisconsin supporters into some action.

In 1881, another athletic association was formed on the Wisconsin campus and student members planned to get possession of the pasture between State Street and the lake to turn it into a campus suitable for baseball and other sports. However, the fairgrounds at Camp Randall were secured instead and the Wisconsin nine defeated Beloit. In 1882, Wisconsin and Ann Arbor (Michigan) formed a league and played twice, with Michigan winning 20–8 and 16–6.

In 1883, Wisconsin sent a representative to the Western Intercollegiate Baseball Meeting and gained membership for the 1883 season. Two losses to Northwestern eliminated Wisconsin from championship consideration. By 1884, Wisconsin was the champion, winning five of six games, and in 1885, the Badgers repeated with key road wins over Racine and Northwestern.

Crew continued to grow in popularity on the campus with the founding of the Madison Boat Club in 1886. Its sponsors—six professors—were united in their belief that "the natural opportunities for boating at the University are unrivaled by those at any other college in the country."

Football's debut was inauspicious, to say the least. Under Coach Alvin Kletsch—the first "official" coach in UW history—Wisconsin played two games in 1889 and scored nary a point, losing to the Calumet Club 27–0 in Milwaukee and at Beloit 4–0.

WISCONSIN TIMELINE

1880: Thomas Edison received a patent for his electric incandescent light

1881: The first U.S tennis championships were played in Newport, RI

1882: The first hydroelectric power plant in the United States was opened in Appleton, WI

1885: Mark Twain's "Adventures of Huckleberry Finn" was published

1887: The first game of softball, invented by George W. Hancock, was played in Chicago's Farragut Boat Club

1888: The National Geographic Society was incorporated in Washington, D.C.

1889: Paris's Eiffel Tower was opened to the public

Crew
1894
Amos W. Marsh
1895-96
Andrew O'Dea

Football
1890
Ted Mestre
1891
Herb Alward
1892
Frank Crawford
1893
Parke Davis
1894-95
H.O.Stickney

Track and Field
1893
R.G.Booth
1894
M.J.Gillen
1895
W.B.Overson
1896
Charles Craigie

The Big Event

Football, track teams develop, succeed

While baseball and crew continued to flourish at Wisconsin in the early-to-mid 1890s, football and track teams were formed and quickly found success.

The baseball Badgers again won a title in 1890 when they posted a 5–1 record. By 1891, the first University of Wisconsin athletic association was organized by the merger of the baseball, football and tennis associations along with the University Boat Club. The UW baseball team swept through the league in 1891, winning all its games. The 1893 club finished 12–3 with Michigan, Illinois and Chicago now among its opponents. The 1894 team went 10–4 and counted among its wins an 11–9 bottom-of-the-ninth-inning victory over one of Michigan's truly great teams.

Track and field began to develop in 1893 with the formation of the Western Intercollegiate Track and Field Association. It included Chicago, Michigan, Northwestern and Wisconsin. The Wolverines outscored the Badgers 52–45 to win the first meet. Wisconsin was second in both 1894 and 1895. James Maybury, the first real sprinter of note at Wisconsin, was third in the 100–yard dash and second in the 220. Maybury won the 100 in 10 seconds and the 220 in 22.4 seconds in the 1896 meet won by Wisconsin with 46 points.

In 1892, Wisconsin rowers beat Chicago in a race at Oconomowoc's Lac LaBelle. By 1894, they had a coach, Amos W. Marsh, who had captained the crew at Cornell. Under his guidance, the rowers defeated the Delaware Boat Club and narrowly lost to the Minnesota Boat Club. Andrew O'Dea took over as coach in 1895 and split again with Delaware and Minnesota, but by 1896 the Badgers had defeated Yale and Minnesota for the first time.

Wisconsin had six football coaches in the 1890s, with Ted Mestre gaining credit for the first win in 1890, a 106–0 shellacking of Whitewater Normal to open a 1–3 season. New coaches followed annually as did winning records each season from 1891–1895.

WISCONSIN TIMELINE

1890: New York World Reporter Nellie Bly completed a trip around the world in 72 hours, 6 days, 11 minutes, beating the fictional 80–day trip of Jules Vernesi Phileas Fogg.

1891: Wisconsin recorded its first football victory, a 106–0 victory over UW-Whitewater.

1892: James J. Corbett knocked out John L. Sullivan in the 21st round to win the world heavyweight crown in New Orleans.

1895: President James Smart of Purdue called a meeting of seven midwestern universities to consider regulation and control of intercollegiate athletics.

Wisconsin won its first Big Ten outdoor track championship under Coach Charles Craigie.

WISCONSIN HEADLINER

J. F. A. (SUNNY) PYRE
FOOTBALL

A fiery spirit and reckless abandon characterized J. F. A. (Sunny) Pyre, who may have been Wisconsin's first real sports hero. Although he played in the days of "beef trust" football and never weighed more than 175 lbs., and often less, Pyre played right tackle for the Wisconsin football teams of 1891 and 1894–96 Press accounts of the day said he was "lightning fast" across the line and knew "how to use his hands and magnificently muscled arms as few linemen did." He also rowed on varsity crew teams of 1893 and 1894. During those latter three football seasons Pyre was also an instructor in English at the UW, carrying a full teaching load as well as working on his doctorate in English. Pyre's best season was probably his last, 1896, which was also Phil King's first year at Wisconsin. That team went unbeaten until a tie with Northwestern and a loss to the Carlisle Indians. As a professor after his playing days, Pyre remained connected with sports as a member of succeeding athletic committees and boards. He served from 1912–1931 as the UW faculty representative to the Big Ten Conference.

WISCONSIN HEADLINER

CHARLES KENDALL ADAMS
PRESIDENT
UNIVERSITY OF WISCONSIN

A strong proponent of athletics and advocate of the formation of a midwestern athletic conference was Charles Kendall Adams, Wisconsin's president from 1892–1901. In the 1895 and 1896 meetings at which the Big Ten was formed, Adams was emotionally involved and eager to get the Conference established. Adams attended Wisconsin games and cheered on the teams, going so far as to help encourage unmotivated students to go out for teams. He also acquired Camp Randall for the UW as a playing field. Born in Vermont in 1835, Adams moved to Iowa with his family as a young man and enrolled at Michigan in 1857, graduating in 1861. He remained in Ann Arbor as a graduate student and hen became a history professor before becoming president at Cornell, where he remained for seven years until accepting the lost at Wisconsin. Ill health forced his resignation from the presidency in 1901 and he died a year later.

THE LIST

WISCONSIN VS. MINNESOTA

Wisconsin's (and the nation's) longest continuous football rivalry, with Minnesota, didn't start too well for the Badgers but by the turn of the 20th century the UW had evened its budding series with the Gophers. Going into the 1998 season and the teams's 108th game, the UW trailed 57–42–8.

The first 10 games:
1890: Minnesota 63, Wisconsin 0
1891: Minnesota 26, Wisconsin 12
1892: Minnesota 32, Wisconsin 4
1893: Minnesota 40, Wisconsin 0
1894: Wisconsin 6, Minnesota 0
1895: Minnesota 14, Wisconsin 10
1896: Wisconsin 6, Minnesota 0
1897: Wisconsin 39, Minnesota 0
1898: Wisconsin 29, Minnesota 0
1899: Wisconsin 19, Minnesota 0

A  FIRST

Badgers among charter members of Western Conference

President Charles Kendall Adams of Wisconsin joined presidents from Chicago, Illinois, Michigan, Minnesota, Northwestern and Purdue in a meeting at Chicago on January 11, 1895, adopted 12 rules for a Midwestern athletic conference. That conference officially became the Intercollegiate Conference of Faculty Representatives and would later become known as the Western Conference and, eventually, as is the case today, as the Big Ten.

The first of the Conference rules, which strengthened the notion of faculty control of athletics, said that "Each college and university which has not already done so shall appoint a committee on college athletics which shall take general supervision of all athletic matters. . . and which shall have all responsibility of enforcing the college or university rules regarding athletics and all intercollegiate sports. Other rules mandated that college athletes be full-time, bona fide students, forbade professionals from playing college sports, prohibited pay for play and mandated that games be played at sites under college control.

BADGER BIG TEN FINISHES...

Football: 1st
coached by Phil King

Baseball: 3rd
coached by Phil King

Outdoor Track: 1st
coached by E.W. Moulton

The Big Event

Wisconsin wins first Big Ten football title

Wisconsin won the Western Conference's first football championship soon after the formation of the Conference, which would soon become popularly known as the "Big Ten."

After opening the season with seven wins, Coach Phil King's team was tied 6–6 by Northwestern and then lost to the Carlisle Indians. Despite that late-season slump, the Badgers claimed the first league title with a 2–0–1 record and a 7–1–1 overall mark. The season-ending loss to Carlisle was the first night and indoor game in UW history played at the Chicago Coliseum.

Defense was the key to the Badgers' success, as six of their wins were shutouts.

Wisconsin's record:	Big Ten, overall records:
UW 34, Lake Forest 0	1–0
UW 18, Madison High School 0	2–0
UW 50, Rush Medical 0	3–0
UW 54, Grinnell 6	4–0
UW 6, Beloit 0	5–0
UW 24, Chicago 0	1–0, 6–0
UW 6, Minnesota 0	2–0, 7–0
UW 6, Northwestern 6	2–0–1, 7–0–1
Carlisle Indians 18, UW 8	2–0–1, 7–1–1

WISCONSIN TIMELINE

1896:   The first modern Olympic Games were held in Athens.

The "Intercollegiate Conference of Faculty Representatives," to become known as the Big Ten, was formed, with Wisconsin as one of seven charter members along with Chicago, Illinois, Michigan, Minnesota, Northwestern and Purdue.

Wisconsin claimed first outright Big Ten football title with a 7–1–1 record for Coach Phil King.

1897:   The famous "Yes, Virginia, there is a Santa Claus" editorial appeared in the *New York Sun*.

BADGER BIG TEN FINISHES...

Football: 1st
coached by Phil King

Outdoor Track: 1st
coached by James Temple and Charles Craigie

The Big Event

Badgers unbeaten in Big Ten, win second straight football title

Coach Phil King guided the Badgers to their second straight Big Ten football championship on the foot of Australian Pat O'Dea, the famed "Kangaroo Kicker," who kicked 14 field goals to lead the team. Key victories in Wisconsin's 9–1 season were the wins over Minnesota, Chicago and Northwestern that gave Wisconsin a 3–0–0 Big Ten record—the first of only four times that the UW would be undefeated and untied in Conference play.

The '98 team would also post a 9–1 record, losing only to Chicago 6–0 to finish third in the Big Ten with a 2–1 slate.

Wisconsin's 1897 season:

UW 30, Lake Forest 0	UW 39, Minnesota 0
UW 8, Madison High School 0*	UW11, Beloit 0
UW 28, Rush Medical 0	UW 25, Chicago 8
UW 20, Platteville Normal 0	UW Alumni 6, UW 0
UW 29, Madison High School 0	UW 22, Northwestern 0

called at halftime because of rain

WISCONSIN TIMELINE

1897: The Big Ten voted to require a year's residence after changing institutions

Coach Phil King's football team outscores its opponents 210–14 en route to a 9–1–1 campaign and second straight Big Ten crown

1898: The U.S. battleship Maine was blown up in Havana harbor, killing 260 crewmen

The Presidents' Committee devised and printed a set of football rules for Conference teams

WISCONSIN HEADLINER

EDWARD R. COCHEMS
FOOTBALL

Edward Cochems starred at both end and halfback during four stellar seasons with the Badgers' fledgling football program around the turn of the century. The Sturgeon Bay native competed in football, track and baseball, but it was on the gridiron that he excelled for Wisconsin teams that posted a 35–4–1 mark during his playing career. Cochems played at end for his first two seasons but then switched to the backfield. He scored four touchdowns in a 1900 win over Notre Dame and three TDs in 1901 against Chicago–including a 100-yard kickoff return. Cochems moved into the coaching ranks immediately after graduation, heading the North Dakota State program in 1902 and 1903. He served as an assistant at Wisconsin in 1904, moved to Clemson as head coach in 1905 and then to St. Louis University in 1906, where he became known as the "father" of the forward pass. Cochems was inducted into the Madison Sports Hall of Fame in 1968 and into the UW Athletic Hall of Fame in 1994.

WISCONSIN HEADLINER

ANDREW O'DEA
ROUTING COACH

Andrew O'Dea, though sometimes overshadowed in the newspaper spotlight of the era by the exploits of his younger brother Pat, Wisconsin's famed "Kangaroo Kicker," was a stellar athlete and coach in his own right. He came to the United States in the early 1890s from his native Australia, where he had worked with livestock on his father's Melbourne farm, first went to Minneapolis, where he coached the Lurlines, amateur rowing club in the Twin Cities. By 1895, O'Dea had come to Madison, where he soon assumed a role as one Wisconsin's great athletes, excelling in rowing and football. The latter sport, though new to him, was not difficult for him to pick up as he had played rugby in his native land. Andrew's brother Pat came to the U.S. in 1895 and became one of Wisconsin's all-time great athletes, but it might be fair to speculate whether the younger brother would have come to Madison without the older already being there.

WISCONSIN HEADLINER

PAT O'DEA
FOOTBALL

Patrick John O'Dea, the fabled "Kangaroo Kicker" who came to Madison from his native Australia, was one of Wisconsin's first athletic heroes. O'Dea played fullback on Wisconsin's 1896–99 football teams, excelling as a drop kicker on field goals. He once made four in one game and 14 in the entire 1897 season. O'Dea made a 65–yard dropkick field goal in an 1898 game in a snowstorm at Northwestern. His first play as a Badger was an 85–yard punt against Lake Forest in 1896, and he unleashed a 110-yard punt against Minnesota the next year. He topped his senior year with a 100-yard touchdown run against Beloit in 1899. Following his playing days, O'Dea coached at Notre Dame and Missouri. He later settled in California under an assumed name. His return to campus in 1934, 35 years after his last game, was a highlight of the Badgers' 7–3 Homecoming victory over Illinois. A member of the Wisconsin State Hall of Fame, O'Dea was inducted as a charter member of the UW Athletic Hall of Fame in 1991.

THE LIST

BIG TEN MEMBERS

Seven universities comprised the original "Intercollegiate Conference of Faculty Representatives." Now, more than a century later, the Big Ten has 14 members, with six of the original seven still members.

Here are years of membership:

University of Chicago	1896–1946
University of Illinois	1896–present
Indiana University	1899–present
University of Iowa	1899–present
University of Maryland	2014–
University of Michigan	1896–1908, 1917–present
Michigan State University	1949–present
University of Nebraska	2011–present
University of Minnesota	1896–present
Northwestern University	1896–present
Ohio State University	1912–present
Penn State University	1990–present
Purdue University	1896–present
Rutgers University	2014–
University of Wisconsin	1896–present

BADGER BIG TEN FINISHES...

Foootball: 3rd
coached by Phil King

Baseball: 5th
coached by Bertrand Husting

Outdoor Track: 4th
coached by John Moakley

The Big Event

UW becomes first "Western" school to be recognized in sports

Many of the established eastern schools looked down on Wisconsin and other midwestern colleges as somehow lacking both in academics and athletics. In fact, the Wisconsin rowers who competed against their eastern brethren were known, probably somewhat derisively, as "Haymakers." The Badger rowing teams of the turn of the century went a long way toward dispelling myths of eastern supremacy in 1899 and 1900.

The UW crews finished second in the famed Poughkeepsie Regatta, at that time the principal collegiate race in the nation and one that was long dominated by eastern schools. That gave Wisconsin credibility and was a warning to the older, established colleges that athletic powers were growing in America's heartland.

WISCONSIN TIMELINE

1898: Wisconsin finished 0–3 in its first basketball season.

1899: George F. Grant received a patent for a golf tee.

Indiana and Iowa were admitted to the Big Ten.

Wisconsin recorded its first basketball win, 25–15 over Wayland Academy.

BADGER COACHES & TEAMS...

Football: 2nd
coached by Phil King

Base ball: 2nd
coached by Phil King

Outdoor Track: 4th
coached by Charles Kilpatrick

The Big Event

Pat O'Dea kicks 62-yard field goal

Pat O'Dea, "The Kangaroo Kicker," routinely did the unbelievable on the football field, but perhaps no more so than in 1899.

Against Minnesota, the Badger safety fielded a punt and, while angling to his left to avoid Minnesota tacklers, got off a right-footed drop-kick that was at least 60 yards away from the goal posts as far as yardage on the field indicated.

The angle really made it more like 65. It sailed cleanly over the crossbars as the longest successful drop-kick in football history. Minnesota end Gil Dobie, who would become a great coach at Cornell and Washington, later called it the greatest play he'd ever seen.

Spectacular as that play was, O'Dea may have topped himself on November 11 of that same season when the Badgers played Illinois at Milwaukee. After a Bill Juneau fair catch following an Illinois punt, O'Dea nailed a place-kick cleanly from 60 yards out.

Actually, his kick really was a good 80 yards because it cleared not only the Illinois goal but also the baseball bleachers behind it and the high fence behind them and landed in the street outside the park.

WISCONSIN TIMELINE

1900: The first auto show in the U.S. opened in New York's Madison Square Garden.

The Conference approved legislation by which any member may object to new legislation within 30 days after such legislation is introduced. This became known as the "White Resolution."

Miler G.R. Keachie and long jumper F.W. Schule are Wisconsin's first Big Ten track and field champions.

1900—01

BADGER BIG TEN FINISHES...

Football: 3rd (tie)
coached by Phil King

Base ball: 4th
coached by Phil King

Outdoor Track: 2nd
coached by Charles Kilpatrick

The Big Event

Badgers second in inaugural Big Ten track championship

Wisconsin finished second to Michigan in the first official Big Ten outdoor track and field championships on June 1, 1901, at Marshall Field in Chicago.

Coach Charles Kilpatrick's squad scored 28 points, 10 behind Michigan, but comfortably ahead of Chicago (17) and Beloit and Minnesota (each with 14) in the nine-team field. The UW had two individual champions, G. R. Keachie in the mile run with a time of 4:34.4 and F.W. Schule in the long jump with a leap of 22'4 4/5". Schule was the Badgers' high scorer, also taking third in the 120-yard high hurdles and third in the 220-yard low hurdles.

Other Wisconsin scorers were George Poage, third in the 440; J. F. Hahn, second in the mile; Edgar McEachron and W. Smith, second and third in the two mile; Meyers, second in the high jump; H. Webster, second in the discus throw; and the mile relay team, which took second.

WISCONSIN TIMELINE

1901: An oil strike in Beaumont, Texas, marked the start of the great Texas oil boom. The first Big Ten outdoor track meet was held at Chicago.

Wisconsin's football team went 9–0 for Badgers' first undefeated season and the Badger baseball team finished 7–3 for its first winning season.

1901–02

BADGER COACHES & TEAMS...

Football: 1st (tie)
coached by Phil King

Baseball: 1st
coached by Oscar Bandelin

Gymnastics: 1st
coached by J.C. Elsom

Outdoor Track: 3rd
coached by Charles Kilpatrick

The Big Event

Wisconsin hosts, wins first Big Ten gymnastics meet

Although the Big Ten didn't officially sponsor a gymnastics champion until 1926, Wisconsin hosted, and won, the first meet of Conference members in 1902.

The meet was also open to teams outside the Big Ten. Wisconsin would go on to win seven of the first 15 titles in the sport. Ironically, the UW never again won a Big Ten gymnastics team title after the sport became part of the Conference's championship slate.

Wisconsin discontinued gymnastics in 1991.

WISCONSIN TIMELINE

1902: The Badgers lost 6–0 to Michigan in football, breaking the UW's 17-game winning streak. Michigan beat Stanford 49–0 in the first Rose Bowl game.

ART CURTIS
FOOTBALL

Four-time letterwinner Art Curtis, according to accounts of the day, rated only superlatives as the right tackle on turn-of-the-century Wisconsin football teams. From his arrival on the field as a freshman in 1898, he had a position won. He never was a second-team player nor did he ever miss a minute of action. He served as captain of Coach Phil King's 1901 team that went 9–0 to become the UW's first undefeated team. That squad outscored the opposition 317–5, defeated every opponent by at least three touchdowns and recorded eight shutouts to share the Big Ten title. Curtis, who was not a big man and never played at more than 178 pounds, was one of the fastest linemen of his day and was the first tackle in the "West" to range widely on the defense. Curtis also starred as a slick fielding first baseman on three UW baseball teams. Following graduation, he coached a year at Kansas, then returned to guide the Badgers to an 11–6–1 mark in the 1903 and 1904 seasons before resigning to complete medical studies. Curtis later became a department head in Northwestern University's school of medicine.

CHRISTIAN STEINMETZ, SR.
BASKETBALL

The "father" of Wisconsin basketball, Milwaukee native Christian Steinmetz starred on Badger teams of 1902–05. In 1904–05, he set a single season scoring record of 462 points for the 18-game schedule, only one of which was played at home. That team played a nine-game tour of the eastern United States, news reports of which helped popularize the game back home in Madison. Steinmetz had a single-game high of 50 points in the opening game of his senior season against Company G, Sparta. He had a record 20 field goals against Beloit College and 26 free throws against the Two Rivers Athletic Club. A member of the Wisconsin State Hall of Fame and the National Basketball Hall of Fame, Steinmetz was one of 35 charter inductees into the UW Athletic Hall of Fame in 1991.

THE LIST

Largest football victory margins
(pre–modern era)

Margin	Opponent	Year	Score
106	Whitewater Normal	1890	106–0
87	Beloit	1903	87–0
85	Marquette	1915	85–0
82	Drake	1904	82–0
82	Lawrence	1915	82–0
76	Dixon (Ill.)	1898	76–0
64	Upper Iowa	1900	64–0
62	Hyde Park (Ill.)	1901	62–0
60	Lawrence	1899	58–0
58	Lawrence	1899	58–0
58	Notre Dame	1904	58–0
57	Arkansas	1912	64–7

NICKNAME

So you want to be a Badger

Not surprisingly, UW sports teams' nickname came from the state of Wisconsin, which had been dubbed the "Badger state," not because of animals but an association with lead miners in Southwestern Wisconsin in the 1820s. Prospectors came to the state looking for minerals and without shelter in the winter had to "live like Badgers" in tunnels burrowed into the hillside.

BADGER BIG TEN FINISHES...

Football: 6th
coached by Phil King

Baseball: 4th
coached by Oscar Bandelin

Outdoor Track: 3rd
coached by Charles Kilpatrick

The Big Event

Wisconsin holds "Point-A-Minute" Michigan to six

Football Coach Phil King's 1902 Badgers finished 6–3 overall, 1–3 in the Big Ten for sixth place, but it was one of those Big Ten losses that made Wisconsin's season memorable.

Michigan had already won games by scores such as 68–0, 119–0, 60–0, 23–0 and 86–0, so little was expected of the Badgers against the grid power. But in a game played before a huge crowd of 18,000 at Chicago, Wisconsin held Coach Fielding Yost's famed "Point-a-Minute" team to just six points, losing 6–0.

It was the closest anyone had come to Michigan in two seasons.

WISCONSIN TIMELINE

1903: The United States and Panama signed a treaty granting the U.S. rights to build the Panama Canal.

First-year coach Emmett Angell saw his Badger cagers rout Sparta's Company C 75–10 as Christian Steinmetz scored 50 points.

BADGER BIG TEN FINISHES...

Football: 8th (tie)
coached by Art Curtis

Baseball: 2nd
coached by Bemis Pierce

Gymnastics: 1st
coached by J.C. Elsom

Outdoor Track: 3rd
coached by Charles Kilpatrick

The Big Event

Wisconsin wins Big Ten gymnastics

The Badgers won their third Big Ten gymnastics title in four years in 1904, winning at home as they had in their two previous triumphs since the meet's inception in 1902.

In those formative days of the Big Ten Conference, gymnastics had joined the "Big Three" of baseball, football and outdoor track as the league's championship events. Coached by J. C. Elsom, who also coached the UW basketball team, the gymnasts scored 40 points to win the meet.

Wisconsin went on to win Big Ten gymnastics championships in 1908, 1913, 1915, 1916, and 1923. After that, the Badgers never again won a league crown in the sport. Wisconsin dropped gymnastics after the 1991 season.

WISCONSIN TIMELINE

1904: The first Olympic Games to be held in the U.S. opened in St. Louis.

The Big Ten ruled that for a student to be eligible for athletic competition, he must have completed a full semester's work in residence; it was termed a radical departure in college athletics.

Wisconsin made its first basketball road trip and comes home 2–6 after games in New Jersey, New York, Pennsylvania, and Ohio.

1904—05

BADGER BIG TEN FINISHES...

Football: 7th (tie)
coached by Art Curtis

Baseball: 3rd (tie)
coached by Bemis Pierce

Gymnastics: 1st
coached by J.C. Elsom

Outdoor Track: 5th (tie)
coached by James Temple

The Big Event

Chris Steinmetz becomes first basketball all-American

Chris Steinmetz, generally regarded as the player who put Wisconsin basketball on the map, became the Badgers' first all-American in 1905. The Milwaukee native—a high scorer in an era when low scores were common—was also named the Helms Foundation player of the year after a season in which he had his single game high 50 points against Company G, Sparta. Called the "father" of UW basketball, Steinmetz was instrumental in establishing the Wisconsin program.

In 1905, as a senior, Steinmetz led the Badgers to a berth in the national championship game, where they lost to Columbia. One of his teammates that year was Bob Zuppke, who would go on to no little fame as the 28-year football coach at Illinois. Steinmetz's career statistics showed 462 points in a season, including 233 free throws (one player could then shoot all a team's free throws).

Steinmetz was the first Badger named to the National Basketball Hall of Fame and also was a charter inductee into the UW Athletic Hall of Fame.

WISCONSIN TIMELINE

1905: Actor Henry Fonda was born in Grand Island, Nebraska.

The Intercollegiate Conference of Faculty Representatives was incorporated in Illinois; it eventually became popularly known as the Big Ten.

1905—06

BADGER BIG TEN FINISHES...

Football: 5th (tie)
coached by Phil King

Cross Country: 3rd
(no coach)

Basketball: 2nd
coached by Emmett Angell

Outdoor Track: 4th
coached by George Downer and Emmett Angell

The Big Event

Coach Angell leads UW to second in Big Ten as player Angell tops all scorers

Wisconsin's Emmett Angell showed versatility the likes of which has never again been seen in the Big Ten—or perhaps anywhere in the nation—when as player-coach he led the Badgers to a runner-up finish in the inaugural season of Big Ten Conference basketball.

Angell, a student of the game as well as a teacher of it, scored 96 points for a 6.9 average in 14 games to pace Wisconsin to a 12–2 record. The Badgers' 6–2 Big Ten mark was good for second behind Minnesota.

Angell served as coach from the 1904–05 through 1907–08 seasons, compiling a 43–15 mark for a .741 winning percentage, best in Wisconsin history. His last two teams tied for Big Ten titles.

WISCONSIN TIMELINE

1906: The federal penitentiary in Leavenworth, Kansas was completed.

The "Angell Conference"—named after Michigan president A.A. Angell—set far–sighted rules and regulations for the Big Ten.

The Badgers finished 5–0 and won the Big Ten football championship.

BADGER COACHES & TEAMS...

Football: 1st (tie)
coached by C.P. Hutchins

Cross Country: 2nd
(no coach)

Basketball: 1st (tie)
coached by Emmett Angell

Baseball: 6th
coached by C.P. Hutchins

Gymnastics: 2nd
coached by Emmett Angell

Outdoor Track: 3rd
coached by Emmett Angell

The Big Event

UW shares football title in shortened season

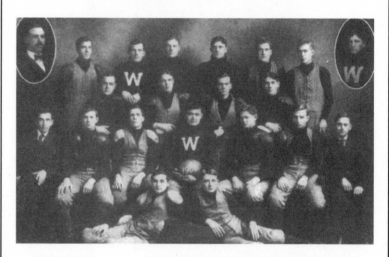

Wisconsin shared a notable Big Ten first in 1906 when its football team went unbeaten over a limited schedule to claim a share of the Conference title with Michigan and Minnesota. Each claimed a share based on its undefeated Big Ten season—Wisconsin at 3–0, Minnesota at 2–0 and Michigan at 1–0. It marked the only time in Big Ten history that three teams were perfect in Conference play.

Wisconsin didn't play traditional powers Michigan, Minnesota or Chicago enroute to its perfect 5–0 mark; a short-lived faculty reform movement had limited the number of games the team could play. Nonetheless, Coach C.P. Hutchins' team, paced by all-league center Ewald Stiehm, notched victories over Iowa, Illinois and Purdue by a combined 63–15 score.

WISCONSIN TIMELINE

1907: The Big Ten raised the limit on football games per season from five to seven. Oklahoma became the 46th state in the Union.

WISCONSIN HEADLINER

J.C. ELSOM
BASKETBALL COACH

J.C. Elsom was one of those coaching pioneers who set the stage for generations of Big Ten coaches to follow. As coach of fledgling UW basketball teams in the years just prior to Conference basketball competition, Elsom was at the forefront of what would become a golden era of basketball excellence in Madison. Building on the tradition established by Elsom's teams, Wisconsin (coached by Walter Meanwell) won 12 Big Ten hoop titles between 1906 and 1929. Elsom, who also served as a professor of physical therapy from 1894–1936, compiled a 25–14 record in six seasons. His first team went 0–3 in 1899 but he never again had a losing record and, in fact, Wisconsin teams would post winning marks until 1918. His best squad was his last one, which posted an 11–4 mark. Elsom died in 1949.

A W FIRST

Bringing home the bacon

One of the first trophies of any kind in college football was the "Slab of Bacon" trophy which served as the prize in the Wisconsin-Minnesota football series. According to the Wisconsin football media guide, the trophy was apparently presented to the winning school in any given year by a sorority from the losing school. The trophy was discontinued in the 1940s and was discovered in an athletic department storage room in 1994. It's now in the football office at Wisconsin.

THE LIST

WISCONSIN'S LONGEST FOOTBALL WINNING STREAKS

Number	First win	Broken by
17	Notre Dame (1900)	Michigan (1902)
14	Indiana (2006)	Illinois (2007)
11	Ohio State (1999)	Northwestern (2002)
10	San Diego State (1998)	Michigan (1998)
9	Central Florida (2004)	Michigan State (2004)
9	Lawrence (1912)	Purdue (1913)
8	Iowa (1894)	Illinois (1895)
8	Lake Forest (1897)	UW Alumni (1897)
8	Minnesota (1920)	Michigan (1921)
8	Purdue (1951)	Ohio State (1952)

A W FIRST

Badgers held out of "big" games

College football was under the gun, figuratively, soon after the turn of the century. The Big Ten had been founded on the principle of faculty control and, in 1906, it was the Wisconsin faculty that asserted itself. Upset by the "proselytizing" and "subsidizing" of athletes, the faculty voted to abolish football. Protests followed and the decision was reversed, to a degree. The UW team was limited to a five-game schedule and prevented from playing its major rivals—Minnesota, Michigan and Chicago. As those were the only games that made any sort of money, revenue fell to $3,400 from $35,000 the previous season. But Wisconsin did have a perfect 5–0 mark and shared the Big Ten title with two of the teams—Michigan and Minnesota—which it was not allowed to play. The faculty relented and allowed the traditional rivals back on the schedule, one at a time.

1907—08

BADGER BIG TEN FINISHES...

Football: 2nd
coached by C.P. Hutchins

Cross Country: 2nd
(no coach)

Basketball: 1st (tie)
coached by Emmett Angell

Baseball: 4th
coached by J. C. Elsom

Outdoor Track: 2nd
coached by Emmett Angell

The Big Event

Badgers are Big Ten gymnastics champs again

Led by all-around champion Felix Zeidelhack, Wisconsin claimed its fourth Big Ten gymnastics championship in six tries in the meet at Madison.

Coach J.C. Elsom's team easily outdistanced runner-up Chicago, which had 10 points, as well as Minnesota (7) and Nebraska (5).

Zeidelhack won his second straight all-around title. He also won three other events: the rings, the parallel bars and the horizontal bar, the latter two for the second straight season.

WISCONSIN TIMELINE

1908: The first Boy Scout troops were organized by Sir Robert Baden-Powell in England.

Michigan withdrew from the Conference to protest "retroactive provisions" of certain Conference enactments.

WISCONSIN HEADLINER

JOHN MESSMER
FOOTBALL, TRACK AND FIELD, BASEBALL

Milwaukee native John Messmer was a three-sport star for Badger football, track and baseball teams of the first decade of the 20th century. The East Side High School product won nine major "W" awards in the three sports, but achieved his greatest success in football. Captain of the 1907 Wisconsin team, Messmer was a first-team all-Big Ten pick and a second-team Walter Camp all-American at guard in 1908. Messmer also won the discus throw in the Big Ten outdoor track meets of 1907 and 1908 and was a member of the UW baseball team that toured Japan in 1909. He was president of the athletic board in 1908 as a student member. Inducted into the Wisconsin State Athletic Hall of Fame in 1959, Messmer was named to the UW Athletic Hall in 1993.

WISCONSIN HEADLINER

FELIX ZEIDELHACK
GYMNASTICS

Felix Zeidelhack dominated events at the 1908 Big Ten gymnastics championship, winning the all-around title for the second straight season. He also won the horizontal bars and parallel bars to lead Wisconsin to its fourth team title.

Zeidelhack had won the same events, plus the pommel horse, in pacing the Badgers to the 1907 championship.

WISCONSIN HEADLINER

HARLAN BETHUNE
"BIDDY" ROGERS
FOOTBALL, BASKETBALL
AND BASEBALL

His play in all three sports was characterized by "consistency with coolness in emergencies," say accounts of the time of Harlan Bethune "Biddy" Rogers. The Portage, Wis., native starred in football, basketball and baseball for the Badger teams at the end of the 20th century's first decade, winning nine letters. A three-year regular at left end, Rogers recovered the kick for the winning touchdown in Wisconsin's 6–5 win over Iowa in 1907. A basketball forward, "Biddy" captained the 1908 team that tied for the Big Ten title. He was a centerfielder on the Badger nine that ended his collegiate career with an exhibition trip to Japan in 1909. The Harlan B. Rogers Scholarship has been established in his memory. A member of the Wisconsin State Hall of Fame, Rogers was one of 35 members in the initial class inducted into the UW Athletic Hall of Fame in 1991.

THE LIST

WISCONSIN'S RECORD AT BOWL GAMES

Bowl	Years	Record
Rose	'53, '60, '63, '94, '99, '00, '11, '12, '13	3-6
Garden State	'81	0-1
Independence	'82	1-0
Hall of Fame	'84, '95	1-1
Copper	'96	1-0
Outback	'98, '05, '08	0-3
Sun	'01	1-0
Alamo	'02	1-0
Music City	'03	0-1
Capital One	'06, '07	2-0
Champs	'08, '09	1-1

BADGER BIG TEN FINISHES...

Football: 3rd
coached by J.A. Barry

Cross Country: 3rd
(no coach)

Basketball: 3rd
coached by Haskell Noyes

Baseball: 5th
coached by Tom Barry

Outdoor Track: 4th
coached by E.W. Moulton

The Big Event

Wisconsin third in first cross country championship

Wisconsin, which today has won more Big Ten cross country team and individual titles than any other school, finished third behind Nebraska and Purdue in the first official Conference meet.

Nebraska (non-Conference teams were then allowed to compete) scored 41 points to upend Purdue while the Badgers—without the benefit of a coach—were third with 59 points.

Top finisher for Wisconsin over the five-mile course at Chicago was William Hover in third place. Hover would take second the next time around although the UW would finish fifth in the team standings.

WISCONSIN TIMELINE

1909: Orville Wright set a record by staying aloft in an airplane for 72 minutes, 40 seconds, over Virginia.

Conference members took an active part in the new National Collegiate Athletic Association.

BADGER BIG TEN FINISHES.......

Football: 3rd
coached by J.A. Barry

Cross Country: 5th
coached by J. C. Elsom

Basketball: 3rd
coached by Haskell Noyes

Baseball: 5th
coached by Tom Barry

Outdoor Track: 6th
coached by Charles Hutchins
& James Lathrop

The Big Event

Beck writes "On, Wisconsin"

A Wisconsin student who was forced to drop out of school for a year used that time to forge a tradition. Carl Beck, who had enrolled at the UW in 1908, withdrew from school to work in Chicago and earn money to further his education. There he met William T. Purdy, who knew music and had started to write music for a song to be entered in a University of Minnesota contest. But Beck suggested that they do a song for Wisconsin, so Purdy wrote the music and Beck the words to provide one of the most famous college songs.

Introduced at a pre-game rally before the Wisconsin-Minnesota game in the fall of 1909, it was instantly a hit with students and townspeople. Beck returned to Madison in 1911, was graduated and became one of the founders of the Wisconsin Alumni Club of New York.

Over the years, it grew in popularity but the need for words which would fit occasions other than football had long been recognized. The original words included a reference to "run the ball clear 'round Chicago." In 1955, Beck composed some new, "all-purpose" lyrics for the famous song, noting in a letter that "These new words are to meet numerous requests for words for possible use on occasions other than football. Instead of stringing out a lot of words, brevity, as in the original, is their aim, having swing and action in keeping with the music and title."

The new lyrics, as written in 1955:

On, Wisconsin! On, Wisconsin!
Stand up, Badgers, sing!

"Forward" is our driving spirit
Loyal voices ring.

On, Wisconsin! On, Wisconsin!
Raise her glowing flame!

Stand, Fellows, let us now
Salute her name!

WISCONSIN TIMELINE

1910: A cork-center baseball was used in the World Series.

The first Big Ten Conference tennis championship was held at Chicago.

Clarence Cleveland (2 mile) and L.W. Johnson (high jump) become Wisconsin's first Big Ten indoor track champions.

BADGER BIG TEN FINISHES......

Football: 5th
coached by J.A. Barry

Cross Country: 1st
coached by Charles Wilson

Basketball: 5th
coached by Haskell Noyes

Indoor Track: 4th (tie)
coached by Charles Wilson

Baseball: 6th
coached by Tom Barry

Gymnastics: 3rd
coached by H.D. MacChesney

Outdoor Track: 5th
coached by Charles Wilson

The Big Event

Wisconsin wins first cross country title

There was a home course advantage of sorts for Coach Charles Wilson's 1910 UW cross country team. The Badgers, running in Madison, scored a low 33 points to win their first Big Ten team title.

Irvin Dohman, who covered the 4.75-mile route in 26:21, became Wisconsin's second individual champ. Wisconsin would go on to win three of the next four Big Ten meets and eight more between that first title and 1927.

It was the start of a streak that by 1997 had seen the Badgers win 33 Conference crowns.

WISCONSIN TIMELINE

1911: The first Indianapolis 500-mile race was won by Ray Harroun.

The first Conference indoor track and swimming championships were held.

1911–12

BADGER BIG TEN FINISHES...

Football: 3rd
coached by J.R. Richards

Cross Country: 2nd
coached by Charles Wilson

Basketball: 1st
coached by Walter Meanwell

Indoor Track: 2nd
coached by Charles Wilson

Swimming: 3rd
coached by Chaunce Hyatt

Baseball: 1st
coached by Gordon Lewis

Outdoor Track: 5th
coached by Charles Wilson

The Big Event

Badgers share basketball crown with Purdue

Wisconsin won its second Big Ten basketball title in 1911–12, sharing the Conference championship with Purdue. The Badgers had previously tied with Minnesota and Chicago for the new Conference's second basketball title in 1906–07. Leading Coach Walter Meanwell's team was Otto Stangel, who scored a Big Ten record 177 points.

WISCONSIN TIMELINE

1911: Led by Jim Thorpe, the United States won the most medals in the Olympic Games in Stockholm.

Ohio State University was admitted to membership in the Big Ten.

The Badgers' last unbeaten football team (7–0) won its fifth Big Ten title for rookie coach Bill Juneau.

OTTO STANGEL
BASKETBALL

Otto Stangel led the Big Ten in scoring with 177 points in the Badgers' Conference championship season of 1911–12, a mark that would stand as the league record for eight seasons. Stangel, a native of Two Rivers, Wis., scored 13 field goals in a 38–12 Wisconsin win over Iowa that year. The team was one of Wisconsin's best and was named national champion for 1912 by the Helms Athletic Foundation. Stangel was inducted into the UW Athletic Hall of Fame in 1995.

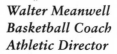

LEADING THE WAY

*Walter Meanwell
Basketball Coach
Athletic Director*

Dr. Walter E. "Doc" Meanwell presided over a golden era in Badger basketball, compiling a 246–99–1 record and winning eight Big Ten titles in 20 years as the Badgers' head coach. A native of Leeds, England, who came to the United States in 1885 at 3 years of age, Meanwell received his medical degree from Maryland in 1909. He joined the UW in 1911 as director of gymnasium and wrestling coach. He became basketball coach with the 1911–12 season and posted a 44–1 mark en route to three straight Big Ten titles as well as the 1915–16 crown before leaving for the same post at Missouri, where he coached the Tigers to two titles in three seasons. Meanwell returned to Madison for the 1920–21 campaign and guided the Badgers to the conference title, which his teams also won in 1923, 1924 and 1929. Meanwell served as Wisconsin's athletic director from 1933–35. A member of the National Basketball Hall of Fame, the Wisconsin State Hall of Fame and the Madison Pen and Mike Club-Bowman Sports Foundation Hall of Fame, Meanwell was a charter inductee into the UW Athletic Hall of Fame in 1991.

THE LIST

*Winningest UW
Football Coaches*

Coach (Years)	Career Victories
Barry Alvarez (1990–2005)	118
Phil King (1896–1902, 1905)	65
Bret Bielema (2006-2012)	60
Milt Bruhn (1956–66)	52
Dave McClain (1978–85)	46
Harry Stuhldreher (1936–48)	45
Ivy Williamson (1949–55)	41
John Jardine (1970–77)	37
J.R. Richards (1911, 1917, 1919–22)	29
Glenn Thistlewaite (1927–31)	26
William Juneau (1912–15)	18

A  FIRST

Badgers win first baseball title

Playing an unbalanced Big Ten schedule, Wisconsin—under first-year coach Gordon "Slim" Lewis—won its first Conference baseball championship in 1912, going 6–1 for an .857 winning percentage. It was enough to edge two-time defending champion Illinois, which had a 10–1 mark and .833 winning percentage.

BADGER BIG TEN FINISHES...

Football: 1st
coached by William Juneau

Cross Country: 1st
coached by Clarence Cleveland

Basketball: 1st
coached by Walter Meanwell

Indoor Track: 2nd
coached by Thomas Jones

Swimming: 2nd
coached by Chauncey Hyatt

Wrestling: 6th
coached by E.B. Nolte

Baseball: 7th
coached by William Juneau

Gymnastics: 1st
coached by H.D. MacChesney

Outdoor Track: 2nd
coached by Thomas Jones

The Big Event

Wisconsin becomes a football power

Wisconsin became a football power in 1912 as Coach Bill Juneau's team won all seven of its games en route to the Badgers' fifth Big Ten championship. Wisconsin scored 246 points and allowed only 29 while in conference play it outscored its five opponents by a combined 169–22.

So domineering was Wisconsin that *Chicago Tribune* sports editor Walter Eckersall picked nine Badgers on his all-Western team, including Joe Hoeffel and Hod Ofstie at ends; Robert "Butts" Butler and Ed Samp at tackles; Ed Gelein and "Tubby" Keeler at guards; Eddie Gillette at quarterback; John Van Riper at halfback; and Al Tandberg at fullback. Butler and Keeler were named all-Americans.

Following Wisconsin's season-ending 28–10 victory at Iowa, there was agitation for the Badgers to meet Harvard for the national championship; the 9–0 Crimson had won the Big Three title and had impressive wins over Yale and Princeton. But John Wilce, 1909 UW captain and the school's graduate manager, said that talk about matching teams for the national title was just that and there would be no such game. Wilce said that such a post-season game was contrary to Western Conference regulations and that, furthermore, the Wisconsin faculty would never approve.

Game scores:
Wisconsin 13, Lawrence 0
Wisconsin 56, Northwestern 0
Wisconsin 41, Purdue 0
Wisconsin 30, Chicago 12
Wisconsin 64, Arkansas 7
Wisconsin 14, Minnesota 0
Wisconsin 28, Iowa 10

WISCONSIN TIMELINE

1913: The first crossword puzzle was published in the Sunday supplement of the *New York World*.

The Big Ten prohibited post-season basketball games.

Tom Jones guided the Badgers to seconds in both the Big Ten indoor and outdoor track meets in the first of his 36 seasons at the helm.

WISCONSIN HEADLINER

ROBERT PARKER "BUTTS" BUTLER FOOTBALL

Robert "Butts" Butler was an all-American tackle on the Badgers' 1912 football team that was undefeated and won the Big Ten championship. In the 1912 season finale against Minnesota, Butler and his 10 teammates played the entire game. He was Wisconsin's first consensus all-American and was named to Walter Camp's first team as a junior and second team as a senior. A native of Glen Ridge, N.J., Butler was a three-time "W" award-winner on Wisconsin teams that posted a 15–4–2 mark over his playing career. Twice an all-Big Ten selection, Butler played professionally for the Canton Bulldogs—with the legendary Jim Thorpe as a teammate—following his graduation in 1914. He was named to the National Football Foundation Hall of Fame in 1972 and was inducted into the UW Athletic Hall of Fame in 1992.

LEADING THE WAY

William J. Juneau Football Coach

William Juneau compiled an 18–8–3 record in four seasons as Wisconsin football coach from 1912–15, including an undefeated campaign in 1912. The Badgers won their fourth Big Ten title and at 7–0 were the last UW team to post a perfect record. Led by consensus all-America (and future UW Athletic Hall of Famer) Robert "Butts" Butler, the Badgers placed a school-record nine players *Chicago Tribune* sports editor Walter Eckersall's all-Western team. Juneau enrolled at Wisconsin in 1899 and won major "W" awards in football the next four years, starring at halfback and end. He also won letters in track in 1900 and 1901, competing in the pole vault, hammer throw and 440-yard dash. He was third in the pole vault in the 1900 Western Intercollegiate meet at Chicago. Juneau also coached at Colorado College, South Dakota State and Marquette before coming to Wisconsin and after his UW stint coached at Texas and Kentucky. Juneau died in 1949 at age 70 in Milwaukee.

THE LIST

WISCONSIN'S MEN'S CONFERENCE MEDAL OF HONOR WINNERS

In 1914, the Big Ten Conference endowed a Medal of Honor to be awarded at each member institution to a student in the graduating class who demonstrated proficiency in scholarship and athletics.

1915

Martin Thomas Kennedy

1916

William Dow Harvey

1917

Meade Burke

1918

Ebert Edward Simpson, Jr.

1919

Charles H. Carpenter

A FIRST

Four Badgers among all-Big Ten cagers

Legendary Wisconsin basketball coach Walter "Doc" Meanwell had the kind of team in the 1912–13 season that most coaches only dream about. Four of his players—Gene Van Gent, Allan Johnson, Carl Harper and John Van Riper—were named to the all-Big Ten first team. It was a season to remember for the Badgers, who won the second of three straight Big Ten championships in a golden era of UW basketball. They were unbeaten through 14 games—11 in the Big Ten—until losing 23–10 at Chicago in the season finale. Their closest game prior to that was a 16–15 win at Illinois.

1913–14

BADGER BIG TEN FINISHES...

Football: 6th (tie)
coached by William Juneau

Cross Country: 1st
coached by Thomas Jones

Basketball: 1st
coached by Walter Meanwell

Indoor Track: 2nd
coached by Thomas Jones

Swimming: 4th
coached by Harry Hindman

Wrestling: 2nd
coached by Fred Schlatter

Baseball: 3rd
coached by Gordon Lewis

Gymnastics: 2nd
coached by H.D. MacChesney

Outdoor Track: 4th
coached by Thomas Jones

The Big Event

Badgers are national basketball champs

For the second time in three seasons, Wisconsin celebrated national and Big Ten basketball championships. Under Coach Walter "Doc" Meanwell, the UW rattled off 15 wins without a loss to claim best-in-the-nation honors. Its 12–0 Big Ten mark also gave Wisconsin its first undisputed Conference crown. Noteworthy was the only shutout in Big Ten basketball history: The Badgers blanked Parsons 50–0 on January 6, 1914, at home.

Wisconsin's record, season:

Wisconsin 48, Knox 15*

Wisconsin 45, Beloit 15*

Wisconsin 50, Parsons 0*

Wisconsin 26, Illinois 25

Wisconsin 57, Indiana 15

Wisconsin 28, Minnesota 7*

Wisconsin 16, Chicago 14

Wisconsin 38, Northwestern 9*

Wisconsin 25, Purdue 20 (OT)*

Wisconsin 33, Northwestern 26

Wisconsin 29, Illinois 16*

Wisconsin 46, Indiana 24*

Wisconsin 27, Minnesota 9

Wisconsin 25, Chicago 18*

Wisconsin 27, Purdue 13

*Home games

WISCONSIN TIMELINE

1914: Britain declared war on Germany and the United States declared its neutrality in World War I.

The Conference Board of Directors put aside $2,000 for the endowment of the ICAA Medal (Medal of Honor).

RAY KEELER
FOOTBALL

Three-time letterwinner Ray Keeler was a consensus all-American lineman for the Wisconsin football team of 1913, which posted a 3–3–1 mark for second-year Coach William Juneau. Keeler, nicknamed "Tubby" in "recognition" of his 185–lb. frame, earned all-American recognition in his junior season from the International News Service. Keeler also won three major "W" awards in track and field. He was captain of the 1914 football team and also served on the athletic board in 1914 and 1915. Keeler went on to coach the Wisconsin-LaCrosse football team to a 45–24–15 record.

BADGER MOMENT

A basketball blanking— one for the record books

It was a basketball game for the ages, at least in the minds of Wisconsin fans. Everyone knew that the Badgers could score and, after all, they had only lost one game in the two prior seasons. And Coach Walter Meanwell's Badgers had racked up a lot of points (for the day) in beating Knox 48–15 and Beloit 45–15 to start their season. But a shutout, still the only one in Big Ten annals, was unexpected to say the least. Nonetheless, it was in the books as one of those games to be remembered: Wisconsin 50, Parsons 0, on January 6, 1914, at Madison.

Wahl jumps to Big Ten victories

High jumper Robert Wahl became Wisconsin's first three-time Big Ten track and field champion in 1914, winning the high jump at 6'1/2" in the Conference indoor meet at Evanston. The Badgers finished second to Illinois for the third straight season. Wahl won the high jump at 5'10" in 1912 and had tied for the crow the event at 5'11 1/2" in the 1913 meet. He also took the high jump titles at the Big Ten outdoor championships in 1913 and 1914.

The Badgers' first Big Ten championships

Sport	1st UW title	1st year championship held
Baseball	1901–02	1895–96
Basketball	1906–07	1905–06
Cross Country	1910–11	1908–09
Fencing	1954–55	1925–26
Football	1896–97	1896–97
Golf	1956–67	1919–20
Gymnastics	1901–02	1901–02
Hockey	1971–72	1958–59
Soccer	1995–96	1991–92
Swimming	none	1910–11
Tennis	none	1909–10
Outdoor Track	1914–15	1900–01
Indoor Track	1926–27	1910–11
Wrestling	none	1911–12

1914—15

BADGER BIG TEN FINISHES...

Football: 4th (tie)
coached by William Juneau

Cross Country: 5th
coached by Thomas Jones

Basketball: 3rd
coached by Walter Meanwell

Indoor Track: 4th
coached by Thomas Jones

Swimming: 4th
coached by Harry Hindman

Wrestling: 4th
coached by Fred Schlayywe

Baseball: 2nd
coached by Gordon Lewis

Gymnastics: 1st
coached by H.D. MacChesney

Outdoor Track: 1st
coached by Thomas Jones

The Big Event

Wisconsin takes Big Ten track title by one point

Wisconsin won its first Big Ten outdoor track and field championship under the tutelage of Coach Tom Jones as the Badgers edged Chicago 38–37 on June 5, 1915, at Champaign, Illinois. It was the first of five one-point decisions in the annals of Big Ten outdoor track. Wisconsin had three champions, all in the field events.

Arlie Mucks, Sr., claimed titles in the shot put (46'3") and discus throw (137'7") while Phil Stiles won the long jump at 23'9" Mucks also added a third in the hammer throw as the Badgers made every point count, scoring in 10 of the 15 events.

It was the first of 20 Big Ten championships that Jones-coached teams would win over the next three decades.

WISCONSIN TIMELINE

1915: The U.S. House of Representatives rejected a proposal to give women the right to vote. Coach H.D. MacChesney's Wisconsin gymnasts won their sixth Big Ten title.

1915—16

BADGER BIG TEN FINISHES...

Football: 6th
coached by William Juneau

Cross Country: 1st
coached by Fred G. Lee

Basketball: 1st
coached by Walter Meanwell

Indoor Track: 2nd
coached by Thomas Jones

Swimming: 4th
coached by Harry Hindman

Wrestling: 6th
coached by Art knott

Baseball: 6th (tie)
coached by Gordon Lewis

Gymnastics: 1st
coached by H.D. MacChesney

Outdoor Track: 1st
coached by Thomas Jones

The Big Event

Badgers win national basketball crown again

None of the great Wisconsin basketball teams of the first decade and one-half of the 20th century may have been as dominating as the Badgers of 1915–16. Coach Walter Meanwell's team posted a 20–1 overall mark and went 11–1 in the Big Ten to coast to the league title.

Undefeated in 10 home games, the Badgers were named the Helms Athletic Foundation national champions, the third UW (and Meanwell-coached) team to be so honored. The 1915–16 Wisconsin five was also the first Big Ten team to win 20 games in a season, a feat that would not be duplicated until 1940 .

Leading the Badgers were all-American (and two-time all-Big Ten) performer George Levis along with his running mates, William Chandler, Mel Haas, Paul Meyers and Harold Olsen. Illinois handed Wisconsin its only loss by a 27–20 count at Champaign to break the Badgers' 12-game winning streak.

WISCONSIN TIMELINE

1916: The Supreme Court ruled that the federal income tax was constitutional.

Wisconsin won four Big Ten championships: cross country, basketball, gymnastics and outdoor track.

HOWARD "CUB" BUCK
FOOTBALL

Called the finest lineman he had ever played with by pro football teammate Jim Thorpe, Howard "Cub" Buck played tackle on Wisconsin's 11–8–2 football teams of 1913–15. Buck, an Eau Claire native, captained the 1915 squad, earning all-Big Ten and all-American honors that season. He is a member of Wisconsin's all-time football team. He played professionally with the Canton Bulldogs from 1915–19 and with the Green Bay Packers from 1921–25, with assistant coaching stops at Wisconsin and Carleton College sandwiched between his pro football stints. Buck later became head coach at Lawrence College (1824–25) and Miami of Florida (1926–28). A member of the Wisconsin State Hall of Fame (1956) and the Green Bay Packers Hall of Fame (1977), Buck was a charter inductee of the UW Athletic Hall of Fame in 1991.

GEORGE LEVIS
BASKETBALL

All-American forward George Levis was one of the mainstays of the 1916 Wisconsin basketball team that compiled a 20–1 mark enroute to the Big Ten championship. Levis, a Madison native, earned all-Conference honors at forward in both 1915 and 1916; he gained all-America status in 1916 after scoring 109 points in 12 Big Ten games in that era of low scores. Levis also was a third baseman for the Badgers' baseball squad. Levis later coached basketball at Indiana for two seasons in the early 1920s, compiling a 25–16 record. He later played a prominent role in developing basketball's glass backboards for his family's firm, Illinois Glass Company. Levis was one of 35 charter inductees into the UW Athletic Hall of Fame in 1991.

THE LIST

WISCONSIN'S BIG TEN FENCING CHAMPIONS

Since Al Stirns won the Big Ten foil title in 1915, 24 Badgers won 33 fencing championships until 1986 when the Big Ten discontinued fencing Wisconsin dropped the sport after the 1991 season.

Foil

Al Stirns (1915), Edward Hampe (1941), Jack Heiden (1955), Jerry Bodnar (1958), Richard Green (1959), Bruce Taubman (1967–68), Neal Cohen (1970, 1972), Harry Chiu (1973), Bob Tourdot (1975), Dean Rose (1978–79), Michael Pedersen (1985)

Epee

Bob Series (1953), Paul Mortonson (1955), Pat Laper (1967), Steve Vandenberg (1977–78), Mike Glennon (1980), Tim Gillham (1983–84–85)

Sabre

Art Kaftan (1935–36), Fred Kaftan (1937–38), Ron LeMieux (1959), Tom Giaimo (1971), Dave DeWahl (1976), Joe Kroeten (1981–82), Mark Draeger (1984)

A  FIRST

Badger teams win four Big Ten titles

Paced by the national champion basketball team, 1915–16 marked one of the great years in Wisconsin sports history, with four Wisconsin teams claiming Big Ten championships. Coach Walter Meanwell's cagers posted a 20–1 overall record and 11–1 Big Ten mark to earn not only the Big Ten crown but also recognition by the Helms Athletic Foundation as national champions. Not to be outdone, the Badger gymnasts, under Coach H.D. MacChesney, won the Conference title. Coach Tom Jones' track and field squad garnered four individual titles and the mile relay crown in the Big Ten outdoor track meet at Evanston to take a 49–35 win over Illinois. And the UW cross country team, coached by Fred Lee and led by Arlie Schardt's third-place finish, scored a low 38 points to win the Big Ten.

BADGER BIG TEN FINISHES...

Football: 6th (tie)
coached by Paul Withington

Cross Country: 6th
coached by Irvin A. White

Basketball: 4th
coached by Walter Meanwell

Swimming: 4th
coached by Harry Hindman

The Big Event

Badgers post mildly successful season in all sports

Wisconsin had mixed success during the 1916–17 campaign.

The football Badgers won their first four games—all at home—under one-year Coach Paul Withington against lightly regarded foes. However, the UW was 0–2–1 in its last three games against Big ten opposition, losing 14–13 to Ohio State and 54–0 to Chicago before playing Illinois to a scoreless tie.

Coach Walter Mean well's national basketball champions "slipped," barely, to 15–3 and a 9–3 fourth-place finish in the Big Ten. However, three players, guards Paul Meyers and Harold Olsen and center Bill Chandler, were all-Conference picks, the latter two for the second consecutive season.

The Badgers placed seventh in Big Ten cross country. In track and field, Wisconsin was third in the Conference indoor meet, with sprinter Carman Smith and miler Arlie Schardt winning their specialties, but didn't compete in the outdoor meet.

The Badgers were fourth of four in the Big Ten swimming and diving championships.

WISCONSIN TIMELINE

1917: Rev. Edward Flanagan founded Boys Town near Omaha.

Michigan resumed its membership in the Big Ten.

Only four Wisconsin teams competed in Big Ten championship play, with the football and cross country teams each sixth in the Conference and the basketball and swimming teams fourth.

BADGER BIG TEN FINISHES...

Football: 3rd (tie)
coached by J.R. Richards

Cross Country: 3rd
coached by Thomas E. Jones

Basketball: 1st
coached by Guy Lowman

Indoor Track: 3rd
coached by Thomas Jones

Swimming: 3rd
coached by Harry Hindman

Baseball: 6th (tie)
coached by Guy Lowman

Outdoor Track: 5th
coached by Thomas Jones

The Big Event

Lowman guides Badgers to Big Ten cage crown

Guy Lowman didn't miss a beat when he took over Wisconsin's basketball coaching reins for the 1917–18 season with Walter Meanwell's departure for military service. The UW chalked up a 14–3 mark overall, with its 9–3 Big Ten slate good enough to give Wisconsin its seventh Big Ten title.

The Badgers, acclaimed as national champions for three of the previous six seasons by the Helms Athletic Foundation, had dropped to an uncharacteristic fourth in the Big Ten standings in 1916–17, albeit with 15–3 overall and 9–3 Big Ten records. But Lowman, who would coach the UW for three seasons until Meanwell's return, got the Badgers off to a quick start with five straight wins to open the campaign.

After a loss at Northwestern, a four-game win skein followed before a 23–21 loss at Chicago. The Badgers recouped and won five in a row again before falling 19–11 to Minnesota in the season finale.

WISCONSIN TIMELINE

1918: Units of the U.S. 1st Division, in the first American offensive of World War I, captured the area around Cantigny, France, from the Germans.

The Conference tendered to the War Department "its services in carrying on athletic activities in and among its members."

Guy Lowman's Badgers won their sixth Big Ten basketball championship in 12 years.

ARLIE MUCKS, SR.
FOOTBALL, TRACK
AND FIELD

"Great" is a word that can't be tossed around lighly, but in the case of Arlie Mucks, Sr., it hardly does the man justice. A football all-American, an Olympic silver medalist as a teenager, Mucks boasted an athletic resume that wasn't far removed from that of Jim Thorpe. The Oshkosh native was an all-Big Ten and all-America guard for the Badgers in 1914, but he had already made his mark. As a teen in 1912, he won the silver medal in the discus in the Stockholm Olympics. Prior to that, he had played tackle on his three-time state champion high school football team. Unbeaten in the shot put and discus as a collegian, Mucks won national titles in the shot and discus three consecutive years, the only manevertodoso. He won U.S. Olympic trials in the shot in 1916, 1920 and 1924 and was Penn Relays shot and discus champ in 1916. Mucks served as a Big Ten football official after his playing career ended. He was named to Wisconsin's all-time football team in 1969, to the Wisconsin State Hall of Fame and, in 1991, as a charter member of the UW Athletic Hall of Fame.

ARTHUR C. NIELSEN , SR.
TENNIS

Even over 80 years after his graduation, Arthur C. Nielsen, Sr., remains one of the great tennis players in Wisconsin history. Nielsen captained the UW tennis teams of 1914–15 through 1917–18. He teamed with Edwin Hammen to win the Big Ten doubles title in 1918. Nielsen later teamed with his son, Arthur, Jr., to win two national titles in father-son doubles competition. He also won the national U.S. hard court title in father-daughter competition. Nielsen was elected to the National Lawn Tennis Hall of Fame in 1971. A 1918 graduate in electrical engineering, Nielsen founded and spent 50 years with A.C. Nielsen Co., the largest firm in marketing and television audience research. His contribution also made possible the 1968 construction on the UW campus of a tennis stadium named for him. Nielsen received an honorary doctorate from Wisconsin in 1974. He was named to the UW Athletic Hall of Fame in 1992.

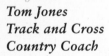 # LEADING THE WAY

Tom Jones
Track and Cross
Country Coach

If any name is synonymous with Wisconsin track and field, it's that of Tom Jones, a coach whose stellar teams from 1913–48 defined the UW's great tradition in track and cross country. And although he had great success, Jones believed more in the amateur spirit and development of men than in victories. Nonetheless, victories were numerous. Jones coached 20 Big Ten championship teams and the 1948 Olympic team. Seven of his teams finished among the top 10 in the NCAA championships, with the Chuck Fenske-led team of 1938 topping that group with a fourth-place national collegiate finish. He guided 137 athletes to Big Ten titles and five to NCAA crowns. Named to halls of fame by the Helms Foundation, the Wisconsin State hall, the Madison Pen and Mike Club-Bowman Foundation and the Drake Relays coaches hall, Jones was inducted as a charter member of the UW Athletic Hall of Fame in 1991. He died in 1969 at age 91.

# A W FIRST

Camp Randall Stadium opens

Wisconsin's famed Camp Randall Stadium is the oldest football stadium in the Big Ten. Now seating 76,027, the stadium sits on a site used variously as a training site for Union soldiers during the Civil War, as a prison for Confederate troops and as a state fair grounds. When the Wisconsin state legislature donated the land to the University, veterans groups prevailed upon the school to call it Camp Randall rather than Randall Field so as to honor veterans buried in a nearby cemetery. Originally seating 10,000, the facility was built for $15,000 and has been expanded nearly a dozen times since then. Wisconsin beat Minnesota 10–7 in its opening game there for the 1917 Homecoming celebration.

1918—19

BADGER BIG TEN FINISHES...

Football: 7th
coached by Guy Lowman

Cross Country: 1st
coached by George T. Bresnahan

Basketball: 10th
coached by Guy Lowman

Indoor Track: 8th
coached by Thomas Jones

Swimming: 4th
coached by Harry Hindman

Baseball: 7th
coached by Maury Kent

Outdoor Track: 9th (tie)
coached by Thomas Jones

The Big Event

Doughboys come home from war

The "war to end all wars" didn't put a stop to intercollegiate athletics, but it certainly slowed things down a bit and teams were admittedly sub-par. The Big Ten Conference had suspended its activities as a "controlling body" and had tendered to the War Department "its services in carrying on athletic activities in and among its members."

With the return of young men from the European theater of operations, college coaches could again turn their attention to sports rather than war. Illinois, which won the 1919 Conference football title via a last-minute upset of Ohio State, lost 14–10 to the Badgers.

Wisconsin center Charles Carpenter earned all-American honors. In basketball, Wisconsin fell from its national championship heights of a year earlier and ended 5–11 overall and 3–9 in the Big Ten for its first last-place finish.

WISCONSIN TIMELINE

1919: A federal amendment to give women the right to vote was passed by the U.S. House of Representatives.

Wisconsin, coached by George Bresnahan, won the "unofficial" Big Ten cross country title with a low 24 points as Bernardo Elsom became the Badgers' fifth individual champion in 27:13 for the five-mile course. No official meet was held because of World War.

1919—20

BADGER BIG TEN FINISHES...

Football: 4th
coached by J.R. Richards

Cross Country: 2nd
coached by George T. Bresnahan

Basketball: 5th
coached by Guy Lowman

Indoor Track: 3rd
coached by Thomas Jones

Swimming: 3rd
coached by Joe Steinauer

Baseball: 7th
coached by Maury Kent

Golf: 7th
(no coach)

Outdoor Track: 3rd
coached by Thomas Jones

The Big Event

Badgers 5–2 in football for 4th in Big Ten

In his first year of his third stint as Badger football coach, John Richards returned from World War I to guide Wisconsin to a 5–2 season in 1919. The UW shut out its first two opponents, Ripon (37–0) and Marquette (13–0), and beat Big Ten rivals Northwestern (10–6) and Illinois (14–10) before dropping its next two.

Minnesota beat the Badgers 19–7 and Ohio State squeaked by the UW 3–0. Wisconsin rebounded to beat Chicago 10–3 in its last game. Two-time all-American center Charles Carpenter, the first UW all-American at his position, captained the 1919 team.

WISCONSIN TIMELINE

1920: New York-to-San Francisco air mail service was inaugurated.

The first Big Ten golf tournament was held at Olympia Fields Country Club in suburban Chicago.

Lloyd Wilder won the pole valt to become Wisconsin's first NCAA track and champion.

BADGER BIG TEN FINISHES...

Football: 2nd
coached by J.R. Richards

Cross Country: 5th
coached by George T. Bresnahan

Basketball: 1st (tie)
coached by Walter Meanwell

Indoor Track: 3rd
coached by Thomas Jones

Swimming: 5th
coached by John Steinauer

Wrestling: 2nd
coached by George Hitchcock

Baseball: 3rd
coached by Guy Lowman

Outdoor Track: 3rd
coached by Thomas Jones (5th, NCAA)

The Big Event

Badgers return to top of Big Ten basketball

After two years away from the top of the Big Ten basketball standings, the Badgers made a triumphant return to Conference supremacy in the 1920-21 season. Wisconsin had slipped to 10th and fifth place finishes in the Big Ten in the two intervening years.

Coach Walter Meanwell, back after a three-year hiatus because of World War I, took over from Guy Lowman and guided the UW to a 13–4 overall record. The Badgers' 8–4 Big Ten mark was good for a tie for the championship.

Wisconsin split its first eight conference games but snared a share of its eighth Big Ten title with a road win over Ohio State and home victories over Chicago, Minnesota and the Buckeyes.

WISCONSIN TIMELINE

1921: Iowa became the first state to impose a cigarette tax.

Official action against post-season football games was taken by the Conference.

Ice hockey officially became a sport at Wisconsin, with the first game a 4–1 loss to the Milwaukee Athletic Club.

WISCONSIN HEADLINER

FRANK L. WESTON
FOOTBALL, BASKETBALL

Frank Weston was a two-time all-Big Ten end for Badger football teams of 1917, 1919 and 1920 and was a second-team Walter Camp All-American in 1921. The Mason City, Iowa, native captained that 1920 Wisconsin team, which posted a 6–1 mark. He also earned a "W" award in basketball in 1919 and 1920. Weston went on to an illustrious career, receiving his medical degree from Rush Medical College. He served as president of the Wisconsin Medical Alumni Association for 1964–65 and received the outstanding alumnus award from the Wisconsin Alumni Association in 1956. He also was a member of the Wisconsin Athletic Board from 1948–63. Weston was inducted into the Madison Sports Hall of Fame in 1965 and into the UW Athletic Hall of Fame in 1994.

WISCONSIN HEADLINER

PAUL MEYERS & CHARLES CARPENTER
FOOTBALL

End Paul Meyers and center Charles Carpenter each earned all-America football honors in 1916 and again in 1919. Meyers, an all-Big Ten choice those same years who played for three different coaches, received first-team all-America honors from Walter Eckersall for his senior season. Eckersall had named him third-team all-America in 1916. Carpenter, the Wisconsin recipient of the Big Ten Medal of Honor in 1919, also made Eckersall's third and first team all-America units in the same years as Meyers. The first all-American center at Wisconsin, Carpenter was captain of the 1919 team. A Madison native, he later served as president of the UW Athletic Board.

WISCONSIN HEADLINER

GEORGE BUNGE
FOOTBALL

George Bunge was a two-time all-American in 1920 and 1921 for Coach J.R. Richards, Wisconsin football teams. Bunge, a center, was a first-team all-America choice in 1920 by Consolidated Press. He earned third-team all-America honors on 1921 from Charles Parker and International News Service. The Badgers posted a three-year mark of 16–4–1, including a runner-up finish in the Big Ten in 1920, during Bunge's career.

WISCONSIN HEADLINER

RALPH SCOTT
FOOTBALL

Ralph Scott, a 210-lber., starred at tackle for the Badgers' 6–1 team of 1920, which finished second in the Big Ten under coach J.R. Richards. Scott was an all-Conference pick as well as a first-team all-American selection on the Walter Camp Team. Scott was noted for his blocking ability on offense and also played tackle on defense.

WISCONSIN HEADLINER

ROLLIE WILLIAMS
FOOTBALL, BASKETBALL, BASEBALL

Rollie Williams, an Edgerton, Wisconsin, native who excelled in football, basketball and baseball in high school, continued to shine at Madison. He earned nine letters for the Badgers and was an all-Big Ten choice as a football halfback in 1922 and a basketball guard for the 1922–23 season. His 75-yard run from scrimmage helped the Badgers defeat Minnesota in the 1921 Homecoming game. He played on Big Ten basketball championship teams as a sophomore and senior and in the spring was an outfielder for the Badger nine. Following his graduation, Williams served as head basketball coach at Millikin University for a season before heading to Iowa for a five-year stint as assistant football and basketball coach. He became head basketball coach at Iowa in 1929 and served through the 1941–42 season and also for the 1950–51 campaign, guiding Hawkeye teams to a 147–139 record. Williams also served as an assistant director of athletics. A member of the Wisconsin State Hall of Fame, Williams was a charter member of the UW Athletic Hall of Fame in 1991.

LEADING THE WAY

John R. Richards Football Coach

John R. Richards was one of Wisconsin's greatest athletes and coaches. The Lake Geneva native starred on early Badger teams in the last decade of the 19th century, playing end for the Badgers in 1892 and fullback from 1893–96. He also earned five track letters as a hurdler and another in crew. Richards had three different terms as Wisconsin's football coach, guiding the team a 5–1–1 mark in 1911 and third in the Big Ten (2–1–1). He coached football at Ohio State in 1912 and then returned to Madison in 1917, where his team went 4–2–1. He left for World War I service and then returned again in 1919 four a four-year stint. His best squad was the 1920 unit that went 6–1 and finished second in the Big Ten. Among the many UW stars he coached were Guy Sundt, "Red" Weston, Chuck Carpenter, George Bunge and "Rowdy" Elliott. After leaving Wisconsin, Richards became a partner in a California investment firm. He died at age 72 in 1947.

THE LIST

BADGERS IN THE COLLEGE FOOTBALL HALL OF FAME

1955	Coach George Little
1955	Dave Schreiner
1958	Coach Harry Stuhldreher *(elected as a Notre Dame player)*
1962	Coach Phil King *(elected as a Princeton player)*
1962	Pat O'Dea
1972	Robert Butler
1974	Elroy Hirsch
1975	Alan Ameche
1988	Marty Below
1993	Pat Harder
1996	Pat Richter
2010	Coach Barry Alvarez
2013	Ron Dayne

A  FIRST

Wilder wins first NCAA pole vault title

Lloyd Wilder was Wisconsin's—and the Big Ten's—first NCAA pole vault champion in the inaugural NCAA outdoor track and field championships at Chicago. Wilder, who lettered only that season for Coach Tom Jones, shared the vault title at 12'0" with Longino Welch of Georgia Tech, Eldon Jenne of Washington State and Truman Gardner of Yale. The Badgers finished fifth in the meet with 9 points as Illinois won the first NCAA team championship. Wilder remains the only Badger to win an NCAA vault crowt is one of only three men—javelin thrower Bob Ray and high jumper Pat Matzdorf are the others—to win a field event in the field event in the NCAA outdoor meet.

BADGER BIG TEN FINISHES...

Football: 4th
coached by J.R. Richards

Cross Country: 3rd
coached by Meade Burke

Basketball: 2nd (tie)
coached by Walter Meanwell

Indoor Track: 2nd
coached by Thomas Jones

Swimming: 2nd
coached by Joe Steinauer

Wrestling: 5th
coached by George Hitchcook

Baseball: 3rd
coached by Guy Lowman

Golf: 3rd
(no coach)

Gymnastics: 2nd
coached by Fred Schlatter

Outdoor Track: 6th
coached by Thomas Jones

The Big Event

UW gridders go 5-1-1, fourth in the Big Ten

Wisconsin started well but finished not so well in the 1921 Big Ten football season. Coach J.R. Richards' team only allowed 13 points in its seven games, but 10 of them came in the final two games of the season.

The Badgers won their first five convincingly, blanking Lawrence 28–0 in the opener before allowing South Dakota State three points in a 28–3 win. Shutouts of Big Ten opponents Northwestern (27–0), Illinois (20–0) and Minnesota (35–0) followed.

But Michigan and Wisconsin tied at 7–7 in the penultimate game before the Badgers lost a 3–0 heartbreaker to Chicago in the season finale.

Four UW players earned all-America honors, with center George Bunge a third-team choice of International News Service; back Alvah Elliott a second-team pick by Walter Eckersall; tackle R.H. Brumm a second unit Consolidated Press selection; and tackle Jimmy Brader a third-team choice by Football World.

WISCONSIN TIMELINE

1922: The Lincoln Memorial in Washington was dedicated.

The Big Ten established the office of Commissioner of Athletics and elected Maj. John L. Griffith to the post.

BADGER BIG TEN FINISHES...

Football: 4th
coached by J.R. Richards

Cross Country: 2nd
coached by Meade Burke

Basketball: 1st (tie)
coached by Walter Meanwell

Indoor Track: 8th
coached by Thomas Jones

Swimming: 3rd
coached by Joe Steinauer

Baseball: 4th
coached by Guy Lowman

Golf: 3rd
(no coach)

Gymnastics: 1st
coached by Frank Leitz

Outdoor Track: 3rd
coached by Thomas Jones

The Big Event

Wisconsin wins its last gymnastics title

The Badgers scored 1,114 points to win the 1923 Big Ten gymnastics championship under the direction of one-year coach Frank Leitz. It was Wisconsin's eighth and last title in the sport.

No other records exist from that year's meet in Big Ten or Wisconsin archives. When Wisconsin dropped the sport almost 70 years later, the Badgers showed an all-time list of 21 individual event champions and five all-around winners to go with their eight team titles.

WISCONSIN TIMELINE

1923: The tomb of King Tut was opened by archeologists in Egypt's Valley of the Kings. The Big Ten raised the limit on football games from seven to eight.

1923–24

BADGER BIG TEN FINISHES...

Football: 7th
coached by Jack Ryan

Cross Country: 3rd
coached by Meade Burke

Basketball: 1st (tie)
coached by Walter Meanwell

Indoor Track: 8th
coached by Thomas Jones

Swimming: 5th
coached by Joe Steinauer

Baseball: 3rd
coached by Guy Lowman

Golf: 4th
(no coach)

Gymnastics: 4th
coached by Fred Schlatter

Outdoor Track: 5th
coached by Thomas Jones

The Big Event

Badgers lose 6–3 to Michigan in wild game

Leading mighty Michigan 3–0 before 20,000 fans at Camp Randall Field, Wisconsin was on the verge of salvaging its 1923 football season. Coach Jack Ryan's first Wisconsin football team had opened the 1923 season in fine fashion, winning three straight games. But a scoreless tie with Minnesota and a 10–0 loss at Illinois had put the Badgers on downward spiral.

What some called "the biggest robbery ever pulled off in Madison" changed everything and gave the Wolverines a 6–3 win and share of the Big Ten title. Wisconsin had punted and Michigan quarterback and safety Tod Rockwell had returned the ball about 20 yards before being tackled by two Badgers near the sidelines at midfield.

Rockwell remained on the ground for several seconds before he got up and walked nonchalantly out of a group of players who had gathered. He then sprinted madly for the end zone, with all watching stupefied.

The official judgment, from referee Walter Eckersall, was that he had not blown his whistle to stop the play and that Colonel Mumma, the field judge, had ruled that forward progress had not been stopped. The touchdown was upheld while Ryan, the Wisconsin bench and the UW fans went into a "mass seizure," as accounts described it.

Eckersall needed an escort of Wisconsin players to leave the field safely and over the following days, in his other role as the *Chicago Tribune's* football writer, defended his decision again and again.

WISCONSIN TIMELINE

1924: Congress granted citizenship to all American Indians.

The UW basketball team tied for the Big Ten championship with an 8–4 mark. Coach Walter Meanwell's Badgers were 11–5 overall, with the rare tie a triple-overtime 25–25 deadlock at home against DePauw.

WISCONSIN HEADLINER

MARTIN P. "MARTY"
BELOW
FOOTBALL

No less an authority than Red Grange said that Marty Below "was the greatest lineman I ever played against." It was high praise indeed for the Oshkosh native, who had been a football and basketball star and captain at Oshkosh High School. He served with the U.S. Marine Corps in World War I and then enrolled at Oshkosh State Teachers College, where he played on championship football and basketball teams. Below transferred to Wisconsin in 1922 and promptly became a first-team all-Big Ten pick in 1922 and 1923 on Badger teams that went 7–5–2. In 1923, Below captained the Badgers and earned all-America honors as a lineman. He was named to the National Football Foundation Hall of Fame in 1988 and to the UW Athletic Hall of Fame in 1992.

LEADING THE WAY

Guy Lowman
Baseball, Basketball and Football Coach

It was only fitting that a three-sport winner in college should have become a three-sport coach. That was Guy Lowman's unique resume at Wisconsin, where he served variously as coach of the baseball, basketball and football teams as well as director of the professional course in physical education from 1917–43. Lowman, a native of Griswold, Iowa, attended Iowa State Teachers, Drake University and the Springfield (Mass.) School of Physical Education. Prior to his arrival in Madison in 1917, Lowman made basketball, baseball and football coaching stops from 1906 at Warrensburg (Missouri) Normal, Missouri, Alabama and Indiana. He coached the UW football team to a 3–3 season in 1918; the Badger basketball teams of 1918–20, winning the Big Ten title in 1920; and Wisconsin baseball teams in 1918 and again from 1921–32, capturing the Conference championship in 1930. Lowman directed the department of physical education for 26 years until his death in Madison at age 66 in 1943. The varsity baseball field on Walnut Avenue near Lake Mendota was named in his honor in 1952.

LEADING THE WAY

Edward H. Templin
Wrestling

Ed Templin was one of Wisconsin's first wrestling stars, winning major "W" awards in 1921, 1922 and 1923. The Baraboo native wrestled as a middleweight for the Badgers, placing second in the 1922 Big Ten meet at 158 lbs. and also taking runner-up honors in 1923 at 175 lbs. He served as the Badgers' team captain as a senior. Templin was inducted into the UW Athletic Hall of Fame in 1995.

A W FIRST

Gage becomes first "SID"

Les Gage became the first sports information director, commonly called the "SID," at Wisconsin in 1923 and served six years as publicist for Badger teams. Gage, along with contemporaries Mike Tobin of Illinois, Jim Hassleman of Michigan State, Eric Wilson at Iowa and Walter Paulison at Northwestern, was one of the pioneers in a profession that has become an integral element of intercollegiate athletics.

BADGER BIG TEN FINISHES...

Football: 10th
coached by Jack Ryan

Cross Country: 1st
coached by Meade Burke

Basketball: 9th
coached by Walter Meanwell

Indoor Track: 2nd
coached by Thomas Jones

Swimming: 2nd
coached by Joe Steinauer

Wrestling: 3rd
coached by George Hitchcook

Baseball: 8th
coached by Guy Lowman

Golf: 5th
(no coach)

Outdoor Track: 2nd
coached by Thomas Jones

The Big Event

First Midwest football broadcast: Wisconsin vs. Michigan

It was a year of firsts for Big Ten football, and Wisconsin played a prominent role in one of them. The Badgers lost 21–0 at Michigan in the first college football game broadcast in the Midwest. WWJ Radio's Ty Tyson and Doc Holland called the action at Michigan Stadium.

In that same year, the *Chicago Tribune* began presenting its "Silver Football" *award* to the football player voted the Big Ten's most valuable player by coaches and media. Red Grange of Illinois was the first winner. It's an award still given today.

WISCONSIN TIMELINE

1925: Tennessee biology teacher John Scopes was arrested for teaching the theory of evolution in violation of a state statute.

It was a year of contrast for the Badgers, with three of the "major" sports, football, baseball and basketball, finishing 10th, eighth and ninth, respectively, in the Big Ten. The other big sport, track, was second both indoors and outdoors while cross country (second), swimming (second) and wrestling (third) upheld UW honor.

1925—26

BADGER BIG TEN FINISHES...

Football: 2nd (tie)
coached by George Little

Cross Country: 1st
coached by Meade Burke

Basketball: 8th (tie)
coached by Walter Meanwell

Indoor track: 3rd
coached by Thomas Jones

Wrestling: 3rd
coached by George Hitchcock

Baseball: 2nd
coached by Guy Lowman

Golf: 5th
coached by Joe Steinauer

Outdoor Track: 5th
coached by Thomas Jones

The Big Event

Badgers win Big Ten cross country title

Led by Victor Chapman, Wisconsin won its second straight Big Ten cross country championship at Ann Arbor, Michigan. It was the Badgers' seventh Conference title. Chapman covered the five-mile course in 26:12 to become the UW's seventh individual champion.

Coach Tom Jones's team scored 39 points to Ohio State's 75 and Illinois's 78. Chapman was awarded the Bill Goldie Trophy as Wisconsin's most valuable runner.

WISCONSIN TIMELINE

1926: The National Broadcasting Company made its debut as a radio network of 24 stations.

The first Big Ten championships in fencing, gymnastics and wrestling were held at Purdue.

Wisconsin played its first international game in ice hockey, losing 7–0 to the University of Manitoba.

WISCONSIN HEADLINER

CHARLES MCGINNIS
TRACK AND FIELD

Charles McGinnis, who enrolled at Wisconsin out of Kansas City, Missouri, won six Big Ten titles during his three-year Badger career. McGinnis claimed the Conference high jump title at 6'2" as a sophomore and then in 1926 earned all-American honors in the event, placing sixth in the NCAA meet. The next two seasons would be his best, however, as McGinnis won the 60-yard high hurdles (7.6 seconds), the high jump (6'5") and the pole vault (12'9") as Wisconsin won its first Big Ten indoor track title in 1927. Outdoors, it was more of the same as McGinnis captured wins in the 120-yard high hurdles (15.2 seconds) and in the pole vault (13'3"). He capped his career with a bronze medal in the 1928 Olympics in Paris by clearing 12'11" in the pole vault. McGinnis was inducted into the UW Athletic Hall of Fame in 1993.

LEADING THE WAY

George E. Little
Football Coach, Athletic Director

In seven years as director of athletics at Wisconsin, George E. Little proved a doer and a builder. In 1925, Little took over a UW football team that had won only one of 12 Big Ten games over the three previous seasons and transformed Wisconsin into a winner. Only a loss to Michigan and tie with Minnesota marred the '25 season, when the Badgers finished 6–1–1 and ended second in the Big Ten. Little's two teams were 11–3–2. After the '26 season Little devoted full-time to his director's duties and began upgrading Wisconsin's facilities. The Wisconsin Fieldhouse was built during his tenure. Additional thousands of seats were added to Camp Randall Stadium. Practice fields for various sports were developed and intramurals became an important part of the UW's physical activity program. Little left Wisconsin in 1932 to become athletic director at Rutgers. He was later named to the National College Football Hall of Fame.

THE LIST

WISCONSIN'S MEN'S CONFERENCE MEDAL OF HONOR WINNERS

1920	Anthony G. Zulfer
1921	Allan C. Davey
1922	George Bunge
1923	Gustave K. Tebell
1924	Harold J. Bentson
1925	Lloyd Vallely
1926	Stephen H. Pulaski
1927	Jefferson DeMent Burrus
1928	Louis Behr
1929	Teodore A. Thelander

A  FIRST

Badgers, Hawks in "Snow Bowl"

The modern-era "Ice Bowl" game in Green Bay between the Packers and Dallas Cowboys in 1967, was pre-dated by Wisconsin and Iowa in 1925 in a "snow bowl" of sorts in Madison. The Badgers won the early November game, 6–0, but the most interesting statistic was the 34 fumbles, 18 in the first quarter alone. The teams had an excuse: blowing snow obliterated the sidelines and every yardline marker.

1926—27

BADGER BIG TEN FINISHES...

Football: 5th
coached by George Little

Cross Country: 1st
coached by Thomas Jones

Basketball: 4th (tie)
coached by Walter Meanwell

Indoor Track: 1st
coached by Thomas Jones

Swimming: 4th
coached by Joe Steinauer

Baseball: 7th
coached by Guy Lowman

Golf: 5th
coached by George Levis

Gymnastics: 2nd
coached by Arpad Masley

Outdoor Track: 3rd
coached by Thomas Jones

The Big Event

Wisconsin wins harrier crown again

Coach Tom Jones's Badger harriers won the third in a string of four straight Big Ten Conference cross country championships in 1926.

Running at Minneapolis, Wisconsin scored 34 points to easily outdistance Ohio State (63) and Iowa (65). Defending champion Victor Chapman of Wisconsin lost his title to Iowa's Jock Hunn, but his fourth-place effort still paced the Badgers to their eighth overall Conference triumph.

WISCONSIN TIMELINE

1927: Charles Lindbergh reached Paris in his monoplane, the Spirit of St. Louis, completing the first solo trans-Atlantic flight.

The Conference ruled that athletes should not engage in athletic writing nor use their names for commercial advertising.

ROLLAND BARNUM
FOOTBALL,
BASKETBALL, BASEBALL

Rolland Barnum, a native of Evansville, Wisconsin, was a nine-time letterwinner for the Badgers in football, basketball and baseball from 1924–27. A full-back and punter in football and a catcher and outfielder in baseball, Barnum most distinguished himself in basketball. He was an all-Big Ten choice at guard in 1926 and captained the 1926–27 Badger cagers. Following college, he played basketball as one of the original Oshkosh All-Stars and also played semi-pro baseball with the Madison Blues. He officiated both Big Ten basketball and football, the latter for 21 years, during which Barnum officiated the 1958 College All-Star Game and the 1952 Rose Bowl. A member of the Madison Pen and Mike Club-Bowman Sports Foundation Hall of Fame, Barnum was named a charter member of the UW Athletic Hall of Fame in 1991.

A W FIRST

McGinnis a winner on track and in field

Charles McGinnis became the first Wisconsin track and field athlete to win Big Ten Conference championships in the same meet on both the track and in the field. McGinnis won the 60-yard high hurdles in 7.6 seconds in the indoor meet at Evanston and also claimed titles in the high jump (6'5") and pole vault (12'9"), leading Tom Jones's team to the championship. McGinnis just about repeated the feat in the outdoor championships in Madison, with the Badgers finishing third in the team battle. He won the 120-yard high hurdles in 15.2 and tied for the pole vault title at 13'3". The UW accomplishment would not be equaled until 1994 when freshman Reggie Torian won the 55-meter high hurdles and the long jump in the Conference indoor meet at Ann Arbor.

THE LIST

WISCONSIN SWIMMING COACHES

In the 103-year history of men's swimming at Wisconsin, only nine men have served as coach. Two— Joe Steinauer and Jack Pettinger— coached Badger swimmers for 56 seasons.

They are:

1911–13	Chauncey Hyatt
1913–19	Harry Hindman
1919–51	Joe Steinauer
1951–69	John Hickman
1969–93	Jack Pettinger
1993–94	John Davey
1994–1999	Nick Hansen
1999–2011	Eric Hansen
2011–Present	Whitney Hite

A W FIRST

Kratz wins NCAA swimming title

Winston Kratz became Wisconsin's first NCAA swimming champion in 1927, winning the 200-yard breaststroke in 2:46.3 in the third national collegiate swim meet. He also was named the Badgers' first swimming all-American. Kratz also won the now-discontinued event in 2:43.3 in the Big Ten meet that year for Coach Joe Steinauer's team, which placed a distant fourth. Kratz is a member of the Wisconsin swimming program's Hall of Fame. Fred Westphal, who won the 50–freestyle in 1959, is the only other Badger male to have previously won an NCAA swim title.

BADGER BIG TEN FINISHES...

Football: 9th (tie)
coached by Glenn Thistlethwaite

Cross Country: 1st
coached by Thomas Jones

Basketball: 3rd (tie)
coached by Walter Meanwell

Indoor Track: 3rd (tie)
coached by Thomas Jones

Wrestling: 2nd
coached by George Hitchcock, (5th, NCAA)

Baseball: 3rd
coached by Guy Lowman

Gymnastic: 2nd
coached by Arpad Masley

Outdoor Track: 6th
coached by Thomas Jones

The Big Event

UW wins in Big Ten cross country

It truly was a golden era for Wisconsin cross country teams. Coach Tom Jones's Badgers pulled off the "four-peat" in 1927, scoring 51 points in the Big Ten meet at Ann Arbor for their fourth consecutive Conference victory.

John Zola, who ran 24:57 for the five-mile course, became Wisconsin's eighth individual Conference titlist. It was the tightest of the UW's four victories from 1924-27; Illinois was close behind with 57 points.

WISCONSIN TIMELINE

1928: The first respirator, or iron lung, was used at a Boston hospital.

Construction began on the Wisconsin Field House.

Wisconsin was 10–7–2 in hockey, its only 10–win season of the pre-modern era.

1928-29

BADGER BIG TEN FINISHES...

Football: 2nd
coached by Glenn Thistlethwaite

Ctoss Country: 4th
coached by Thomas Jones

Basketball: 1st (tie)
coached by Walter Meanwell

Indoor Track: 3rd
coached by Thomas Jones

Swimming: 4th
coached by George Hitchcock

Baseball: 3rd
coached by Guy Lowman

Golf: 5th
coached by George Levis

Gymnastics: 3rd
coached by Arpad Masley

Outdoor Track: 7th
coached by Thomas Jones

The Big Event

Badgers post first 10-win season in ice hockey

Coach John Farquhar's Badger hockey team recorded its first 10-win season, going 11–7–2 despite a season-ending four-game winless string. It marked a sharp turnaround from the UW's initial season in 1921–22, when the Badgers were 0–8, and from the next six seasons, when the UW only had one winning campaign.

Wisconsin opened the season with a 1–1 tie against Houghton School of Mines (to become future WCHA rival Michigan Tech) and then rattled off five straight wins over the Marquette (Michigan) Owls, the Wausau Hockey Club, the Chicago Athletic Assn. and the North Dakota Aggies (twice).

The Badgers didn't fare as well against Big Ten and Western Intercollegiate Hockey League (WIHL) foes Michigan and Minnesota. The UW was 1–2–1 against the Wolverines and 1–3 against the Gophers. Farquhar had a 21–20–7 record in his three seasons as coach.

WISCONSIN TIMELINE

1929: Pluto was discovered by astronomer Clyde Tombaugh as he worked in the Lowell Observatory in Flagstaff, Arizona.

The University of Iowa was suspended from Conference membership due to infractions of an athletic nature.

WISCONSIN HEADLINER

LLOYD LARSON
FOOTBALL, BASEBALL

A later generation may have known Lloyd Larson as "Mr. Wisconsin," the long-time sports editor of the *Milwaukee Sentinel*, where he spent 50 years chronicling pro and college sports and five times was named Wisconsin "Sports Writer of the Year." But his time as a Badger came well before his induction into the UW Athletic Hall of Fame in 1993. Larson enrolled at the UW out of Milwaukee South Division High School, where he was an all-city quarterback. He won "W" awards in football in 1924 and 1925 and in baseball in 1925, 1926 and 1927, captaining the latter team. Larson also became a Big Ten football and basketball official and officiated the 1951 Rose Bowl game. Always an active participant in things related to the UW, Larson served as president of the National W Club (1959) and was named that group's "Man of the Year" in 1974. He also served as 1962–63 president of the Wisconsin Alumni Association, from which he received the Distinguished Service award in 1967.

LEADING THE WAY

Glenn Thistlewaite
Football Coach

One of Wisconsin's top coaches in the 1920s was football coach Glenn Thistlewaite. His .611 winning percentage in his five seasons as Badger mentor still ranks him eighth on the all–time UW list. His five seasons in Madison produced a 26–16–3 record, including a 7–1–1 mark and runner-up finish in the Big Ten (3–1–1) in 1928. All-Americans he coached at Wisconsin included tackle Rube Wagner, tackle Milo Lubratovich and guard Greg Kabat. Thistlewaite came to Madison after five years at Northwestern (23–16–1), where he guided the Wildcats to two Big Ten titles. Prior to that, he had spent nine years at Oak Park (Illinois) High School, where he compiled a 78–9 record. Thistlewaite was a 1908 graduate of Earlham (Indiana) College, where he captained the football team, played baseball and competed in track. He began his coaching career with a one-year stint at Illinois College before returning to Earlham, where his teams went 22–7–1 in four seasons before Thistlewaite left for Oak Park.

THE LIST

CONSENSUS FOOTBALL ALL-AMERICANS

Year	Player	Year	Player
1912	Robert "Butts" Butler, T	1981	Tim Krumrie, NG
		1994	Cory Raymer, C
1913	Ray "Tubby" Keeler, G	1998	*Tom Burke, DE
		1998	Aaron Gibson, T
1915	Howard "Cub" Buck, T	1999	*Ron Dayne, RB
		1999	*Chris McIntosh, T
1919	Charles Carpenter, C	2000	Jamar Fletcher, DB
1920	Ralph Scott, T	2004	Erasmus James, DE
1923	Marty Below, T	2006	*Joe Thomas, T
1930	Milo Lubratovich, T	2010	*Gabe Carimi, T
1942	*Dave Schreiner, E	2010	Lance Kendricks, TE
1954	*Alan Ameche, RB	2011	Montee Ball, RB
1959	*Dan Lanphear, T	2012	Montee Ball, RB
1962	Pat Richter, E		
1975	Dennis Lick, T		*Unanimous Consensus All-Americans

A W FIRST

Sprachen ze English?

Multilingualism is not something generally associated with football, but there was a new twist to the announcing in the season-ending Wisconsin-Minnesota game on November 24, 1928, in Madison. The UW announcer called the game in five languages—Norwegian, Swedish, German, Yiddish and Chinese—and, presumably, English. A 19–19 tie with Purdue and a 6–0 loss to Gophers were the only blemishes on Wisconsin's 7–1–1 season. In any language, the loss was still a loss.

BADGER BIG TEN FINISHES...

Football: 10th
coached by Glenn Thistlethwaite

Cross Country: 2nd
Coached by Thomas Jones

Basketball: 2nd
coached by Walter Meanwell

Indoor Track: 1st
coached by Thomas Jones

Swimming: 5th
coached by Joe Steinauer

Baseball: 1st
coached by Guy Lowman

Golf: 5th
coached by George Levis

Outdoor Track: 3rd
coached by Thomas Jones

The Big Event

Badger nine wins Big Ten title; trackmen take indoor crown

The stock market had crashed in October, 1929, but Wisconsin fortunes in two sports rose in 1930. Coach Guy Lowman's Badgers won their first Big Ten baseball championship in 18 years in 1930, posting a 9–1 Big Ten mark to edge Illinois by a game.

It was the third title ever for the UW. Pacing the UW were Moe Winer, the shortstop and team captain, and pitchers Nello Pacetti and Art Sommerfield.

In track, another Tom Jones-coached team won its second Conference indoor track championship in four seasons, scoring 21 points in the meet at Minneapolis to hold off Illinois (18) and Indiana (17).

Three Badgers won their events: Bill Henke in the 440-yard dash in 51.1; Sammy Behrinthe shot put with a throw of 46'1"; and Ted Shaw in the high jump with a leap of 6'1".

WISCONSIN TIMELINE

1930: American novelist Sinclair Lewis won the Nobel prize in literature. Iowa resumed its membership in the Conference.

The Wisconsin Field House was dedicated on December 18 as the Badger cagers defeat Penn 25–12.

WISCONSIN HEADLINER

JOHN F. (BOBBY) POSER
BASEBALL, BASKETBALL

Bobby Poser was a two-sport star for Wisconsin in the early 1930s, earning "W" awards in baseball (1930–31) and basketball (1931–33). The Columbus, Wisconsin, native earned both bachelor's and medical degrees from Wisconsin. As a pitcher and outfielder on the 1930 Big Ten Championship team, Poser hit .391 to lead the team in hitting en route to all-Conference honors. He captained the basketball team as a senior in 1932–33. Following graduation, he coached the 1935 and 1936 Wisconsin baseball team and also pitched for the Chicago White Sox and the St. Louis Browns. In 1933, while playing for Des Moines, Poser had nine RBIs to set a single game Western Minor League record. He also served as president of the National "W" Club in 1957–58. Poser was inducted into the UW Athletics Hall of Fame in 1996.

A W FIRST

Behr throws to three titles

Sammy Behr claimed a place among Wisconsin's great shot putters with his performances in 1929, 1930 and 1931, becoming the first UW weightman to win three Big Ten titles in the event. Not even the legendary Arlie Mucks, Sr., a two-time Olympian in the discus, won three shot titles. Behr claimed his first win indoors in '29, putting the shot 45'7 1/2", followed in 1930 with a 46'1" throw and then ended his indoor career with a 48'9" heave in '31. He also won outdoor titles in Big Ten meets in 1929 and 1930. Not until Jeff Braun won four Conference shot titles from 1976–79 would a Badger match the feat.

THE LIST

TRACK AND FIELD OLYMPIANS

1904	Emil Breikreutz, 800 meters
	George Poage, 400-meter hurdles
	Frank Waller, 400 meters
1912	Arlie Mucks, Sr., discus
1916	Arlie Mucks, Sr., discus
1920	Arlie Schardt, 3,000-meter relay
1928	Charles McGinnis, pole vault
1948	Don Gehrmann, 1,500 meters
	Tom Jones, coach
	Lloyd LaBeach, 100 & 200 (Panama)
1964	Charles "Rut" Walter, coach
1972	Mike Manley, steeplechase
1980	Steve Lacy, 1,500 meters
1984	Steve Lacy, 1,500 meters
	Cindy Bremser, 1,500 meters
1992	Suzy Favor Hamilton, 1,500 meters
1996	Suzy Favor Hamilton, 800 meters
	Kathy Butler, 5,000 meters (Canada)
	Maxwell Seales, 4x400 relay (St. Lucia)
2000	Pascal Dobert, 3000-meter steeplechase
2008	Matt Tegenkamp, 5,000 meters
2012	Matt Tegenkamp, 10,000 meters
2012	Mohammed Ahmed, 10,000 meters (Canada)
	Evan Jager, 3,000-meter steeplechase

THE LIST

WISCONSIN'S FENCING COACHES

1911
Dr. Walter E. Meanwell

1912–17
H.D. MacChesney

1920–26
Fred Schlatter

1927–51
Arpad L. Masley

1952–72
Archie Simonson

1973–90
Tony Gillham

1990–91
Jerzy Radz

BADGER BIG TEN FINISHES...

Football: 4th (tie)
coached by Glenn Thistlethwaite

Cross Country: 2nd
coached by Thomas Jones

Basketball: 7th (tie)
coached by Walter Meanwell

Indoor Track: 4th
coached by Thomas Jones

Baseball: 5th (tie)
coached by Guy Lowman

Golf: 5th
coached by George Levis

Gymnastic: 2nd
coached by Arpad Masley

Outdoor Track: 1st
coached by Thomas Jones, (6th, NCAA)

The Big Event

UW Field House opens

Discussions of replacing the antiquated Red Gym on Langdon Street began several years before the UW Field House actually opened in 1930. It was not, however, until athletics director George Little, who came to Wisconsin from the University of Michigan in 1925, made upgrading the UW's athletic facilities a top priority that discussions became reality.

By 1927, Little, who served for two years as the Badger football coach, produced a detailed master plan for the general renewal of several facilities, including what would become the UW Field House.

Critics, who felt the proposed facility's seating capacity in excess of 8,000 was far too large, tabbed the project "Little's Folly." Nonetheless, state architect Arthur Peabody, along with Paul Cret of the Laird and Cret firm, moved forward with their design, which reflected the strong influences of Lathrop Hall, another UW project created by Laird and Cret with Peabody's assistance some 20 years earlier.

Groundbreaking for the project, located at the open end of the Camp Randall horseshoe, took place on September 26, 1929, and the official building dedication occurred a little more than a year later when the Badger basketball team defeated Pennsylvania 25–12 on December 18, 1930, in front of a sellout crowd of 8,600.

The Field House, one of the last buildings constructed before the stock market crash of 1929, cost $453,756, with $51,000 to be repaid by the Division of Intercollegiate Athletics through revenues and private gifts over the following 10 years. The UW had established a facility that was comparable in merit to any of its kind in the country.

WISCONSIN TIMELINE

1931: "The Star Spangled Banner" became the national anthem.

Coach Glen Thistlewaite's Wisconsin football team posted a 6–2–1 record, winning all six of its games at home, four by shutouts, but tied Ohio State and lost to Purdue and Northwestern on the road.

BADGER BIG TEN FINISHES...

Football: 6th
coached by Glenn Thistlethwaite

Cross Country: 2nd
coached by Thomas Jones

Basketball: 8th (tie)
coached by Walter Meanwell

Indoor Track: 5th
coached by Thomas Jones

Baseball: 3rd (tie)
coached by Guy Lowman

Golf: 7th
coached by Joe Steinauer

Outdoor Track: 7th
coached by Thomas Jones

The Big Event

Badgers struggle through so-so seasons

No Badger teams won Big Ten championships during the 1931–32 campaign. Wisconsin finished 5–4–1, 3–3 in the Conference, in football coach Glenn Thistlewaite's last year at the reins while Tom Jones's harriers placed second to Indiana, which was in the middle of a six-year championship run.

The Badger cagers didn't fare any better, chalking up an 8–10 overall mark and 3–9 Big Ten eighth–place finish. The UW golfers finished seventh in the Conference tourney while the baseball Badgers tied for third in the Big Ten with a 6–4 slate.

In the 1932 track meets, Wisconsin finished fifth indoors and dropped to seventh in the Big Ten after winning the Conference the previous season. High jumper Robert Murphy was the Badgers' sole indoor champ while teammate Ted Shaw claimed the outdoor high jump crown for the UW's only win.

WISCONSIN TIMELINE

1932: The Summer Olympics opened in Los Angeles.

Art Thomsen took over as Wisconsin hockey coach and led the team until the 1935 season.

1932—33

BADGER BIG TEN FINISHES...

Football: 3rd
coached by Clarence Spears

Cross Country: 5th
coached by Thomas Jones

Basketball: 8th
coached by Walter Meanwell

Indoor Track: 6th (tie)
coached by Thomas Jones

Swimming: 7th
coached by Joe Steinauer

Baseball: 7th
coached by Irv Uteritz

Golf: 5th
coached by Joe Steinauer

Outdoor Track: 8th
coached by Thomas Jones

The Big Event

Wisconsin begins boxing program

Over the course of its 28-year history, the NCAA boxing scene was dominated by Wisconsin, with a 134–28–18 overall dual mark, eight NCAA team titles and 38 individual championships.

Two men deserve most of the credit for this splendid record. They were George F. Downer, athletic publicity director at the UW until his death in 1941, and John J. Walsh, a Madison attorney, who coached the team for 23 years.

Downer is known as the "father" of intercollegiate boxing at Wisconsin. He was the first to see the possibilities of boxing as a successful intercollegiate sport at the UW and he turned his vision into reality by organizing the first university team in 1933.

Downer's first team fought its first match with St. Thomas College of St. Paul, Minn, in Madison on March 21, 1933. Walsh was the St. Thomas coach and one of the members of that team that battled the Badgers to a 4–4 draw. The impression Walsh made on Downer that day was such that, through the latter's efforts, Walsh was hired as Wisconsin's coach in 1934.

The George F. Downer Award became the most coveted honor a Wisconsin boxer could attain. It was presented to the boxer coming closest, in the coach's estimation, to Downer's ideals of a champion, including scholarship, sportsmanship, boxing ability and competitive spirit.

WISCONSIN TIMELINE

1933: The first motion picture drive-in opened in Camden, New Jersey.

Because of the Great Depression, hockey is dropped as an intercollegiate sport, but the Badgers continued to play until 1935.

WISCONSIN HEADLINER

WALTER F. (MICKEY) MCGUIRE
FOOTBALL

Walter F. (Mickey) McGuire lettered for Wisconsin football teams of the early 1930s that posted a 17–7–3 record from 1930–32, including third place in the Big Ten and a 6–1–1 overall mark in 1932, McGuire's senior season. The Honolulu native, who had a stellar prep career at Honolulu High School, led the 1932 Badgers with 36 points and scored all three Wisconsin touchdowns in the UW's 20–13 win over Minnesota. He was also named the Big Ten's most valuable player and was the top punter in the Conference with a 43.0 average. After graduation, McGuire went on to a noteworthy career in business, athletics and government. For 30 years, he was managing director of the Hula Bowl and past president and director of Honolulu Stadium. McGuire also served as managing director of the 1979 NFL Pro Bowl Game. He served five terms in the Territorial House of Representatives and was a special assistant to the president of United Airlines. He was inducted into the UW Athletics Hall of Fame in 1996.

WISCONSIN HEADLINER

MILO LUBRATOVICH
FOOTBALL

Three–time letterwinner Milo Lubra-trovich starred at tackle for the Badgers in 1930, earning all–America honors two years after he broke his leg as a sophomore in a game against Alabama. By his senior season, Lubratovich had rebounded nicely. He had become a consensus all-America end and played in the annual East-West Game. He received all-America mention from 10 different authorities, including the Newspaper Enterprise Association, United Press and Hearst. Lubratovich played professional baseball in the Brooklyn Dodger organization from 1931–35.

WISCONSIN HEADLINER

GREGORY KABAT
FOOTBALL, TRACK AND FIELD

Gregory Kabat was an all-Big Ten lineman for Wisconsin football teams that piled a 17–7–3 record from 1930–32. He also served as the Badgers' captain in his senior season. The Milwaukee native earned major "W" awards three times in football and twice in track. He won the discus throw at the 1931 Big Ten outdoor track and field championships with a throw of 150'10 1/2" and also earned all-America honors that year in the event. Kabat was inducted into the UW Athletic Hall of Fame in 1995.

WISCONSIN HEADLINER

TED SHAW
TRACK AND FIELD

Two-time Big Ten high jump champion Ted Shaw was a mainstay of Coach Tom Jones Wisconsin track teams of the early 1930s. The native of River Forest, Illinois, who prepped at Elgin Academy where he starred in football and track, held the national high school record in his specialty during his junior and senior years. As a UW sophomore in 1930, Shaw set a national record of 6'6 3/16". A three-time "W" award-winner, he was the Wisconsin track captain in 1932 and later that year competed in the U.S. Olympic trials in Los Angeles.

1933—34

BADGER BIG TEN FINISHES...

Football: 8th (tie)
coached by Clarence Spears

Cross Country: 2nd
coached by Thomas Jones

Basketball: 2nd (tie)
coached by Walter Meanwell

Indoor Track: 9th
coached by Thomas Jones

Baseball: 3rd (tie)
coached by Irv Uteritz

Golf: 9th
coached by Joe Steinauer

Tennis: 6th
coached by Arpad Masley

Outdoor Track: 5th (tie)
coached by Thomas Jones

The Big Event

Badgers rebound to second in Big Ten basketball

After three straight second division finishes in the Big Ten, Wisconsin's 1933–34 basketball team posted a 14–6 overall record and 8–4 Big Ten mark, good for second in the Conference. The season marked the end of Walter Meanwell's basketball coaching career at the UW, a tenure that had begun with the 1911–12 season and been continuous save for his three–year absence during World War I.

The Badgers, who had ended the 1932–33 campaign with nine losses in its final 10 games, did an about-face to start the next campaign. Wisconsin won its first five games in December, slumped with losses at Marquette, Illinois and Iowa right after the first of the year, but then won seven of its last eight.

That finish set the table for the Badgers' return to the top of the Big Ten the following season as co-champs under Meanwell's successor, Harold "Bud" Foster. Rolf Poser paced the Badgers, earning the first of his two all-Big Ten mentions.

WISCONSIN TIMELINE

1934: Elzire Dionne gave birth to quintuplets in a farmhouse near Callander, Ontario.

Harold "Bud" Foster took over as men's basketball coach.

Wisconsin placed ninth in the Big Ten indoor track meet, its worst finish to date under Coach Tom Jones, but the Badgers rebounded to take fifth outdoors.

1934-35

BADGER BIG TEN FINISHES...

Football: 5th (tie)
coached by Clarence Spears

Cross Country: 1st (tie)
coached by Thomas Jones

Basketball: 1st (tie)
coached by Harold Foster

Indoor Track: 3rd
coached by Thomas Jones

Swimming: 7th
coached by Joe Steinauer

Wrestling: 8th
coached by Paul Gerling

Baseball: 6th
coached by Robert Poser

Golf: 4th
coached by Joe Steinauer

Tennis: 8th
coached by Arpad Masley

Outdoor Track: 3rd
coached by Thomas Jones

The Big Event

Men's basketball shares Big Ten title

Wisconsin's 1934–35 men's basketball team was long on experienced players—in fact, the entire team returned from the previous season's squad—but short on experienced coaching. In fact, it was to be Bud Foster's first season guiding the Badgers, for whom he was an all-American in 1930.

With veterans such as Rolf "Chub" Poser, Gilly McDonald, Nick DeMark, Ed Stege, Bob Knake, Pete Preboski and Ray Hamann, Wisconsin was met with high expectations as the season began.

After losing a practice game to the school's freshman squad, the Badgers began the season with four straight wins before dropping back-to-back outings against Marquette and Pittsburgh. A win over Michigan State (not yet a Big Ten member) concluded the non-conference portion of the season.

The Conference campaign began with a 19–18 loss to Purdue. Wisconsin rebounded, however, with a stellar defensive effort in a 12–9 win over then-Conference favorite Northwestern. Two more wins followed before the Wildcats got their revenge with a 36–31 victory over the Badgers. That loss left Wisconsin with a 3–2 mark in league play.

Wisconsin, however, went on to win six of its final seven games, including a 37–27 overtime thriller over Indiana at the UW Field House. The Badgers finished the season tied with Illinois and Purdue for the Big Ten title. Poser and McDonald were named all-Big Ten.

WISCONSIN TIMELINE

1935: The first automatic parking meters were installed in Oklahoma City.

The Big Ten adopted regulations governing broadcasting rights to home games.

The Badgers won the Big Ten basketball title with a 15–5 record under new head coach "Bud" Foster.

1935—36

BADGER BIG TEN FINISHES...

Football: 9th (tie)
coached by Clarence Spears

Cross Country: 3rd
coached by Thomas Jones

Basketball: 8th
coached by Harold Foster

Indoor Track: 2nd
coached by Thomas Jones

Baseball: 7th
coached by Robert Poser

Golf: 5th
coached by Joe Steinauer

Tennis: 4th
coached by William Kaeser

Outdoor Track: 4th
coached by Thomas Jones, (6th, NCAA)

The Big Event

Harry Stuhldreher hired as football coach

After four seasons under Clarence Spears daring which Wisconsin football fortunes had declined from a 6–1–1 mark to a 1–7 ninth–place Conference finish, Harry Stuhldreher was hired to resuscitate the UW program starting with the 1935 season.

As one of Notre Dame's famed "Four Horsemen," Stuhldreher had a name that resonated gridiron glory. In 13 years at the Badger helm, he never won a Big Ten title, but he restored some respect to the Wisconsin program. His best team, the 1942 unit, had an 8–1–1 record and finished second in the Conference at 4–1.

Three other Stuhldreher-coached teams posted winning records and his 45 career victories are fifth highest in Wisconsin football annals. Three of his players at Wisconsin—end Dave Schreiner (1941–42), fullback Marlin "Pat" Harder (1942) and quarterback Earl "Jug" Girard (1944)—earned first-team all-American honors.

WISCONSIN TIMELINE

1936: Jesse Owens won four gold medals in the Olympic Games in Berlin.

The Conference voted to accept a resolution by the University of Wisconsin that its faculty considers itself in control of athletic affairs.

Chuck Fenske won the NCAA 1,500–meter run in the NCAA track meet, beginning a legacy of Badger excellence in the 1,500 and mile.

WISCONSIN HEADLINER

JOHN GERLACH
BASEBALL

"Good field, good hit." That was John Gerlach, who starred at shortstop for Wisconsin baseball teams of the late 1930s. The Shullsburg, Wisconsin, native won three "W" awards in 1936, 1937 and 1938 and served as captain of the Badger nine his junior and senior seasons. His errorless play at shortstop was a key to the team's success; the Badgers were 44–27 in his three varsity years, with third-place Big Ten finishes in the latter two seasons. But Gerlach's hitting was no less remarkable as he batted .415 in 1936 and .320 in 1938. Gerlach saw action in the major leagues with the Chicago White Sox in 1938 and 1939. He served as a major with a pilot–troop carrier command group in World War II. Gerlach was named to the Madison Sports Hall of Fame in 1972 and inducted into the UW Athletic Hall of Fame in 1994.

WISCONSIN HEADLINER

ROLF "CHUB" POSER
BASKETBALL, BASEBALL

Two-time all-Big Ten guard Rolf Poser enrolled at the Madison campus out of Columbus, Wisconsin, in 1932 and eventually earned three major "W" awards each in basketball and baseball. Nicknamed "Chub," he served as captain of the 1933–34 cagers who placed second in the Big Ten. He was also captain and leading scorer on the 1934–35 unit that tied for the Big Ten title. Poser was named all-Conference for his junior and senior seasons and also was an All-Western pick at guard in 1934–35. He was the 1935 Wisconsin recipient of the Big Ten Medal of Honor for proficiency in scholarship and athletics. Poser was inducted into the UW Athletic Hall of Fame in 1993.

WISCONSIN HEADLINER

EDWARD "EDDIE" JANKOWSKI
FOOTBALL

Edward "Eddie" Jankowski was a standout fullback and linebacker on three Wisconsin teams of the mid–1930s. The Milwaukee native, out of Riverside High School, was the Badgers' MVP in 1935–36. He played in the East-West Shrine Game of 1936 and in the 1937 College All-Star Game. A first-round selection of the Green Bay Packers in the 1937 National Football League draft, Jankowski went on to a stellar professional career and eventually was named to the Packers' Hall of Fame. He was inducted into the UW Athletic Hall of Fame in 1992.

WISCONSIN HEADLINER

ROBERT FADNER
BOXING

Wisconsin boxer Bob Fadner made history with his NCAA title in 1936. The 125-lber. was the first winner in that particular weight class in the 1936 championship tournament at Charlottesville, Virginia. More important, however, is his place in Wisconsin boxing annals as the first of an NCAA-record 38 men who would win national collegiate finals bouts for the Badgers. Since the NCAA discontinued the sport after the 1960 championships, Wisconsin's hold on that record is secure.

BADGER BIG TEN FINISHES...

Football: 8th (tie)
coached by Harry Stuhldreher

Cross Country: 1st (tie)
coached by Thomas Jones

Basketball: 8th (tie)
coached by Harold Foster

Indoor Track: 3rd
coached by Thomas Jones

Swimming: 8th
coached by Joe Steinauer

Baseball: 3rd (tie)
coached by Lowell Douglas

Golf: 4th
coached by Joe Steinauer

Tennis: 4th (tie)
coached by William Kaeser

Outdoor Track: 5th
coached by Thomas Jones, (10th, NCAA)

The Big Event

Fenske wins NCAA mile run championship

Chuck Fenske, Wisconsin's "Monarch of the Mile," lived up to that nickname as he became the school's first NCAA champion on the track in 1937. He won the mile run in 4:13.9 in the national collegiate meet at Berkeley, California.

It was the second NCAA individual track and field title for the UW since the meet's inception in 1921; pole vaulter Lloyd Wilder tied for the victory in that first-ever meet. Fenske was a three-time Big Ten mile champion and at one time held world records in the 1,000-yard run (2:09.3) and three-quarter mile run (2:59.7).

WISCONSIN TIMELINE

1937: The Golden Gate Bridge across San Francisco Bay was opened.

Pole vaulter Al Haller successfully defended his Big Ten indoor and outdoor championships and became the Badgers' only four-time Conference pole vault champ.

BADGER BIG TEN FINISHES...

Football: 4th (tie)
coached by Harry Stuhldreher

Cross Country: 2nd
coached by Thomas Jones

Basketball: 7th
coached by Harold Foster

Indoor Track: 2nd
coached by Thomas Jones

Swimming: 7th
coached by Joe Steinauer

Wrestling: 4th
coached by George Martin

Baseball: 3rd (tie)
coached by Lowell Douglas

Golf: 6th
coached by Joe Steinauer

Tennis: 7th
coached by Roy Black

Outdoor Track: 2nd
coached by Thomas Jones, (4th, NCAA)

The Big Event

Badgers place third in Big Ten indoor and outdoor track meets

Four champions in both the indoor and outdoor Big Ten track and field championships propelled the Badgers to second-place finishes behind Michigan. Only once before (1927) had Wisconsin had as many as four champs and only in 1913 had the Badgers won five events.

Earning Conference titles in the indoor meet at Chicago were Chuck Fenske, a double winner in the 880-yard run (1:55.4) and mile (4:11.1); Walter Mehl in the two-mile run at 9:18.3; and pole vaulter Milt Padway at 13'4". Michigan won the meet with 32 1/3 points followed by Coach Tom Jones's Badgers (26) and Iowa (20 1/3).

Outdoors, four champions were again the order of the day for Wisconsin in the meet at Columbus, Ohio. The same foursome reprised their indoor victories, with Fenske at 1:52.9 in the 880 and 4:10.9 in the mile; Mehl at 9:10.4 in the two mile; and Padway at 13'8" in tying for the pole vault crown. Wisconsin's 37 points placed it well behind Michigan's 61 but were enough to edge Ohio State (31).

WISCONSIN TIMELINE

1938: Cincinnati Reds left–hander Johnny Vander Meer became the only major leaguer to pitch successive no-hit, no-run games.

The Big Ten affirmed a ruling that the football season end the last Thursday before Thanksgiving Day.

WISCONSIN HEADLINER

CHARLES H. FENSKE
TRACK AND FIELD,
CROSS COUNTRY

Wisconsin had its own "king," at least in track and field, prior to World War II. Chuck Fenske, known as the "Monarch of the Mile," was three-time Big Ten mile champion from 1936–38 and the NCAA outdoor titlist in the event in 1937. He also held world records in the 1000-yard run (2:09.3) and the three-quarter run (2:59.7). Fenske also set an indoor mile record of 4:07 the famed Wanamaker Mile. He captained the Badgers' cross country and track teams in 1937–38, his senior season, and wor Big Ten Conference Medal of Honor that year. Fenske was na "Miler of the Year" in 1940 after he went unbeaten in eight prestigious races against the best runners in the world. Named to halls of fame at the Drake Relays, the State of Wisconsin and the Pen and Mike Club-Bowman Sports Foundation, Fenske was a charter member of the UW Athletic Hall of Fame in 1991.

WISCONSIN HEADLINER

HOWARD WEISS
FOOTBALL

A three-sport star in high school at Fort Atkinson in football, basketball and, golf, fullback Howard Weiss earned all-Big Ten and all-America recognition in 1938 as well as Big Ten MVP honors.
To top it off, he also was class president and twice the Badgers' most valuable player. An outstanding runner, effective and effective blocker, Weiss played linebacker on defense. To this day, his 40-yard run at Northwestern in 19 ranks as one of the greatest in Badger annals. He played in East West Shrine Game in 1938 and the College All-Star Game in 1939. Picked by the Detroit Lions in the 1939 NFL draft, Weiss played two seasons in the professional ranks. He was one of 35 charter members named to the UW Athletic Hall of Fame in 1991.

THE LIST

WISCONSIN'S MEN'S
CONFERENCE MEDAL
OF HONOR WINNERS

1930	Donald W. Mieklejohn
1931	Louis E. Oberdeck
1932	Harvey H. Schneider
1933	Nello Anthony Pacetti
1934	Robert A. Schiller
1935	Rolf Falk Poser
1936	Howard Thurston Heun
1937	Leonard L. Lovshin
1938	Charles H. Fenske
1939	Walter I. Bietila

A  FIRST

*Badgers post best NCAA
track finish*

Wisconsin placed fourth in the NCAA outdoor track and field championships, its best finish ever under Coach Tom Jones and a standing that would not be equaled until 59 years later. Leading the Badgers were champion Walter Mehl (5,000-meter run) and all-Americans Milt Padway (second, pole vault) and Chuck Fenske (fourth, 800 meters, and third, 1,500 meters).

1938—39

BADGER BIG TEN FINISHES...

Football: 6th
coached by Harry Stuhldreher

Cross Country: 2nd
coached by Thomas Jones

Basketball: 7th
coached by Harold Foster

Indoor Track: 2nd
coached by Thomas Jones

Swimming: 5th
coached by Joe Steinauer

Baseball: 6th (tie)
coached by Lowell Douglas

Golf: 9th
coached by Joe Steinauer

Tennis: 7th
coached by Roy Black

Outdoor Track: 2nd
coached by Thomas Jones, (5th, NCAA)

The Big Event

Boxers win Wisconsin's first NCAA team title

Just six years after Wisconsin established a varsity boxing program, it had its first national collegiate championship in the sport. It marked also the first official NCAA title won by any Wisconsin team.

The Badgers of Coach John Walsh had been building momentum toward a team title. They had gone unbeaten and untied in 1935, but the first NCAA championships were not held until 1937 at the University of California at Davis. After another unbeaten and untied season in 1938, but no NCAA title, the third boxing tournament in 1939 proved the magic one for Walsh and his team. The Badgers were ready, winning four championships.

Gene Rankin at 135 lbs., Omar Crocker at 145, Woodrow Swancutt at 155 and Truman Tbrgerson at 175 all won titles, giving the Badgers 25 points and the team championship. Rankin would go on to become a three-time champ while Swancutt would successfully defend his title in 1940.

WISCONSIN TIMELINE

1939: Lou Gehrig called himself "the luckiest man on the face of the Earth" in his farewell speech at Yankee Stadium.

William R. Reed was hired to establish the Big Ten Service Bureau as the "Modern Era" of Conference competition began.

WISCONSIN HEADLINER

WOODROW P. "WOODIE" SWANCUTT
BOXING

The "Fightin'est Fighter" in the 1938 All-University Tournament, Woodrow P. "Woodie" Swancutt was a two-time NCAA champion for the great Badger boxing teams of the late 1930s and early 1940s. Born in 1915 in Edgar, Wisconsin, Swancutt prepped at both Stevens Point and LaCrosse high schools before enrolling at the UW. He won the 1939 national collegiate 155-lb. title as the Badgers won the team championship. Swancutt successfully defended his title in 1940 but enlisted in the Air Force in 1941, passing up his final year of eligibility when due to enter medical school. He was inducted into the UW Athletic Hall of Fame in 1992.

BADGER MOMENT

Var-sity! Var–sity!

The traditional arm-waving at the end of the song, "Varsity," came from the University of Pennsylvania, where students waved their caps after losing a game. In 1934, UW band leader Ray Dvorak instructed students to salute UW President Glenn Frank after each game. It led to one of the most famous college alma maters.

The words:
Var-sity! Var-sity!
U-rah-rah! Wisconsin!
Praise to thee we sing
Praise to thee our Alma Mater
U-rah-rah, Wisconsin!
Our Team is RED HOT!

THE LIST

WRESTLING COACHES' RECORDS

Coach (Seasons)	Years	Record
E.R. Finley (1911–12)	2	0–0–2
E.B. Nolte (1913)	1	1–0–0
Fred Schlatter (1914–15)	2	3–0–1
Art Knott (1916–17)	2	1–5–0
Joe Steinauer (1919–20)	2	2–2–0
George Hitchcock (1921–33)	13	28–37–1
Paul Getting (1934–35)	2	1–14–0
George Martin (1936–42,46–70)	32	181–166–12
John Roberts (1943)	1	4–2–0
Frank Jordan (1944–45)	2	1–5–1
Duane Kleven (1971–82)	12	132–46–5
Russ Hellickson (1983–86)	4	70–22–1
Andy Rein (1987–93)	7	69–35–3
Barry Davis (1994–Present)	19	195–144–11

A  FIRST

Badgers make first West Coast trip

Wisconsin's football team made its first trip to the West Coast in 1938, bringing national recognition to Harry Stuhldreher's third team. The Badgers, ranked 15th nationally after winning four of their first six games, defeated UCLA 14–7. The UW ended its season 5–3 after losing 21–0 at home to Minnesota in the season finale. Pacing the Badgers was first–team all–American halfback Howard Weiss, the Big Ten's most valuable player.

1939—40

BADGER BIG TEN FINISHES...

Football: 9th (tie)
coached by Harry Stuhldreher

Cross Country: 1st
coached by Thomas Jones

Basketball: 9th
coached by Harold Foster

Indoor Track: 3rd
coached by Thomas Jones

Wrestling: 7th
coached by George Martin

Baseball: 6th
coached by Art Mansfield

Golf: 6th
coached by Joe Steinauer

Tennis: 7th
coached by Roy Black

Outdoor Track: 3rd
coached by Thomas Jones

The Big Event

Badgers win Big Ten cross country

Wisconsin won the 1939 Big Ten cross country championship, its first since its four straight victories from 1924–27. Indiana had won six consecutive crowns from 1928–32 and in 1938. No meets were held from 1933–37. Wisconsin scored a low 28 points to upend the defending champion Hoosiers at Chicago.

Walter Mehl, who went on to win the NCAA title later that fall, won his only Big Ten harrier race in 20:34.7 over the four–mile course. The Badgers' 28–point score, more than 70 years later, still stands among the top 20 on the Conference's list of all–time lowest winning scores.

WISCONSIN TIMELINE

1940: The United States began its first peacetime draft lottery.

The Big Ten voted to permit nine football games per season, six Conference games to be required and at least two at each home institution.

Wisconsin won its only NCAA basketball championship as John Kotz is named tournament MVP.

WISCONSIN HEADLINER

WALTER J. "WALLY" MEHL
CROSS COUNTRY, TRACK

That Walter J. "Wally" Mehl's name is legendary in track annals at Wisconsin, where many great milers have run over the decades, shows just how good this Wauwatosa native was. He competed for the Badgers from 1935–39, winning the 1939 NCAA and Big Ten cross country titles his senior season after taking second in both as a junior. He won the NCAA two–mile run in 1938 after taking indoor and outdoor Conference crowns in that event, but it was in the mile that Mehl really made his name. He won the Big Ten indoor and outdoor mile titles in 1939 and then, following his graduation, started winning miles with abandon. Mehl was the National AAU indoor champ in 1940 and then took its metric equivalent outdoors. He also won the Penn Relays special mile that year and took the win in the famed Wanamaker Mile in 1941. He later earned a Ph.D. in education from Wisconsin. A member of the Drake Relays Hall of Fame, Mehl was inducted into the UW Athletic Hall of Fame in 1992.

WISCONSIN HEADLINER

OMAR CROCKER
BOXING

Omar Crocker was called "the greatest of all the boxing representatives we ever had" by no less than legendary Badger boxing coach John Walsh. Crocker, a native of Norcross, Minnesota, came to Wisconsin in the late 1930s and proceeded to post a three-year collegiate mark of 22–1–1. He won the 1939 NCAA title at 145 lbs. and lost the 1940 national collegiate title at the same weight on a judge's error. He was the Contender's Tournament champion in 1936 at 135 lbs. Crocker also won all–university titles from 1938–40, the first at 135 lbs. and the latter two at 145 lbs. He won "W" awards in 1938, 1939 and 1940 and was inducted as a charter member of the UW Athletic Hall of Fame in 1991.

THE LIST

FIRST-ROUND NFL & AFL DRAFT CHOICES FROM WISCONSIN

1937	Ed Jankowski, Green Bay Packers
1941	George Paskvan, Green Bay Packers
1944	Pat Harder, Chicago Cardinals
1945	Elroy Hirsch, Cleveland Rams
1947	Don Kindt, Chicago Bears
1948	Earl Girard, Green Bay Packers
1955	Alan Ameche, Baltimore Colts
1960	Dale Hackbart, Minnesota (AFL); Jim Heinke, Dallas Texans (AFL); Bob Nelson, Dallas Texans (AFL); Jerry Stalcup, Minnesota (AFL); Bob Zeman, Los Angeles Chargers (AFL)
1963	Pat Richter, Denver Broncos (AFL)
1976	Dennis Lick, Chicago Bears
1980	Ray Snell, Tampa Bay Buccaneers
1985	Richard Johnson, Houston Oilers; Al Toon, New York Jets; Darryl Sims, Pittsburgh Steelers
1988	Paul Gruber, Tampa Bay Buccaneers
1992	Troy Vincent, Miami Dolphins
1999	Aaron Gibson, 27th, Detroit Lions
2000	Ron Dayne, 11th, New York Giants
2000	Chris McIntosh, 22nd, Seattle Seahawks
2001	Jamar Fletcher, 26th, Miami Dolphins
2001	Michael Bennett, 27th, Minnesota Vikings
2002	Wendell Bryant, 12th, Arizona Cardinals
2004	Lee Evans, 13th, Buffalo Bills
2005	Erasmus James, 18th, Minnesota Vikings
2007	Joe Thomas, 3rd, Cleveland Browns
2011	J.J. Watt, 11th, Houston Texans
2011	Gabe Carimi, 29th, Chicago Bears
2012	Kevin Zeitler, 27th, Cincinnati Bengals
2013	Travis Frederick, 31st, Dallas Cowboys

THE LIST

CAMP RANDALL COACHING RECORDS

Fourteen of UW's 18 football coaches have posted winning records at Camp Randall.

Football Coach (years)	Record
William Juneau (1913–15)	9–4–1
Paul Withington (1916)	4–0–1
J.R. Richards (1917, 1920–22)	15–4–2
Guy Lowman (1918)	2–2
Jack Ryan (1923–24)	4–3–3
George Little (1925–26)	8–2
Glenn Thistlewaite (1927–31)	20–7–1
Clarence Spears (1932–35)	11–7
Harry Stuhldreher (1936–48)	29–31–4
Ivy Williamson (1949–55)	25–7–2
Milt Bruhn (1956–66)	33–20–4
John Coatta (1967–69)	3–13–1
John Jardine (1970–77)	27–19–2
Dave McClain (1978–85)	29–21–1
Jim Hides (1986)	2–4
Don Morton (1987–89)	6–13
Barry Alvarez (1990–2005)	67–32–3
Bret Bielema (2006–12)	44–5
Gary Anderson (2013-present)	

BADGER BIG TEN FINISHES...

Football: 4th (tie)
coached by Harry Stuhldreher

Cross Country: 1st (tie)
coached by Thomas Jones

Basketball: 1st (tie)
coached by Harold Foster (1st, NCAA)

Indoor Track: 5th (tie)
coached by Thomas Jones

Swimming: 9th
coached by Joe Steinauer

Wrestling: 6th
coached by George Martin,
(tie for 5th, NCAA)

Baseball: 6th
coached by Art Mansfield

Golf: 5th
coached by Joe Steinauer

Tennis: 5th
coached by Carl Sanger

Outdoor Track: 5th
coached by Thomas Jones

The Big Event

Badgers win 1941 NCAA basketball title

Wisconsin won its first and only NCAA basketball championship, defeating Washington State 39–34. Coach Harold "Bud" Foster's team ended the season with 15 straight wins, including three in the NCAA tournament, to finish with a 20–3 record.

Leading the Badgers in the title game at Kansas City, Missouri, were Gene Englund with 13 points and tournament MVP John Kotz with 12. The Badgers trailed the Cougars 10–8 and 12–9 early in the game but a pair of baskets by Kotz gave Wisconsin a lead; the Badgers never again trailed and jumped to a six–point lead at 30–24 after WSU had tied the game.

Wisconsin's run to the title began in the NCAA East Regional at the UW Field House when it downed Dartmouth 51–50 in a game in which the lead changed hands five times. Englund and Kotz scored 18 and 15 points, respectively, to lead the UW.

In the regional title game, also at the Field House, the Badgers avenged a 36–34 home loss to Pittsburgh with a 36–30 victory. Although Pitt had a 23–18 lead early in the second period, an Englund basket and four points from Kotz put the Badgers up 24–23, a lead they never relinquished enroute to the NCAA championship game. Englund ended with 11 points and Kotz with 10.

WISCONSIN TIMELINE

1941: The United States entered World War II one day after the Japanese bombing of Pearl Harbor.

The Conference permitted service teams to schedule a limited number of football and basketball games with Big Ten teams.

John Kotz was picked as the Big Ten's most valuable basketball player, marking the second straight season a Badger is so honored.

JOHN KOTZ
BASKETBALL

Two-time all-American John Kotz was one of the stars in an era of Badger basketball excellence. The Rhinelander native, who had an outstanding prep career at Wisconsin Valley and led his team to the 1939 state title, continued his stellar play under Coach Bud Foster at Wisconsin. Only a sophomore when the Badgers won the 1941 NCAA basketball title, Kotz was named outstanding player in the championship game following a season in which he was named all-Big Ten. In 1942, Kotz led the Big Ten in scoring with a record 242 points over a 15-game schedule. He set a single-game mark with 31 points against Iowa. His 841 point career total was then a UW record. Kotz was named a charter member of the UW Athletic Hall of Fame in 1991.

GENE ENGLUND
BASKETBALL

Kenosha native Gene Englund, the Big Ten's most valuable basketball player in 1941, led Bud Foster's Badgers to the conference title and the UW's only NCAA championship in the sport. Englund was named all-Big Ten and all-American at center after a season that saw him finish second in the Big Ten scoring race with a then-Wisconsin record 162 points (for conference games). He scored a career-high 27 points against Purdue that year enroute to a Badger single season scoring record of 304 points; in fact, he led Wisconsin in scoring in 15 of the team's 23 games that championship season. Englund scored 42 points in the three NCAA tournament games, including 18 in Wisconsin's 51–50 first–round victory over Dartmouth. Englund was a charter inductee into the UW Athletic Hall of Fame in 1991.

GEORGE PASKVAN
FOOTBALL,
TRACK AND FIELD

Fullback George Paskvan was a two-time all-Conference choice in 1939 and 1949 and both times was the Badgers' most valuable player. The LaGrange, Illinois native led the UW in rushing in 1939 with 459 yards and in scoring the following year with 30 points. His career rushing total was 1,029 yards. He was named to the second team Associated Press all-American team in 1939 and the United Press third team that season. Drafted by the Green Bay Packers in the first round of the 1941 NFL draft, Paskvan also played in the College All–Star game. He also won the shot-put in the 1941 Big Ten indoor track championships. Paskvan received the Harlan N. Rogers Scholarship awarded to the outstanding student-athlete in the study of the U. S. Constitution. Paskvan was inducted into the UW Athletic Hall of Fame in 1993.

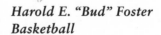

LEADING THE WAY

Harold E. "Bud" Foster
Basketball

Twenty-five year basketball coach Harold E. "Bud" Foster remains a legend in the state as the only coach to guide a team to the NCAA championship. Foster's magic season came in 1940–41 as the Badgers won the Big Ten crown and then took the three-game NCAA tournament. But his playing and coaching careers were more than that one season. He was an all-Big Ten center in 1929 and 1930 for UW and then earned all-America honors in 1930. He also played professionally with the Oshkosh All–Stars. Foster became Wisconsin's freshman coach in 1933 and head coach the following season, where he remained for 25 years, leading Wisconsin to conference titles in 1935 and 1947 as well. His career mark was 265–267. He was a president of the basketball coaches association and also was named to numerous halls of fame, including Helms, the National Basketball Hall, the Wisconsin State Athletic Hall and the Madison Pen and Mike Bowman Sports Foundation Hall. Foster was a charter inductee into the UW Athletic Hall of Fame in 1991.

BADGER BIG TEN FINISHES...

Football: 5th
coached by Harry Stuhldreher

Cross Country: 5th
coached by Thomas Jones

Basketball: 2nd (tie)
coached by Harold Foster

Indoor Track: 5th
coached by Thomas Jones

Swimming: 8th
coached by Joe Steinauer

Wrestling: 6th
coached by George Martin

Baseball: 3th
coached by Art Mansfield

Golf: 6th
coached by Joe Steinauer

Tennis: 8th
coached by Carl Sanger

Outdoor Track: 5th
coached by Thomas Jones

The Big Event

Badgers win another NCAA boxing crown

By the early 1940s, intercollegiate boxing was well into its golden era at Wisconsin. The 1942 Badgers won their second NCAA title and posted their fifth season without a loss or a tie. In the NCAA championships, four UW boxers again won titles for Coach John Walsh.

Gene Rankin won his third 135–lb. crown while Warren Jollymore (145), Cliff Lutz (155) and George Makris (175) also won their championship bouts. The Badgers would again win in 1943, with their five individual winners a mark that another Wisconsin team would equal in 1956.

Winning in '43 were Lutz at 145 lbs., Don Miller at 155, Myron Miller at 165, Makris at 175 and John Verdayne at heavyweight. The Wisconsin boxing teams of 1940–44 ran up a string of 24 consecutive victories and routinely drew large crowds for their matches at the Wisconsin Fieldhouse. Attendance records were set each of the six times Wisconsin hosted the tournament.

WISCONSIN TIMELINE

1942: Glenn Miller's orchestra recorded its hit song "(I've Got a Gal in) Kalamazoo" at Victor Studios in Hollywood.

Certain rules were waived by the Big Ten because of wartime conditions, including inter-freshman team competition.

Wisconsin is named mythical national football champion by the Helms Foundation after its 8–1–1 season.

WISCONSIN HEADLINER

DAVID N. SCHREINER
FOOTBALL

Twice an all–American, Lancaster, Wisconsin, native David N. Schreiner has been called by some one of the finest ends to ever play the game. His No. 80 has been retired by Wisconsin. An all-Big Ten and all-American choice in 1941 and 1942, Schreiner caught three touchdown passes in the second period of a 1942 game against Marquette as the Badgers won 35-7. He was the team's leading pass receiver in 1942 with 18 catches for 386 yards and five touchdowns. He was named both the Big Ten's and Wisconsin's most valuable player. Selected in the second round of the National Football League draft by the Detroit Lions, Schreiner also played in the 1943 East West Shrine Game. A member of the all–time Wisconsin football team and the Wisconsin State Hall of Fame, Shreiner was named to the charter class of the UW Athletic Hall of Fame in 1991. He died in service to his country in Okinawa in 1945. The David N. Schreiner Memorial Scholarship has been established in his memory.

WISCONSIN HEADLINER

GENE RANKIN
BOXING

Gene Rankin remains the only boxer in NCAA history to win three NCAA championships in the same weight class, taking national collegiate titles for the Badgers at 135 pounds in 1939, 1941 and 1942. The '39 and '42 squads—the latter captained by Rankin—won NCAA team titles as well. Rankin, who was born in 1916 in Duluth, Minnesota, graduated from Superior Central High School. He won the 1937 National Diamond Belt title in 1937 in Boston before enrolling at Wisconsin to box under the soon-to-be-legendary John Walsh. Rankin's trademarks in the ring were his speed and finesse. He later saw service in the U.S. Navy during World War II. Rankin was inducted into the UW Athletic Hall of Fame in 1992.

WISCONSIN HEADLINER

JOHN ROBERTS
FOOTBALL, WRESTLING

From his high school days at Valley High School in West Des Moines through his wrestling and football careers at Wisconsin, John excelled. A two-time Iowa state champ as a prep and a football all stater, Roberts continued his winning ways in Madison. He earned "W" awards in both football and wrestling and was a member of the 1942 UW football team that went 8–1–1 en route to a third-place Big Ten finish and No. 3 national ranking. But it was in wrestling that Roberts made his mark, winning Big Ten titles in the 165-lb. weight class in 1941 and at 175 pounds a year later. He also was NCAA runner-up in 1941. Following graduation, Roberts coached the 1943 UW wrestling team and then embarked on a long career in high school athletics. He coached football at Stevens Point High School from 1946–51 and then at UW-Stevens Point from 1952–56. Roberts then served as executive director of the Wisconsin Interscholastic Athletic Association from 1957–85. He was inducted into the UW Athletic Hall of Fame in 1994.

LEADING THE WAY

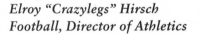

Elroy "Crazylegs" Hirsch
Football, Director of Athletics

Elroy Hirsch was a triple–threat halfback for the 1942 Badgers, carried his talents to Michigan and then became one of the great wide receivers in National Football League history. He became the UW's athletic director in 1969 and over the next 18 years presided over an era of growth, change and success in Wisconsin sports. In 1942, he paced the Badgers to the brink of a national championship as they finished 8–1–1, second in the Big Ten and ranked third nationally. His No. 40 was retired by Wisconsin. He was the MVP in the 1946 College All-Star game and then went on to professional stardom with the Chicago Rockets of the old All-American Conference and later with the Los Angeles Rams. In 1951, he set a pro record of 1,495 yards on 66 receptions and 17 touchdown passes as the Rams won the NFL title. Hirsch was a charter member of the UW Athletics Hall of Fame and a member of the NFL All-Time All-Star team. But it's as an administrator that many alumni of the past 30 years remember him and as a tireless promoter of all things Wisconsin.

BADGER BIG TEN FINISHES...

Football: 2th
coached by Harry Stuhldreher

Cross Country: 5th
coached by Thomas Jones

Basketball: 4th (tie)
coached by Harold Foster

Indoor Track: 2nd
coached by Thomas Jones

Swimming: 7th
coached by Joe Steinauer

Wrestling: 9th
coached by John Roberts

Baseball: 2nd
coached by Art Mansfield

Golf: 6th
coached by Joe Steinauer

Tennis: 3rd
coached by Carl Sanger

Outdoor Track: 5th
coached by Thomas Jones

The Big Event

Badgers second in Big Ten football, ranked third nationally

Wisconsin's 1942 football team, coached by Harry Stuhldreher and featuring standouts Elroy "Crazylegs" Hirsch and Dave Schreiner, put together one of the best seasons in school history and was named mythical national champion by the Helms Foundation. The Badgers compiled an 8–1–1 overall record and No. 3 national ranking by the Associated Press.

Wisconsin started the season 6–0–1, the only blemish being a 7–7 tie with Notre Dame in the second game of the year. It was in that game that Hirsch earned his nickname when a local writer, commenting on a 60–yard touchdown run, said, "his crazy legs were gyrating."

Also included in the seven–game unbeaten string was the UW's first-ever win over a No. 1-ranked opponent. The Badgers toppled Coach Paul Brown's Ohio State Buckeyes 17–7 in the UW's homecoming game on October 31.

The following week, however, Wisconsin (after moving up to No. 2 in the Associated Press rankings) was upset 6–0 before a homecoming crowd at Iowa. That loss kept the Badgers from the Big Ten title and possibly the national championship. The UW concluded the season with victories over Northwestern and Minnesota to finish second in the Conference race.

Schreiner, an end, was named the Big Ten MVP and earned consensus first-team all-American acclaim. Fullback Marlin "Pat" Harder, along with Hirsch, also earned all-America mention.

WISCONSIN TIMELINE

1943: American bombers staged the first air raid on Germany in World War II.

The Conference allowed freshmen to play on varsity teams for the duration of the war.

End Dave Schreiner and fullback Marlin "Pat" Harder become the first pair of Badgers since 1920 to earn all-America honors in the same season. Schreiner, honored for the second time, was the UW's first two-time All-American while Harder led the Big Ten in scoring.

MARLIN "PAT" HARDER
FOOTBALL

One of the all-time Wisconsin football greats is Marlin "Pat" Harder, who starred on nationally ranked Badger teams as well for two National Football League champions. A Milwaukee native out of Washington High School, Harder led the Big Ten in rushing (590 yards) and scoring (58 points) as a sophomore in 1941. He was an all-American and all-Conference fullback on the Badgers' 1942 unit that was second in the Big Ten and ranked third nationally. In the 1943 College All-Star game, Harder was named MVP after scoring on a 37-yard pass play and a 33-yard run in the collegians' 27–7 win over the Washington Redskins. He played professionally with the Chicago Cardinals and Detroit Lions, leading the NFL in scoring in 1947 and 1948 and tying for scoring honors in 1949. Harder became an NFL official following his playing career. A member of the Wisconsin State Athletic Hall of Fame, Harder was a charter inductee into the UW Athletics Hall of Fame in 1991.

WISCONSIN HEADLINER

FREDERICK W. NEGUS
FOOTBALL, BASEBALL

Fred Negus, a first-team all-Big Ten center for Wisconsin football teams in 1942 and 1946, also earned similar honors for Michigan in 1943. Like many servicemen during World War II, Negus attended Michigan for a year in conjunction with the Marine Corps' V-12 program; he also ran on the Wolverines' Big Ten title-winning mile relay team in 1944. The Martins Ferry, Ohio native starred immediately at Wisconsin and was named a member of the Associated Press sophomore All-American team in 1942. Following his service time, Negus returned to Madison and again earned all-Conference honors at center as well as the Badgers' MVP award. He was a member of the 1947 College All-Stars who defeated the Chicago Bears. After receiving his B.S. degree from Wisconsin, Negus played professionally with the Chicago Rockets of the All-America Football Conference from 1947–49 and with the NFL's Bears in 1950. He tied an AAFC record with a 97-yard fumble return for a touchdown in 1948. Recipient of the Fort Atkinson (WI) Chamber of Commerce Small Business Person Award in 1997, Negus was inducted into the UW Athletic Hall of Fame in 1998.

LEADING THE WAY

Harry Stuhldreher, Football Coach, Director of Athletics

All-American quarterback Harry Stuhldreher contributed to intercollegiate athletics as head football coach and director of athletics in his 15–year tenure at Wisconsin. A member of the famed Notre Dame "Four Horsemen", the native of Massillon, Ohio, earned all-American honors in 1923 and 1924 for the Fighting Irish. He then compiled a 65–25–10 record as head coach at Villanova before coming to Madison in 1936. As head football coach at the UW for 13 years, his record of 45–62–6 was not a winning one, but his philosophy as athletic director of "Athletics for All" was a winner as his leadership produced well-rounded development of all sports and facilities. His 1942 Badger team was second in the Big Ten (8–1–1) and ranked third nationally. He also coached the College All-Stars to a 27–7 win over the NFL champion Washington Redskins in 1943. He received the A.A. Stagg Award in 1965 for his contributions to college football Foundation Hall of Fame, Stuhldreher was inducted into the UW Athletic Hall of Fame in 1994.

A FIRST

Five Badgers win NCAA boxing titles

Winning its second straight NCAA boxing title—and third ever—to conclude the 1942–43 season was impressive enough for Wisconsin's dominant boxing team, but even more noteworthy than that were the individual achievements that made that championship possible. Five Badgers won NCAA crowns, a first in the sport's history and a record that would not be matched until another Wisconsin quintet turned the trick in 1956. Winning in 1943 for Coach John Walsh's team were Cliff Lutz at 145 lbs., Don Miller at 155, Myron Miller at 165, George Makris at 175 and John Verdayne at heavyweight. They were the second NCAA wins for Lutz and Makris.

BADGER BIG TEN FINISHES...

Football: 8th
coached by Harry Stuhldreher

Cross Country: 5th
coached by Thomas Jones

Basketball: 2nd (tie)
coached by Harold Foster

Indoor Track: 8th
coached by Thomas Jones

Swimming: 6th
coached by Joe Steinauer

Wrestling: 3rd
coached by Frank Jordan

Baseball: 7th
coached by Art Mansfield

Golf: 5th
coached by Joe Steinauer

Tennis: 6th
coached by Harold A. Taylor

Outdoor Track: 8th
coached by Thomas Jones

The Big Event

Athletes at war

The war that fathers of athletes of the 1940s had fought in a little more than a generation earlier unfortunately wasn't the last one that would affect American life and intercollegiate athletics.

The Big Ten and its member schools tried their best to maintain a semblance of normalcy in their programs but finally acknowledged the haphazardness of applying rules in a time of war.

Initially, the Conference removed eligibility restrictions on freshmen and then waived all eligibility rules for students in the military attending member institutions. Finally, all eligibility rules were discarded, save those requiring a student-athlete's regular enrollment and maintenance of amateur status.

One of the most famous Badgers of them all, Elroy "Crazylegs" Hirsch, would compete, and star, at Michigan between playing stints at Wisconsin because of wartime service. Another Badger star, NCAA champion boxer Cliff Lutz, would have his collegiate career split because of military service.

Most sports were affected in some way. No Big Ten gymnastics or fencing championships were held from 1943–46 and the league's golf tournament was shortened to 36 holes in 1944 and 1945.

WISCONSIN TIMELINE

1944: D–Day: Allied forces began the invasion of Europe.

The University of Chicago announced its withdrawal from scheduling athletic championships for 1944–45.

Big Ten Commissioner John L. Griffith died.

WISCONSIN HEADLINER

CLIFF LUTZ
BOXING

One of only two three–time NCAA boxing champions in an era dominated by Wisconsin boxers, Cliff Lutz won his first national collegiate title in 1942 and his third five years later because of World War II. The Badgers, under legendary coach John Walsh, won the NCAA crown each of those three seasons. Lutz won at 155 pounds in 1942, dropped a class to 145 lbs. and won again in 1943 and then again in 1947 at the lighter weight. The Appleton native was the "Fightin'est Fighter" in the All–University Tournament in 1941 and 1942. Lutz was inducted into the UW Athletic Hall of Fame in 1993.

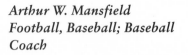

LEADING THE WAY

Arthur W. Mansfield
Football, Baseball; Baseball
Coach

The name of Arthur W. "Dynie" Mansfield is another that's synonymous with Wisconsin. The Cleveland, Ohio, native enrolled at the UW in 1925 and spent nearly all of the next 45 years on the Madison campus. A versatile athlete, Mansfield won major "W" awards in 1926 and 1928 and baseball letters from 1927–29. He was also the all-university heavyweight boxing champion in 1928 and 1929. He played baseball in the New York Giants organization and semi-pro football with the Madison Blues in the early 1930s before joining the Wisconsin physical education faculty in 1936. In 1940, Mansfield became the Badgers' baseball coach, a post he would hold through 1970, compiling a 441–339 record and Big Ten titles in 1946 and 1950. Mansfield also coached Wisconsin's 1947 and 1948 150-lb. football teams. Mansfield was a member of the 1956 U.S. Olympic baseball committee and was elected in 1970 to the American Association of Baseball Coaches Hall of Fame. He was inducted into the UW Athletic Hall of Fame in 1998.

THE LIST

UW BASEBALL'S
.400 HITTERS

These Badgers hit
.400 in Big Ten play:

1940-Bob Smith, .441

1942-John Kasper, .431

1944-Merlin Brinker, .455

1945-Jim Ackeret, .429

1949-Bob Shea, .410

1952–Harvey Kuenn, .444*

1963–64-Rick Reichardt, .471*

1965-Joe Romary, .400

1968-Geoff Baillie, .400

1970-Mike Johnson, .415

1973-Lee Bauman, .400

1973-Tom Shipley, .446

1974-Steve Bennett, .458

1975-Lee Bauman, .457

1975-Duane Gustavson, .408

1977-John Hnath, .409

1977-Randy Johnson, .406

1982-Joe Scime, .404

1983-Joe Scime, .426

1983-Mike Verkuilen, .419

1985-Joe Armentrout, .464

*led Big Ten

THE LIST

WISCONSIN'S NCAA
BOXING CHAMPIONS

1936: Robert Fadner, 125 lbs.
1939: Gene Rankin, 135 lbs.
1939: Omar Crocker, 145 lbs.
1939: Woodrow Swancutt, 155 lbs.
1939: Truman Torgerson, 175 lbs.
1940: Woodrow Swancutt, 155 lbs.
1940: Nick Lee, Hwt.
1941: Gene Rankin, 135 lbs.
1942: Gene Rankin, 135 lbs.
1942: Warren Jollymore, 145 lbs.
1942: Cliff Lutz, 155 lbs.
1942: George Makris, 175 lbs.
1943: Cliff Lutz, 145 lbs.
1943: Don Miller, 155 lbs.
1943: Myron Miller, 165 lbs.
1943: George Makris, 175 lbs.
1943: Verdayne John, Hwt.
1947: Cliff Lutz, 145 lbs.
1947: John Lendenski, 165 lbs.

1948: Donald Dickinson, 148 lbs.
1948: Steve Gremban, 148 lbs.
1948: Calvin Vernon, 176 lbs.
1948: Vito Parisi, Hwt.
1951: Dick Murphy, 155 lbs.
1951: Bob Ranck, Hwt.
1952: Bob Morgan, 147 lbs.
1952: Bob Ranck, Hwt.
1953: Pat Sreenan, 147 lbs.
1953: Ray Zale, 178 lbs.
1954: Bob Meath, 156 lbs.
1956: Dean Plemmons, 112 lbs.
1956: Dick Bartman, 139 lbs.
1956: Vince Ferguson, 156 lbs.
1956: Orville Pitts, 178 lbs.
1956: Truman Sturdevant, Hwt.
1959: Charles Mohr, 165 lbs.
1960: Brown McGhee, 132 lbs.
1960: Jerry Turner, 156 lbs

BADGER BIG TEN FINISHES...

Football: 7th
coached by Harry Stuhldreher

Cross Country: 1st
coached by Thomas Jones

Basketball: 6th (tie)
coached by Harold Foster

Indoor Track: 8th
coached by Thomas Jones

Swimming: 8th
coached by Joe Steinauer

Wrestling: 9th
coached by Frank Jordan

Baseball: 2nd
coached by Art Mansfield

Golf: 6th
coached by Joe Steinauer

Tennis: 5th (tie)
coached by Harold A. Taylor

Outdoor Track: 6th
coached by Thomas Jones

The Big Event

Big Ten cross country title goes to Wisconsin

Wisconsin hadn't won a Big Ten cross country championship in five years, almost unconscionably long given the UW tradition in the sport. But the 1944 meet at Chicago ended a three-year string of fifth-place finishes as the Badgers scored 44 points to Indiana's 52.

Bill Lawson claimed the individual win in 21:16 for the four-mile course. He was Wisconsin's 10th Big Ten champion and Coach Tom Jones's first winner since Walter Mehl led the UW to the '39 team title.

Wisconsin would go on to win the next two Big Ten meets and begin a run of six titles in seven years, with the top UW runner each of those years placing first, second or third.

WISCONSIN TIMELINE

1945: President Franklin D. Roosevelt died; less than a month later, the war in Europe ended.

Big Ten Conference faculty approved Kenneth L. (Tug) Wilson, Northwestern's Athletic Director, as commissioner.

Wisconsin boxers lose their first match in the Field House to an Iowa Pre-Flight team, snapping a 57-match winning streak for the Badgers.

1945–46

BADGER BIG TEN FINISHES...

Football: 6th
coached by Harry Stuhldreher

Cross Country: 1st
coached by Thomas Jones

Basketball: 9th
coached by Harold Foster

Indoor Track: 3rd
coached by Thomas Jones

Swimming: 8th
coached by Joe Steinauer

Wrestling: 10th
coached by George Martin

Baseball: 1st
coached by Art Mansfield

Golf: 7th
coached by Joe Steinauer

Tennis: 8th
coached by Carl Sanger

Outdoor Track: 8th
coached by Thomas Jones, (5th, NCAA)

The Big Event

Badgers first in Big Ten baseball

Wisconsin returned to the top of the Big Ten baseball standings in 1946, posting a 9–2 record to take the title by 11/2 games over defending champion Michigan.

It was the UW's first Conference baseball championship since 1930. Coach Dynie Mansfield's team had set the stage for its climb to the top with an 8–4 campaign in 1945.

Four-time letterwinner Gene Jaroch, the Badgers' most valuable player, became the first pitcher in Big Ten history to win six games in a season.

WISCONSIN TIMELINE

1946: The United States defeated Australia 5–0 in the Davis Cup, the worst defeat ever for a defending champion.

The University of Chicago formally withdrew from the Big Ten.

The Big Ten championship Badgers took third place in the NCAA basketball East Regional in New York.

1946—47

BADGER BIG TEN FINISHES...

Football: 6th
coached by Harry Stuhldreher

Cross Country: 1st
coached by Thomas Jones

Basketball: 9th
coached by Harold Foster

Indoor Track: 3rd
coached by Thomas Jones

Baseball: 1st
coached by Art Mansfield

Golf: 7th
coached by Joe Steinauer

Tennis: 8th
coached by Carl Sanger

Outdoor Track: 8th
coached by Thomas Jones, (5th , NCAA)

The Big Event

Badger cagers climb from cellar to Big Ten title

Just a year earlier they were cellar-dwellars. Coach Bud Foster's Wisconsin men's basketball team went from a last-place finish in 1946 (4–17 overall, 1–11 in league play) to a 15–5 overall regular-season record and 9–3 Conference slate that was good for the 1947 Big Ten title and an invitation to the 1947 NCAA Tournament.

The Conference crown was Wisconsin's first since 1941 when Foster guided the Badgers to their first and only NCAA title. Paced by forward Bob Cook, the team's leading scorer, and guard Glen Selbo, the team and Big Ten MVP, Wisconsin remained in first place all season and led the league in scoring with 677 points behind 248 field goals and a then-Big Ten standard 181 free throws. Wisconsin also led the league in field goal percentage at 29.8 percent.

Cook scored 70 field goals and 47 free throws, while shooting 34.7 percent from the field. Cook and guards Walt Lautenbach, the team captain, and Selbo were first-team all-Big Ten selections.

The Badgers lost their first game in the NCAA East Regional in New York City, 70–56, to City College of New York before defeating Navy 50–49 in the consolation game.

Among the games the Badgers played in 1947 was a 54–42 win over Northwestern at Chicago Stadium on February 15. The crowd of 19,165 for that contest was the largest for the Badgers in a Big Ten game.

WISCONSIN TIMELINE

1947: Auto pioneer Henry Ford died at age 83 in Dearborn, Michigan.

Wisconsin, Illinois, Michigan and Ohio State began 150-pound, intercollegiate football competition.

Tom Jones's cross country team won its 15th Big Ten championship, and third straight, as freshman sensation Don Gehrmann took second in the four-mile race at Chicago.

WISCONSIN HEADLINER

THOMAS C. BENNETT
FOOTBALL, TRACK AND FIELD

Six-time letterwinner Tom Bennett starred for Wisconsin's football teams as a receiver and for Badger track squads as a pole vaulter. The Green Bay (West High School) native won "W" awards in football in 1946, 1947 and 1948 and track letters from 1947–49. He was the Badgers' top pass receiver on the '46 and '47 teams and also punted. He won four Big Ten titles in the pole vault from 1947–49 and in both his sophomore and senior seasons tied for the vault title at the Drake Relays. Bennett earned all-America honors in his specialty in 1949 with a second-place effort in the NCAA meet and was also voted "Senior Athlete of the Year" by student "W" Club members. Holder of bachelor's and master's degrees from the UW, Bennett then served as assistant track coach from 1951–69 and as varsity golf coach from 1970–77. In 1963, he authored "The Twentieth Century Track." The 1969–70 state games director for Wisconsin Special Olympics, Bennett was named "Mr. Olympics" in 1972 by Madison service clubs. Bennett was inducted into the UW Athletic Hall of Fame in 1998.

WISCONSIN HEADLINER

ROBERT "BOBBY" COOK
BASKETBALL, BASEBALL

Bobby Cook was a high-scoring forward and two-time all-Big ten selection for four Wisconsin basketball teams during and just after World War II. Cook, a native of Harvard, Illinois, just south of the state line, led the Big Ten in scoring in 1947, totaling 187 points in 12 games, after finishing fourth and sixth in Conference scoring the previous two seasons. He was the top scorer on the 1947 Badger five that won the Big Ten title and took third in the NCAA Eastern Regional. His 847 points in three seasons were then the most UW history. Cook, who drained 8 of 11 field goal attempts in 1948 game against Northwestern for a Big Ten record, was the Badgers' MVP in both 1946 and 1948. A standout third baseman, Cook starred on Wisconsin's 1946 Big Ten co-chamions and earned major "W" awards three times in each of his sports. He later played professionally with the She-boygan Redskins. Cook was named to the UW Athletic Hall of Fame in 1992.

WISCONSIN HEADLINER

GLEN SELBO
BASKETBALL

Glen Selbo is one of only four Wisconsin basketball layers to win the Silver Basketball Award, presented by the *Chicago Tribune* to the Big Ten's top basketball player. Selbo, who lettered from 1944–47, led Coach Harold "Bud" Foster's team to 16–6 overall record and the Big Ten title at 9–3. In the NCAA tourment—in Wisconsin's first appearance since its 1941 championship season—the Badgers lost 70–56 to City College of New york in the regional in New York City. The UW defeated Navy 50–49 the third-place game. Selbo was named to the all-Big Ten team, of course, and was joined on that honor squad by teammates Bob Cook and Walt Lautenbach.

BADGER MOMENT

UW wins its fourth NCAA boxing championship

Wisconsin scored 24 points to earn its fourth NCAA boxing championship in 1947. Leading Coach John Walsh's Badgers, and hardly missing a beat since his return from World War II service, as Cliff Lutz, who won his third title and his second at 145 lbs., following his initial win in 1942 at 155 lbs. Also claiming an individual championship for the Badgers was John Lendenski at 165 lbs.

BADGER BIG TEN FINISHES...

Football: 2nd
coached by Harry Stuhldreher

Cross Country: 2nd
coached by Thomas Jones

Basketball: 3rd (tie)
coached by Harold Foster

Indoor Track: 6th
coached by Thomas Jones

Swimming: 7th
coached by Joe Steinauer

Wrestling: 7th
coached by Art Mansfield

Golf: 8th
coached by Joe Steinauer

Gymnastics: 4th
coached by Dean Mory

Tennis: 3rd
coached by Al Hildebrandt

Outdoor Track: 6th
coached by Thomas Jones

The Big Event

Boxers win again ...
their fifth NCAA title

It never got boring, but it certainly became almost routine. Wisconsin again racked up back-to-back NCAA boxing titles, following its 24-point victory in the 1947 tournament with a 45-point win, scoring its most points to date, in the 1948 national collegiate bouts.

Four Badgers won individual crowns: Donald Dickinson (148 lbs.), Steve Gremban (156), Calvin Vernon (176) and Vito Parisi (heavyweight). The season also marked the continuation of another lengthy winning streak by Wisconsin.

The boxers of 1946–49 went undefeated in 27 straight matches before being stopped by Minnesota, 4 to 3, in the 1950 season opener. Wisconsin also had a home unbeaten streak of 72 wins and 2 ties that lasted until 1950, when Michigan State ended that string.

WISCONSIN TIMELINE

1948: "Kukla, Fran and Ollie" and the rest of the Kuklapolitan players premiered, live, on NBC-TV.

The first Big Ten Records Book was published.

Don Rehlfeldt took 37 shots as the Badgers trounced Iowa 70–47 in basketball; it's still a UW single-game record.

More than 15,000 boxing fans jammed the Field House to see the Badgers battle Washington State.

DON GEHRMANN
TRACK AND FIELD,
CROSS COUNTRY

One of the legendary names in one of Wisconsin's most successful sports is Don Gehrmann, a Milwaukee (Pulaski High School) product who dominated the American middle distance scene from 1947–51. Gehrmann won 39 consecutive major mile races from the 1948 Olympic Games to March 3, 1951. He was a four-time Big Ten outdoor mile champion from 1947–50 and the NCAA mile champ in 1948, 1949 and 1950. Three times he won the outstanding performer award at the Drake Relays and twice he won Big Ten individual cross country titles while the Badgers won team championships overland from 1948–50. Gehrmann is in various halls of fame, including the state of Wisconsin, Drake Relays, Madison Pen and Mike-Bowman Sports Foundation. He was a charter inductee into the UW Athletic Hall of Fame in 1991.

EUGENE A. JAROCH
BASEBALL

Gene Jaroch was a mainstay on the mound for Wisconsin baseball teams from 1944–47. Jaroch, a native of Chicago (Wells High School), earned four major "W" awards. He was a strikeout specialist, striking out 52 batters in 46 1/3 innings in the Badgers' 1946 Big Ten championship season. He set a Conference record with 16 K's in a 7–0 win over Chicago that year. His six wins (against no losses) set a Conference mark and accounted for two-thirds of the UW's Big Ten victories. For his career, Jaroch struck out 156 batters in 138 2/3 innings in Big Ten play. He posted a career mark of 18–13 but was especially tough on Conference foes, against whom he was 15–4. Jaroch earned a B.S. degree in physical education. He was inducted into the UW Athletic Hall of Fame in 1998.

EARL GIRARD
FOOTBALL

Earl "Jug" Girard played two seasons at Wisconsin, 1944 and 1947, and earned first-team all-America honors from Look magazine as a 17-year-old freshman in his first season. Regarded as a triple-threat quarterback, Girard was equally skilled at running, passing and punting. Drafted after his freshman year, he returned to school for the '47 season and scored two touchdowns off 158 yards in punt returns against Iowa. He's still the Wisconsin player to return two punts for touchdowns in a game and his return yardage still stands as a game record. Girard, who also played baseball, was drafted in the first round of the NFL draft by the Green Bay Packers. He also spent some time in the Cleveland Indians' farm system.

LEADING THE WAY

John Walsh
Boxing Coach

Boxing at Wisconsin was THE sport under Coach John Walsh. The Minneapolis native, who as a youth was one of the great boxers in the Twin Cities, coached and boxed at St. Thomas College, which fought the Badgers to a 4–4 tie in 1933. Encouraged the next year by Wisconsin officials to enroll in the UW Law School while coaching boxing, Walsh stayed for 23 years. He guided the Badgers to eight NCAA team titles, most in any sport in UW history. Nine of Walsh's Wisconsin teams were unbeaten and 29 boxers won 35 NCAA championships under his tutelage. His great dedication to boxing and his unique methods of developing young boxers earned him the position of co-coach of the 1948 U.S. Olympic team. He ended his Wisconsin coaching career in 1956, having compiled a 116–22–1 mark. A member of the Madison Pen and Mike Club-Bowman Sports Foundation Hall of Fame, Walsh was a charter member of the UW Athletic Hall of Fame in 1991.

1948—49

BADGER BIG TEN FINISHES...

Football: 9th
coached by Harry Stuhldreher

Cross Country: 1st
coached by Guy Sundt

Basketball: 7th
coached by Harold Foster

Indoor Track: 1st (tie)
coached by Guy Sundt

Swimming: 8th
coached by Joe Steinauer

Wrestling: 8th
coached by George Martin

Baseball: 8th (tie)
coached by Art Mansfield

Golf: 9th
coached by Joe Steinauer

Gymnastics: 4th
coached by Dean Mory

Tennis: 3rd
coached by Al Hildebrandt

Outdoor Track: 3rd
coached by Guy Sundt, (tie for 7th, NCAA)

The Big Event

Badgers win indoor track title for new coach Guy Sundt

Guy Sundt's debut as Wisconsin's track coach and successor to 36-year veteran Tom Jones was an auspicious one. The Badgers claimed their first indoor title since 1930, scoring 38 points at Champaign, Illinois, to share the top spot with defending champ Ohio State.

Distance star Don Gehrmann paced Wisconsin, winning the 880-yard run in 1:53.1 and the mile in 4:16.1. Also winning individual championships for the UW were two-miler Jim Urquhart at 9:25.7 and pole vaulter Tom Bennett with a 14'0" clearance.

The mile relay quartet of Dick Whipple, Mel Goldin, Gehrmann and Bob Mansfield was also victorious in 3:18.6. Gehrmann (mile), Urquhart (two mile) and Bennett (pole vault) repeated their indoor wins outdoors as the Badgers took third in the spring meet.

WISCONSIN TIMELINE

1949: "South Pacific" opened on Broadway.

Michigan State College was admitted to membership in the Conference.

Don Rehlfeldt became Wisconsin's last basketball all-American to date and was picked second in the NBA draft.

WISCONSIN HEADLINER

ROBERT "RED" WILSON
FOOTBALL, BASEBALL

Three-time Wisconsin football MVP Robert "Red" Wilson was the Big Ten's most valuable player in 1949. The former all-state grid star and state discus champ out of Milwaukee, Wisconsin, started on offense as an end and defense as a linebacker for Ivy Williamson's first Wisconsin team in 1949. He had been a center on offense for his first three Badger seasons starting in 1946, winning the first of his three UW MVP honors in 1947. He was later named to Wisconsin's all-time football team. A top catcher for the Badger baseball squad from 1947–50 and MVP in 1948, Wilson hit .342 that year and .426 in 1949. The 1950 Badgers shared the Big Ten title and placed fourth in the NCAA tournament as Wilson was named Wisconsin's Big Ten Medal of Honor recipient. He later went on to a professional career with the Chicago White Sox, Detroit Tigers and Cleveland Indians. A member of the Wisconsin State Hall of Fame and the Madison Pen and Mike Club-Bowman Sports Foundation Hall of Fame, Wilson was a charter inductee of the UW Athletic Hall of Fame in 1991.

LEADING THE WAY

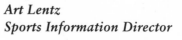

Art Lentz
Sports Information Director

Art Lentz served as sports information director at Wisconsin for 10 years, winning numerous national sports publicity awards during his tenure, including recognition by the Helms Athletic Foundation in 1956. Lentz, a Milwaukee native who was a graduate of the University of Iowa, worked for the *Des Moines Register* and *Tribune* for two years before coming to the (Madison) *Capital Times* in 1933. He became assistant sports editor in 1943, did football, basketball and track play-by-play on radio and left the *Capital Times* in 1946 to become the Badgers' SID. Lentz left Wisconsin in 1956 to become publicity director for the U.S. Olympic Committee and handled press duties at the 1956 Olympics in Melbourne, Australia. He became the USOC's assistant executive director in 1959 and executive director in 1965, a post he held until 1973. He died at 65 in 1973 in New York City.

THE LIST

WISCONSIN'S MEN'S CONFERENCE MEDAL OF HONOR WINNERS

1940	**1945**
Ralph H. Moeller	Ken Chandler
1941	**1946**
Kenneth E. Boxby	Jerry Thompson
1942	**1947**
Burleigh E. Jacobs	Exner Menzel
1943	**1948**
Frederick R. Rehm	Carlyle Fay, Jr.
1944	**1949**
Edward M. Dzirbik	Donald R. Peterson

BADGER MOMENT

Stuhldreher, Jones depart

There were more than a few good moments in the careers of Harry Stuhldreher and Tom Jones. Stuhldreher, the 13-year football coach at Wisconsin, called it quits after the 1948 season. Stuhldreher's 45 wins at Wisconsin are fifth in Badger annals. Veteran track mentor Jones, a fixture in Madison since 1913, also bid adieu. In his 36 years, Jones coached 20 Big Ten championship teams as well as the 1948 U.S. Olympic team.

BADGER BIG TEN FINISHES...

Football: 4th
coached by Ivy Williamson

Cross Country: 1st
coached by Guy Sundt

Basketball: 2nd
coached by Harold Foster

Indoor Track: 5th
coached by Guy Sundt

Swimming: 7th
coached by Joe Steinauer

Wrestling: 6th
coached by George Martin

Baseball: 1st (tie)
coached by Art Mansfield

Golf: 9th
coached by Joe Steinauer

Tennis: 4th
coached by Al Hildebrandt

Outdoor Track: 4th
coached by Guy Sundt

The Big Event

UW beats Michigan twice, shares baseball title

Wisconsin took top honors in Big Ten baseball for the second time in five years in 1950, chalking up a 9–3 mark that was good enough for a share of the title with Michigan. The Badgers handed the Wolverines two of their three losses.

Pacing Coach Dynie Mansfield's nine was one of the Conference's top batteries in pitcher Thornton Kipper and Bob Wilson. The latter was regarded for some 20 years afterward as one of the finest catchers in Big Ten history and once scored six runs and had seven RBIs in a 1949 slugfest against Western Michigan.

Also critical to the Badgers' success were slugging outfielders Paul Furseth and Bruce Elliott, each of whom hit .333 for the season. It was the last Big Ten baseball pennant that Wisconsin would win and the Badgers' only NCAA appearance.

WISCONSIN TIMELINE

1950: The comic strip "Peanuts," created by Charles Schulz, was first published in nine newspapers.

The Big Ten increased the football traveling squad limit from 36 to 40 players.

Don Gehrmann won his third straight 1,500–meter run title in the NCAA track and field championships.

DON REHFELDT
BASKETBALL

Two-time all-Big Ten center Don Rehfeldt was a mainstay of Badger basketball teams in the post-World War II years. Rehfeldt, a Chicago native who enjoyed a great prep career at Amundsen High School, originally enrolled at Wisconsin in 1944, but was called into the service. He returned in early 1947 to join the Badgers' Big Ten championship team of that season. It was in 1949 and 1950 that Rehlfeldt starred, leading the Big Ten in scoring with 229 points in 1949 and 265 in 1950 over the 12-game schedules; only five other players ever scored 200 or more points in a 12-game Conference season. He was named most valuable player in the Big Ten for 1950 and twice was named Wisconsin's MVP. Rehfeldt scored 35 points against Northwestern in 1950, a Wisconsin mark that held up for 15 years. He was picked by the Baltimore Bullets in 1950 as the second choice in the NBA draft. A member of the Illinois Basketball Coaches Hall of Fame, Rehfeldt was named a charter member of the UW Athletic Hall of Fame in 1991.

EDWARD "EDDIE" WITHERS
FOOTBALL

Edward "Eddie" Withers earned all-American honors for the Badgers as a star defensive halfback on the 1950 Badger football team. Prior to enrolling at Wisconsin, Withers starred as an all-city linebacker and as a basketball center for Madison Central High School. In pacing the E gers to a 14–0 win at Iowa in 1950, Withers interecepted three passes for 103 yards off returns of 30, 34 and 39 yards, the first for a touchdown. During his playing career, Wisconsin posted an 18–7–2 mark from 1949–51. Withers, who had eight career interceptions for 200 return yards, also earned all-Big Ten honors as a defensive back in 1951 and was drafted by the Green Bay Packers. He received a degree in physical education from Wisconsin in 1952. Forty years later, he was inducted into the UW Athletic Hall of Fame.

THE LIST

WISCONSIN SPORTS FACILITIES

Camp Randall Stadium   (football)
**Camp Randall Memorial
Sports Center** (The Shell) (track)
Kohl Center   (basketball, ice hockey)
Wisconsin Field House   (wrestling, volleyball)
McClain Athletic Facility   (football & soccer practice)
Nielsen Tennis Stadium   (tennis)
Dan McClimon Memorial Track   (track and field, soccer)
Natatorium   (swimming, diving)
Southeast Recreational Facility (SERF)   (swimming)
Lake Mendota (rowing)
University Ridge Golf Course   (golf)
Goodman Softball Complex   (softball)
Thomas Zimmer Championship Course   (cross country)

A  FIRST

*Rehlfeldt the
first first-rounder*

Don Rehlfeldt was picked second overall and thus became the first UW basketball player selected in the first round of the NBA draft. Four other Badgers were chosen in the first round in subsequent years. Al Henry was 12th overall in 1970; Wes Matthews was 14th in 1980; and Michael Finley and Paul Grant were each taken with the 25th pick in 1995 and 1997, respectively.

BADGER BIG TEN FINISHES...

Football: 2nd (tie)
coached by Ivy Williamson

Cross Country: 1st
coached by Riley Best

Basketball: 4th (tie)
coached by Harold Foster

Indoor Track: 6th (tie)
coached by Riley Best

Swimming: 9th
coached by Joe Steinauer

Wrestling: 6th
coached by George Martin

Baseball: 5th
coached by Art Mansfield

Golf: 3rd
Joe Steinauer

Tennis: 7th
coached by Al Hildebrandt

Outdoor Track: 8th
coached by Riley Best

The Big Event

UW wins Conference cross country

Wisconsin's 1950 Big Ten cross country championship, another in the Badgers' proud tradition, would be noteworthy, although no one would know it at the time.

Under first-year coach Riley Best, who had succeeded the legendary Tom Jones, the Badgers scored 56 points to hold off Big Ten newcomer and national power Michigan State, which had 61.

Walter Deike, a year away from winning his first individual title, placed third. But the win—the UW's 18th Big Ten triumph—would be Wisconsin's last in the sport until 1977.

WISCONSIN TIMELINE

1951: Coast-to-coast dial telephone service began.

The Big Ten renewed its Rose Bowl agreement with the Pacific Coast Conference for a three-year period.

Wisconsin's "Hard Rocks" football team led the nation in total defense en route to a 7–1–1 season.

ALBERT (AB) NICHOLAS
BASKETBALL

High-scoring guard Albert (Ab) Nicholas starred on Badger teams of the early 1950s, twice earning first-team all-Big Ten honors and in 1952 gaining second-team all–American recognition from *Look* magazine. Nicholas had come to Wisconsin from Rockford, Illinois, where he was a second-team Illinois all-stater in 1948. Twice the Badgers' most valuable player, Nicholas scored 982 points in 66 varsity games, making him at that time the highest-scoring guard in UW basketball history. Nicholas was the 1951–52 Harlan B. Rogers scholarship recipient for 1951–52 and was named the 1952 "W" Club "Athlete of the Year." He's a past president and member of the board of directors of the National "W" Club and served on the UW System Board of Regents from 1987–94. President of the Milwaukee-based Nicholas Company, he was a major donor to the new Kohil center, a pavilion which bears his name. Nicholas was inducted into the YW Athletic Hall of Fame in 1994.

PAT O'DONAHUE
FOOTBALL

Pat O'Donahue starred at defensive end on Wisconsin's "Hard Rocks" football teams from 1949–51. The Eau Claire native came to Madison out of St. Patrick's High School, where he earned all-state honors in both football and basketball as a senior in 1947–48. O'Donahue's senior season at the UW was a stellar one. An all-Big Ten pick, he also was a first-team all-America selection of the Football Writers Association, the Associated Press and the Newspaper Enterprise Association. O'Donahue played in the 1951 Blue–Gray Game and was a member of the 1952 College All–Stars. He played professionally with the San Francisco 49ers (1952) and the Green Bay Packers (1955). O'Donahue was inducted into the UW Athletic Hall of Fame in 1993.

LEADING THE WAY

Guy Sundt
Football, Cross Country and Track Coach Athletic Director

Guy Sundt's 35 years at Wisconsin took him from his days as an eight-time "W" award winner in football, track and basketball through coaching stints in five sports and finally to the director's chair. Sundt enrolled at Madison out of nearby Stoughton and made his mark as football team captain and a first-team all-Big Ten pick in 1921. He also was an outdoor track all-American in the longjump. After graduating, Sundt coached football, basketball and track at Ripon College from 1922–24 before returning to Wisconsin, where he served as freshman basketball coach (1924–29), freshman baseball coach (1925–26), assistant football, track and cross country coach (1924–48) and as assistant athletic directory (1936–50). Sundt became head track and cross country coach in 1948 and guided the Badgers to Big Ten cross country title in '48 and '49 and to a co–championship in the 1949 Conference indoor track meet. He then served as Wisconsin's athletic director from 1950–55. Sundt was inducted into the UW Athletic Hall of Fame in 1993.

THE LIST

MEN'S BASKETBALL HONORS

Naismith Hall of Fame
Dr. Walter Meanwell (inducted in 1959)
Harold Olsen (1959)
Chris Steinmetz Sr. (1959)
Harold "Bud" Foster (1964)

All-America (first team)
Chris Steinmetz Sr. (1905)
George Levis (1916)
Harold "Bud" Foster (1930)
Gene Englund (1941)
John Kotz (1942)
Alando Tucker (2007)

Big Ten MVP
Gene Englund (1941)
John Kotz (1942)
Glen Selbo (1947)
Don Rehlfeldt (1950)
Devin Harris (2004)
Alando Tucker (2007)

BADGER BIG TEN FINISHES...

Football: 2nd
coached by Ivy Williamson

Cross Country: 2nd
coached by Riley Best

Basketball: 7th
coached by Harold Foster

Indoor Track: 6th
coached by Riley Best

Swimming: 7th
coached by John Hickman

Wrestling: 5th (tie)
coached by George Martin

Baseball: 3rd
coached by Art Mansfield

Golf: 3rd
coached by John Jamieson

Tennis: 8th
coached by Carl Sanger

Outdoor Track: 9th
coached by Riley Best

The Big Event

Boxers win another NCAA title

Wisconsin's boxers had never gone longer than four years between national collegiate titles and they weren't about to rewrite a successful script in 1952.

Coach John Walsh's team, last a winner in 1948, got back on top with 27 points. It was the UW's sixth championship since 1939 and re-established Wisconsin as the premier collegiate boxing power.

Two men won championship bouts, Bob Morgan in the 147 lb. class and Bob Ranck in the heavyweight division, his second straight NCAA win there.

WISCONSIN TIMELINE

1952: NBC's *Today* show premiered with Dave Garroway as the host.

The Conference approved an 18-game round-robin basketball schedule.

Wisconsin was selected as the Big Ten's representative in the 1953 Rose Bowl after tying Purdue for the Conference title.

WISCONSIN HEADLINER

HARVEY KUENN
BASEBALL

Milwaukeean Harvey Kuenn came full circle in his athletic career from his days as a football, basketball and baseball star at Milwaukee Lutheran High School to his American League pennant-winning stint in 1982 as manager of the Milwaukee Brewers. In between, there was stardom at Wisconsin and a long professional baseball career. Kuenn won major "W" awards at Wisconsin in 1951–52 in basketball and in both the 1951 and 1952 seasons, in baseball. He earned all-Big Ten and all-American honors at shortstop in 1952, his junior season, while captaining the Badgers and leading them to third place in the Conference. Kuenn led the Big Ten with 63 at bats, 28 hits, 16 runs, 6 doubles, 5 triples and 16 RBIs. His single season average of .436 was the third best ever by a Wisconsin ballplayer. His career batting average of .382 was second best in Badger history. Kuenn signed with the Detroit Tigers after his junior year and also played with Cleveland, San Francisco, Philadelphia and the Chicago Cubs. A member of the Wisconsin State Hall of Fame, Kuenn was a charter inductee of the UW Athletic Hall of Fame.

WISCONSIN HEADLINER

HAROLD FAVERTY
FOOTBALL

Harold (Hal) Faverty, an end and linebacker, was a four-time "W" award winner in football over a seven-season span. He earned first-team all-America honors in 1951 from the International News Service. Faverty played for the Badgers in 1945, 1948, 1950 and 1951, with service in the military interrupting his schooling and playing career. As a 25-year-old senior, he was one of the most experienced players on the 1951 Wisconsin team that went 7–1–1 under Coach Ivy Williamson. Faverty, who played on both sides of the ball, was integral to the Badgers as a linebacker on the famed "Hard Rocks" defense, which allowed a school record low 5.9 points per game. He also played in the 1952 College All-Star game in Chicago.

WISCONSIN HEADLINER

WALTER DIEKE
TRACK AND CROSS COUNTRY

Walter Dieke starred for Wisconsin cross country and track teams from 1948–52. Dieke led the Badgers to the 1950 Big Ten championship with a third place finish in the Conference meet and that year also earned all-American honors. He captained the 1951 squad and won the Big Ten individual title. His senior track season in 1952, however, was his best. Dieke became Wisconsin's first NCAA long distance champion, winning the NCAA 10,000 meter run in 32:25.1 in the meet at Berkeley, Cal. He's a member of Wisconsin's track and field "Hall of Honor."

A W FIRST

Koepcke is Big Ten golf medalist

Doug Koepcke became the first of Wisconsin's four Big Ten golf champions in 1952. Koepcke had rounds of 73, 74, 79 and 80 en route to his winning 306 total in the 72-hole tournament at Champaign. Coach John Jamieson's first Wisconsin team finished third behind Michigan and Purdue.

1952-53

BADGER BIG TEN FINISHES...

Football: 1st
coached by Ivy Williamson

Cross Country: 4th
coached by Riley Best

Basketball: 5th
coached by Harold Foster

Indoor Track: 10th
coached by Riley Best

Swimming: 7th
coached by John Hickman

Wrestling: 9th
coached by George Martin

Baseball: 6th
coached by Art Mansfield

Golf: 5th
coached by John Jamieson

Tennis: 8th
coached by Carl Sanger

Outdoor Track: 9th
coached by Riley Best

The Big Event

Wisconsin wins first Big Ten football title in 40 years, goes to Rose Bowl

Wisconsin's 1952 football team earned the first bowl bid in the school's history after winning its first Big Ten title since 1912. Paced by four all-Big Ten selections, back Alan Ameche, tackle Dave Suminski, guard Bob Kennedy and guard George O'Brien, the Badgers posted a 6–3–1 record and made the UW's first Rose Bowl appearance on New Year's Day in 1953.

Coming off a 7–1–1 season in 1951 and a runner–up Big Ten finish, the Badgers were ready for a great season. Ranked seventh in the pre-season polls, Wisconsin stopped Marquette 42–19 in the season opener. And after a 20–6 win over second-ranked Illinois in the next game, fourth-year Coach Ivy Williamson's Badgers were even ranked first nationally—the only time that's happened in Wisconsin history.

Losses to Ohio State and eighth-ranked non-conference foe UCLA were sandwiched around a 42–13 win over Iowa. A non–league win over Rice and victories over Northwestern (24–20) and Indiana (37–14) kept the Badgers in the Big Ten lead and even a 21–21 tie with Minnesota didn't hurt the UW cause. After losing 7–0 to USC in Pasadena, Wisconsin ended the season ranked 10th by United Press International and 11th by the Associated Press

WISCONSIN TIMELINE

1953: President Harry Truman announced that the U.S. had developed a hydrogen bomb.

The Conference reduced football traveling squads to 38 and adopted a 14-game Conference basketball schedule for 1954–55.

Badgers beat top-ranked Illinois 34–7 in football at Camp Randall.

WISCONSIN HEADLINER

DAVE SUMINSKI
FOOTBALL

Dave Suminski, a three-year standout for Wisconsin in the early 1950s, made his debut as a defensive tackle in 1952 a great one. Suminski had started the two previous seasons on the Badgers, offensive line. On defense, he earned all–Big Ten and all–American honors on a Wisconsin team that would win the Conference with a 4–1–1 mark and go on to play in the 1953 Rose Bowl. It was the UW's first bowl appearance. In that game, a 7–0 loss to USC, the Badger defense held the vaunted Trojan offense to just 48 yards rushing. Suminski was selected by the Washington Redskins in the 1953 National Football League draft and later played with the Chicago Cardinals and the Hamilton Tiger Cats of the Canadian Football League.

WISCONSIN HEADLINER

DON VOSS
FOOTBALL

Despite playing only two seasons before a knee injury in the 1953 Rose Bowl ended his career, Don Voss was one of the top ends in Wisconsin history. In his first season, 1951, Voss was named to the Associated Press freshman all-America team and was a member of Wisconsin's "Hard Rocks," the best defensive unit in the nation. A year later he helped guide Coach Ivy Williamson's Big Ten champion Badgers to their first-ever bowl game. He was the youngest member of *Look* magazine's 1952 all-America team.

LEADING THE WAY

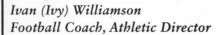

Ivan (Ivy) Williamson
Football Coach, Athletic Director

Ivy Williamson is a name that is synonymous with Wisconsin football excellence as he presided over one of the most successful eras in Badger gridiron history and led the UW to its first Rose Bowl. As a player, Williamson earned all-Big Ten honors at Michigan in 1932, when he captained the Wolverines. He also played on Michigan's 1930 and 1931 teams and lettered in basketball at Ann Arbor in his junior and senior seasons. Following assistant coaching stints at Yale sandwiched around service in World War II, Williamson compiled a 13–5 record in two years at Lafayette College before coming to Madison in 1949. In seven years as head man at Wisconsin, Williamson posted a 41–19–4 mark, 29–13–4 in the Big Ten, and led the 1952 Badgers to the Conference title and 1953 Rose Bowl berth. He also served as chairman of the NCAA Football Rules Committee. Williamson became director of athletics in 1955 and led Wisconsin until his death in 1969. A member of the Wisconsin State Hall of Fame, Williamson was one of the charter inductees into the UW Athletic Hall of Fame in 1991.

THE LIST

BADGERS IN THE BOWLS

1953	Rose:	USC 7, UW 0
1960	Rose:	Washington 44, UW 8
1963	Rose:	USC 42, UW 37
1981	Garden State	Tennessee 28, UW 21
1982	Independence:	UW 14, Kansas State 3
1984	Hall of Fame:	Kentucky 20, UW 19
1994	Rose:	UW 21, UCLA 16
1995	Hall of Fame:	UW 34, Duke 20
1996	Copper:	UW 38, Utah 10
1998	Outback:	Georgia 33, UW 6
1999	Rose:	UW 38, UCLA 31
2000	Rose:	UW 17, Stanford 9
2000	Sun:	UW 21, UCLA 20
2002	Alamo:	UW 31, Colorado 28
2003	Music City:	Auburn 28, UW 14
2005	Outback:	Georgia 24, UW 21
2006	Capital One:	UW 24, Auburn 10
2007	Capital One:	UW 17, Arkansas 14
2008	Outback:	Tennessee 21, UW 17
2008	Champs Sports:	Florida State 42, UW 13
2009	Champs Sports:	UW 20, Miami 14
2011	Rose:	TCU 21, UW 19
2012	Rose:	Oregon 45, UW 38
2013	Rose:	Stanford 20, UW 14

BADGER BIG TEN FINISHES...

Football: 3rd
coached by Ivy Williamson

Cross Country: 3rd
coached by Riley Best

Basketball: 5th (tie)
coached by Harld Foster

Indoor Track: 9th
coached by RIley Best

Swimming: 5th
coached by John Hickman

Wrestling: 5th
coached by George Martin

Baseball: 2nd
coached by Art Mansfield

Golf: 10th
coached by John Jamieson

Tennis: 7th
coached by Carl Sanger

Outdoor Track: 10th
coached by Riley Best

The Big Event

Boxers take seventh
NCAA crown

It took only 19 points and the Badgers had just one championship, but it was enough to give Wisconsin and Coach John Walsh their seventh NCAA boxing title in 1954. Bob Meath claimed the Badgers' lone individual win in the 156 lb. weight class.

WISCONSIN TIMELINE

1954: The world's first atomic submarine, the USS Nautilus, was launched in Groton, CT.

Big Ten directors adopted a procedure for selection of the Rose Bowl representative.

Wisconsin's Alan Ameche won the Heisman Trophy.

1954–55

BADGER BIG TEN FINISHES...

Football: 2nd
coached by Ivy Williamson

Cross Country: 6th
coached by Riley Best

Basketball: 6th (tie)
coached by Harold Foster

Indoor Track: 5th
coached by Riley Best

Swimming: 6th
coached by John Hickman

Wrestling: 4th
coached by George Martin

Baseball: 7th
coached by Art Mansfield

Golf: 3rd
coached by John Jamieson

Tennis: 5th
coached by Carl Sanger

Outdoor Track: 8th
coached by Riley Best

The Big Event

Ameche wins Heisman Trophy

Fullback Alan "The Horse" Ameche in 1954 became the only Badger to ever win the Heisman Trophy—emblematic of college football's best player. The Kenosha native won the trophy after rushing for 641 yards and nine touchdowns.

In the voting by sports writers throughout the nation, Ameche totaled 1,068 points to outdistance Oklahoma linebacker–center Kent Burris (838) and Ohio State halfback Howard "Hopalong" Cassady (810). Ameche, who was sixth in the 1953 voting, dominated in 1954, receiving 214 first-place votes and a majority of votes cast in the east and midwest.

Ameche made first-team all-America squads as picked by the Football Writers Association, *Look* magazine, Newspaper Enterprise Association, Paramount News, All-Academic, *Athletic Publications, Catholic Weekly* and UNICO (National Italian Association).

Besides Ameche, five other Badgers have finished among the top 10 in balloting for the Heisman. They are Howard Weiss, sixth in 1938; Dave Schreiner, 10th in 1942; Dale Hackbart, seventh in 1959; Pat Richter, sixth in 1962; and Ron Vander Kelen, ninth in 1962.

WISCONSIN TIMELINE

1955: The new Air Force Academy was dedicated at Lowry Air Force Base in Colorado.

The Conference approved the pending NCAA TV plan and voted to pool and share equally all proceeds.

Wisconsin won the last of its eight NCAA boxing titles in the tournament held at the Wisconsin Field House.

WISCONSIN HEADLINER

ALAN AMECHE
FOOTBALL

Alan "The Horse" Ameche remains the only Wisconsin football player to have won the Heisman Trophy. Three times an all-Big Ten selection and twice an all-American as a fullback, the Kenosha native was the Conference's most valuable player in 1954. He set a Rose Bowl record of 133 yards on 28 carries in the 1953 game for Ivy Williamson's Big Ten champion Badgers. Ameche was selected by the Baltimore Colts in the first round of the 1955 NFL draft and ran 79 yards for a touchdown against the Chicago Bears on the first play of his pro football career. A member of the National Football Foundation Hall of Fame, Ameche also had his number 35 retired by Wisconsin. He was named a charter member of the UW Athletic Hall of Fame in 1991.

WISCONSIN HEADLINER

RICHARD W. CABLE
BASKETBALL

Dick Cable was one of the Badgers' top basketball performers in the early 1950s, earning major "W" awards from 1952–55. He was a second-team all-Big Ten pick as a senior and earned honorable mention all-Conference status in his first two seasons. The 1955 team captain and most valuable player, Cable scored had career best 31 points against Tulane and later equaled that performance against Notre Dame. He set a Badger single-game mark with 11 against California in 1952. Cable led the Badg scoring in 1953–54 and 1954–55, setting a UW record for field goal accuracy (.436) in his junior campaign. He was the Badgers' career scoring leader when he graduated and still is 12th on the all-time list. Cable was the Badgers' Big Ten Medal of Honor recipient as a senior. Drafted by the NBA's Milwaukee Hawks in the second round, Cable chose to pursue a business career. He served as a volunteer fund–raiser for the Kohl Center project from 1995–98. Cable was inducted into the UW Athletic Hall of Fame in 1998.

LEADING THE WAY

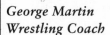

George Martin
Wrestling Coach

George Martin, an NCAA wrestling champion who as a coach stayed in superb condition, guided Wisconsin wrestling fortunes from 1935 until 1970. Wrestling was at a low ebb when he came to Wisconsin but in his first season the UW won more dual matches than in the five previous years combined. Although Martin's UW teams never won a Big Ten championship, the Badgers were competitive and featured such top wrestlers as John Roberts, Clarence Self, Larry Lederman, Rick Heinzelman, Mike iluck and future Badger coach Russ Hellickson. An Iowa native, Martin twice won the Big Six 165–lb. championship for Iowa State, le won the NCAA title at that weight in 1933 and the national AA 175–lb. title in 1934. He captained Iowa State to the 1933 NCAA crown and qualified for the 1936 Olympics, but was disqualified for the Olympic berth when he accepted the Wisconsin coaching position. Martin was inducted into the Helms Hall Wrestling Hall of Fame in 1969. He drowned at age 59 in 1970 while on a canoeing trip in Ontario.

THE LIST

ALAN AMECHE'S
HEISMAN TROPHY-
WINNING SEASON

Game	Carries	Yards	TD
Marquette	18	107	1
Michigan State	17	127	1
Rice	21	90	2
Purdue	18	73	1
Ohio State	16	42	0
Iowa	26	117	1
Northwestern	17	59	1
Illinois	0	0	0
Minnesota	13	26	2

BADGER BIG TEN FINISHES...

Football: 6th
coached by Ivy Willamson

Cross Country: 6th
coached by Riley Best

Basketball: 8th (tie)
coached by Harold Foster

Indoor Track: 7th
coached by Riley Best

Swimming: 9th
coached by John Hickman

Wrestling: 7th
coached by George Martin

Baseball: 3rd
coached by Art Mansfield

Golf: 4th
coached by John Jamieson

Tennis: 9th
coached by Carl Sanger

Outdoor Track: 9th
coached by Riley Best

The Big Event

Boxers win last boxing title

The 1956 NCAA boxing championships marked the end of an era in the collegiate sport. Wisconsin won its eighth and last boxing title as legendary Coach John Walsh neared the end of his coaching career.

The Badgers' 47 points were the most a Wisconsin team had ever scored in the NCAA tournament. And the five individual crowns won by Badger boxers had only been equaled by the Wisconsin team of 1943, another NCAA title-winning unit.

Taking their championship bouts were Dean Plemmons at 112 lbs., Dick Bartman at 139, Vince Ferguson at 156, Orville Pitts at 178 and Truman Sturdevant at heavyweight. All were first-time champions.

WISCONSIN TIMELINE

1956: Don Larsen of the New York Yankees became the first pitcher to throw a perfect game in the World Series, beating the Brooklyn Dodgers 2–0.

The Council of Ten extended Big Ten Commissioner Tug Wilson's contract for a five-year term.

BADGER BIG TEN FINISHES...

Football: 9th
coached by Milt Bruhn

Basketball: 9th
coached by Harold Foster

Indoor Track: 8th
coached by Riley Best

Swimming: 6th
coached by John Hickman

Wrestling: 8th
coached by George Martin

Baseball: 9th
coached by Art Mansfield

Golf: 1st
coached by John Jamieson

Tennis: 9th
coached by Carl Sanger

Outdoor Track: 10th
coached by Rliey Best

The Big Event

Wisconsin wins Big Ten golf, fencing tournaments

Wisconsin emerged with two Big Ten championships during the 1956–57 season.

Coach Archie Simonson's Badgers earned their second fencing title in three years and got the better of fencing power Illinois in doing so. Epee champ Paul Mortensen and his teammate in the same weapon, Chuck Barnum, paced the Badgers along with Frank Tyrell, a scorer in sabre, and Gerry Bedner and Paul Lamba, who scored in foil.

John Jamieson's golfers captured the '57 Conference golf championship at Iowa City. The Badgers totaled 1,512 strokes for the 72–hole tourney, eight strokes ahead of Iowa.

Leading Wisconsin were Roger Rubendall, who carded a 291 (74–76–71–70) to finish third, and Dave Forbes, who came in fourth at 299 off rounds of 79, 76, 70 and 74. It was Rubendall's third consecutive top five finish.

WISCONSIN TIMELINE

1957: Althea Gibson was the women's clay court singles championship, making her the first black player to win a major U.S. tennis crown.

The Conference created a Financial Aids Service to make determinations of financial aid.

1957–58

BADGER BIG TEN FINISHES...

Football: 4th (tie)
coached by Milt Bruhn

Basketball: 10th
coached by Harold Foster

Indoor Track: 9th
coached by Riley Best

Swimming: 7th
coached by John Hickman

Wrestling: 9th
coached by George Martin

Baseball: 5th
coached by Art Mansfield

Golf: 8th
coached by John Jamieson

Tennis: 8th
coached by Carl Sanger

Outdoor Track: 9th
coached by Riley Best

The Big Event

Badger teams generally struggle in transition year

The 1957–58 season was a transition year of sorts for many of Wisconsin's teams, with little success. Second-year Coach Milt Bruhn's football squad tied for fourth in the Big Ten. The Badgers won their first three, dropped their middle three to Iowa, Ohio State and Michigan State and then rebounded to score wins over Northwestern, Illinois and Minnesota in a 6–3 campaign.

Coach Bud Foster's next-to-last basketball team, despite having two honorable mention all-Big Ten picks in most valuable player Walt Holt (15.4 points per game) and Bob Litzow (14.7), suffered through an 8–14 season. The Badgers started out 8–6 but lost their final eight to finish last in the Conference.

It was the end of an era in boxing at Wisconsin as retiring coach John Walsh's last team placed fourth in the NCAA meet. Archie Simonson's fencers were 10–4 in dual meets and placed second in the Big Ten, the best finish by a Wisconsin team this year.

Gerald Bodner won the foil title and also placed fifth in the NCAA meet, leading the UW to eighth place nationally.

Dynie Mansfield's baseball team was 17–12 overall and finished fifth in the Big Ten at 8–7. Leading the Badgers was first-team all-American centerfielder Ron Nieman, who hit .327.

Wisconsin's track teams placed ninth in the indoor and outdoor championships.

WISCONSIN TIMELINE

1958: America's first successful Earth satellite, Explorer I, was launched from Cape Canaveral, Florida.

The Conference approved a 10-game football schedule effective in 1965.

BADGER BIG TEN FINISHES...

Football: 2nd
coached by Milt Bruhn

Basketball: 10th
coached by Harold Foster

Indoor Track: 5th
coached by Riley Best

Swimming: 7th
coached by John Hickman

Wrestling: 6th
coached by George Martin

Baseball: 2nd (tie)
coached by Art Mansfield

Golf: 6th
coached by John Jamieson

Tennis: 9th
coached by Carl Sanger

Outdoor Track: 9th
coached by Riley Best

The Big Event

Westphal wins NCAA 50-freestyle

Fred Westphal became Wisconsin's second—and last, to date-national collegiate champion in swimming in 1959, winning the 50-yard freestyle in the 1959 championships at Cornell. His time, 22.3 seconds, equaled the fifth-best mark ever posted by a winner in the event.

In the qualifying heats, Westphal set NCAA and American records of 21.9 seconds. The Janesville native was a three-time swimming all-American for the Badger teams in the late 1950s, three times placing among the top five in national collegiate meets.

As a high school star, he won an individual state title and led Janesville to the 1955 WIAA state swimming championship. At Wisconsin, he compiled a 28–9 dual meet record swimming 50, 60 and 100-yard freestyle events in collegiate competition while serving as Badger captain in 1958 and co-captain in 1959.

As a sophomore in 1957, Westphal won the 50 free at the Big Ten meet and went on to place second in the NCAA. He was runner-up in the Conference in that event as a junior and senior and also took second in the NCAA in his second year of eligibility. Westphal was a charter member inductee in the UW Athletic Hall of Fame in 1991.

WISCONSIN TIMELINE

1959: Alaska and Hawaii were admitted to the Union as the 49th and 50th states.

The Big Ten revised its summer competition rule to permit limited basketball play.

Wisconsin won its second Rose Bowl berth after rallying to beat Minnesota 11–7.

BADGER BIG TEN FINISHES...

Football: 1st
coached by Milt Bruhn

Basketball: 9th
coached by John Erikson

Indoor Track: 10th
coached by Riley Best

Swimming: 8th
coached by John Hickman

Wrestling: 10th
coached by George Martin

Baseball: 3rd
coached by Art Mansfield

Golf: 6th
coached by John Jamieson

Tennis: 7th
coached by Carl Sanger

Outdoor Track: 10th
coached by Riley Best

The Big Event

Wisconsin wins Big Ten football title

Wisconsin won its first undisputed Big Ten football championship since 1912 with a come-from-behind 11–7 win at Minnesota to clinch the title. It also gave Coach Milt Bruhn's team a return to the Rose Bowl seven years after the Badgers had played in Pasadena for the first time.

Defensive end Dan Lanphear rebounded from an injury-plagued junior season to earn all-America honors for Wisconsin. His fumble recovery and blocked punt for a safety were critical plays in the Badgers' 12–3 win over Ohio State. Also starring for the UW were all-Conference quarterback Dale Hackbart and all-league guard Jerry Stalcup.

Despite losing 44–8 to Washington in the 1960 Rose Bowl, the Badgers finished the season ranked sixth by both the Associated Press and United Press International.

The 1959 season:
Wisconsin 16, Stanford 14*
Wisconsin 44, Marquette 6*
Purdue 21, Wisconsin 0
Wisconsin 25, Iowa 16*
Wisconsin 12, Ohio State 3*
Wisconsin 19, Michigan 10
Wisconsin 24, Northwestern 19
Illinois 9, Wisconsin 6*
Wisconsin 11, Minnesota 7
Washington 44, Wisconsin 8

*Designates home game

WISCONSIN TIMELINE

1960: Sen. John F. Kennedy (D–Mass.) announced his bid for the Democratic presental nomination.

Junior college graduates were made immediately eligible upon enrollment in a Conference university.

DALE L. HACKBART
BASEBALL, BASKETBALL,
FOOTBALL

Madison native Dale Hackbart earned six major "W" awards in three sports, and went on to a distinguished 14-year professional football career with Green Bay, Washington, Minnesota, St. Louis and Denver. He also played for the Vikings in the 1970 Super Bowl against Kansas City. Hackbart, who prepped at Madison East High School, quarterbacked Wisconsin's 1957–59 football teams and was selected by Green Bay in the third round of the 1960 National Football League draft. As a senior, he was an all-Big Ten pick after leading the Conference in total offense with 686 yards. Hackbart scored 134 points in this career off 21 touchdowns and eight extra points. He was a forward on the 1959 Badger basketball squad and as a two-year outfielder for the UW baseball team, he posted a career .290 batting average; he also played in the Pittsburgh Pirates' minor ague system. Hackbart was named to the Madison Pen and Mike Club-Bowman Sports Hall of Fame in 1983 and to the UW Athletics Hall of Fame in 1996.

DAN LANPHEAR
FOOTBALL

Dan Lanphear earned all-America honors as a defensive end for Wisconsin in 1959, atoning for a injury-plagued junior season. The Madison native was accorded first-team all-America honors by *The Associated Press, United Press, News Enterprise Association, The Sporting News,* the American Football Coaches Association and *Look magazine.* His best game may have been the Badgers' 12–3 win over Ohio State in 1959. Lanphear recovered a fumble, blocked a punt for a safety and knocked two OSU running backs out of the game with strong hits. Lanphear played defensive end for the American Football League's Houston Oilers and was a member of their AFL championship teams of 1960 and 1961.

LEADING THE WAY

Milt Bruhn
Football Coach

Milt Bruhn remains the only UW foot-ball coach to lead the Badgers to a pair Big Ten titles in the 20th century, with his 1959 and 1962 teams having accomplished that feat and played in the 1960 and 1963 Rose Bowl games. Bruhn, who in 11 seasons posted a 52-45-6 mark, had three of his squads—1958 (8th), 1959 (6th) and 1960 (2nd)—ranked among the top 10 in final national polls. Those three teams' combined 20–6–1 regular season mark stands as the best for any three–year span since the turn of the century. Bruhn came to Wisconsin from Lafayette College in 1949 with Ivy Williamson after coaching stops at Amherst, Minnesota, Colgate, and Franklin and Marshall. Minnesota native, Bruhn played guard on Minnesota's undefeated 1934 and 1935 national title teams and was a catcher on the Gophers' 1835 Big Ten champion baseball team. He was a charter member of the UW Athletic Hall of Fame in 1991.

A W FIRST

Two UW winners in NCAA boxing championship

It was more a Wisconsin ending than a beginning as a glorious era of Badger sports ended tragically in the final NCAA boxing championships. Under new coach Vern Woodward, who had succeeded John Walsh after the 1958 season, the Badgers finished sixth in the 1959 NCAA tourney and second in 1960. Charles Mohr had claimed the 165 lb. title in '59 and Brown McGhee (132 lbs.) and Jerry Turner (156 lbs.) were the final Wisconsin boxing champions. The sport was discontinued after Mohr died of an injury suffered in the 1960 NCAA championship in a 165 lb. bout with Stu Bartell of San Diego State.

BADGER BIG TEN FINISHES...

Football: 9th
coached by Milt Bruhn

Cross Country: 4th
coached by Tom Bennett

Basketball: 8th
coached by John Erickson

Indoor Track: 9th
coached by Charles Walter

Swimming: 8th
coached by John Hickman

Wrestling: 9th
coached by George Martin

Baseball: 6th
coached by Art Mansfield

Golf: 9th
coached by John Jamieson

Tennis: 8th
coached by Carl Sanger

Outdoor Track: 10th
coached by Charles Walter

The Big Event

Unheralded Miller stars at quarterback

Ron Miller, who wasn't even on the 1960 Badger foot-ball roster, let alone the depth chart, was the surprise of the 1960 season. The junior walk-on became the Big Ten's top passer, completing 72 of 144 attempts and leading the Conference in total offense with 966 yards, only 15 of which were by rushing.

For the season, Miller had 1,395 yards, all except 44 in the air, and eight touchdowns. He had 200-yard-plus games in 1960 against Marquette (224 yards on 9 of 19) and Purdue (223 yards on 12 of 23). Milt Bruhn's Badgers, still a year away from a winning record and two years away from their next Rose Bowl, weren't as effective as their quarterback.

The UW finished 3–6, dropping five of its last six games. Miller again was the Badgers' starter in 1961, passing for 11 touchdowns and 1,487 yards off 104 comple-tions in 198 attempts. But no story could have been greater than his in 1960, when he walked on to Badger football stardom.

WISCONSIN TIMELINE

1961: Two U.S. helicopter companies arrived in Saigon, the first direct support for South Vietnam's battle against communist guerillas.

Kenneth L. (Tug) Wilson retired as commissioner and was succeeded by Bill Reed.

Wisconsin defeated top-ranked Ohio State 86–67 in bas-ketball at the Field House, ending the Buckeyes' 47-game winning streak.

1961-62

BADGER BIG TEN FINISHES...

Football: 5th
coached by Milt Bruhn

Cross Country: 4th
coached by Charles Walter

Basketball: 2nd
coached by John Erickson

Indoor Track: 1st
coached by Charles Walter

Swimming: 9th
coached by John Hickman

Wrestling: 4th
coached by George Martin,
(6th, NCAA)

Baseball: 4th
coached by Art Mansfield

Golf: 5th
coached by John Jamieson

Tennis: 7th
coached by Carl Sanger

Outdoor Track: 2nd
coached by Charles Walter

The Big Event

Hockey returns after 28-year absence

Wisconsin played its first intercollegiate hockey game in 1922, but the program was disbanded 12 years later and did not return to the Madison campus until 1962, thanks to the work of several individuals.

UW Athletics Director Ivan Williamson had become a fan of a local youth hockey team called the Madison Hawks, who were coached by John Riley. Williamson enjoyed the Hawks' games and had visions of returning the game to the UW.

Fenton Kelsey, a successful local businessman interested in promoting and developing the sport in Madison, was instrumental in hastening hockey's return to the area by building Hartmeyer Ice Arena with the hope that the facility would speed up the return of the game on campus and bolster interest locally.

With a first-rate arena now in place, and Williamson's full commitment to the sport, the University's Athletic Board approved hockey's return in March, 1962. Williamson hired Riley as the coach and the program played a number of scrimmages and games against teams of all kinds.

That first year—1962–63—Williamson and Riley laid the foundation for what became Wisconsin's first modern era hockey season in 1963–64.

Wisconsin's first game, played in front of 695 curious fans, resulted in a 13–6 loss to St. Mary's College of Winona, Minn. The Badgers fell behind 12–0 before Tom French scored Wisconsin's first modern-era goal on a penalty shot.

WISCONSIN TIMELINE

1962: Astronaut John Glenn became the first American to orbit the Earth.

Conference offices were moved to the Sheraton-Chicago Hotel.

Second-ranked Badgers made their second Rose Bowl appearance in three years, with their rally falling short in a 42–37 loss to USC.

BADGER BIG TEN FINISHES...

Football: 1st
coached by Milt Bruhn

Cross Country: 3rd
coached by Charles Walter

Basketball: 6th
coached by John Erickson

Indoor Track: 3rd
coached by Charles Walter

Swimming: 7th
coached by John Hickman

Wrestling: 5th
coached by George Martin

Baseball: 5th
coached by Art Mansfield

Golf: 2nd
coached by John Jamieson

Tennis: 8th
coached by David G. Clark

Outdoor Track: 2nd
coached by Charles Walter

The Big Event

Badgers lose most exciting Rose Bowl after Winning Big Ten title

The '62 Wisconsin football team rolled to an 8–1 record, including a win over top-ranked Northwestern on November 10, and the school's second Big Ten title in four years. The Badgers finished the campaign with a consensus No. 2 national ranking after a thrilling meeting with top-ranked USC in the Rose Bowl.

Wisconsin's 23-point fourth quarter explosion wasn't quite enough as it dropped a season-ending 42–37 Rose Bowl encounter to Southern Cal. The Trojans had claimed a 42–14 lead on the first play of the fourth quarter before the huge Badger comeback.

USC raced to a 21–7 halftime lead and extended it on the first play of the third stanza, before Ron VanderKelen led one of the biggest charges in bowl history.

VanderKelen reached paydirt on a 17–yard scamper to reduce the margin to 28–14. USC responded with a pair of TD passes by Pete Beathard and the Trojans led 42–14.

Lou Holland (13–yard run) and Gary Kroner (4–yard reception) tallied for the Badgers within three minutes. A bad center snap on a punt resulted in a UW safety. After the free kick, VanderKelen hit three straight passes, including a 19–yard score to Pat Richter for the final 42–37 margin.

VanderKelen, the game MVP, set both Wisconsin and Rose Bowl records with 401 yards passing. Richter caught 11 of those aerials for 163 yards. The 79 total points was a Rose Bowl record that stood for 28 years.

WISCONSIN TIMELINE

1963: President John F. Kennedy was assassinated in Dallas.

Conference participation in the "Inter-Conference Letter of Intent" plan was approved.

Wisconsin lost 13–6 to St. Mary's (Minnesota) in the first ice hockey game of the modern era; a week later, the Badgers defeated Macalaster 3–2 for their first win.

ROGER EVERHART
GOLF

Roger Everhart became Wisconsin's third Big Ten golf champion in 1963. He carded a 292 over the 72–hole course in Madison off rounds of 73, 73, 68 and 78. But his heroics weren't enough to give Coach John Jamieson's Badgers their second team title. Minnesota scored 1,523 to the UW's 1,524.

WISCONSIN HEADLINER

PAT RICHTER
FOOTBALL, BASKETBALL,
BASEBALL, DIRECTOR
OF ATHLETICS

Pat Richter was the last of Wisconsin's nine-letter winners, earning "W" awards in football, basketball and baseball from 1960–63. Richter had the magic touch, particularly in football and baseball. Twice an all-Big Ten and all-American end, the Madison (East High School) product led the Conference in pass receiving in 1961 and 1962 and as the Badgers' punter led the Conference as a senior. He caught scoring passes in eight straight games in 1962 and set Rose Bowl records with 11 catches for 163 yards in 1963. In baseball, Richter was almost as awesome, three times earning all-Big Ten first- or second-team honors as an outfielder. He hit safely twice in each of 10 straight games in 1962. The UW's Big Ten Conference Medal of Honor winner in 1963, Richter was a first-round draft choice of the Washington Redskins and played professionally for eight seasons. He was an NCAA Silver Anniversary Top Six Award recipient in 1988. Richter was named the UW's athletic director in 1989.

LEADING THE WAY

Bill Aspinwall
Athletic Business Manager

Bill Aspinwall's career at Wisconsin spanned 46 years over six decades. To say that the Hurley, Wis., native knew Wisconsin's coaches well would be an understatement. He served six athletic directors, seven football coaches, six each in baseball, wrestling and track, three in swimming and fencing, four in golf, seven each in boxing and hockey, nine in crew and 11 in tennis. A 1928 UW accounting graduate, Aspinwall had begun working in the athletic department as a student in 1926 and upon graduation became its first full-time accountant. He succeeded George Levis as business manager in 1932 and added the ticket manager's duties 10 years later upon Harry Schwenker's death. The jobs were split in 1956 and Aspinwall reverted to his role as business manager until his retirement in June, 1972. He was the 40-year secretary of the athletic board and was a charter member of the College Athletic Business Managers Association, serving as its president in 1957 and later as its permanent secretary-treasurer. Aspinwall was named CABMA's "Business Manager of the Year" in 1970. He died at age 76 in January, 1983, in Madison.

BUCKY BADGER

From Benny to Regbad to Bucky

Badgers have been recognized for years as the UW mascot. The version currently known as Bucky, sporting a cardinal and white letter sweater, was first drawn in 1940 by artist Art Evans. He went by names like Benny, Buddy, Bernie, Bobby and Bouncey.

Sports publicist Art Lentz had the idea of bringing the Badger to life. Unfortunately, the first live Badger mascot was too difficult to control and once escaped handlers at a game. In the interest of fan and player safety, he was retired to the Madison Zoo. The Badger Yearbook replaced the live Badger with a small raccoon named "Regbad" (badger spelled backwards) and called it a "badger in a raccoon coat."

In 1949, Connie Conrad, a student in the art department, was commissioned to mold a papier-mâché badger head. Bill Sagal, a gymnast and cheerleader, wore the outfit at a homecoming game. A contest was held to name the mascot, with the winning entry, Buckingham U. Badger, or Bucky, apparently coming from song lyrics which urged the football team to "buck right through the line."

Bucky has survived and prospered, weathering even a 1973 attempt by the state attorney general to replace him with a "lovable and productive" Cow, "Henrietta Holstein."

1963—64

BADGER BIG TEN FINISHES...

Football: 5th
coached by Milt Bruhm

Cross Country: 2nd
coached by Charles Walter

Basketball: 10th
coached by john Erickson

Indoor Track: 2nd
coached by Charles Walter

Swimming: 6th
coached by George Martin

Baseball: 4th (tie)
coached by Art Mansfield

Golf: 5th
coached by John Jamieson

Gymnastics: 4th
coached by George Bauer

Tennis: 5th
coached by John Powless

Outdoor Track: 1st
coached by Coached by Charles Walter

The Big Event

Badgers win outdoor track title

It took Coach Charles "Rut" Walter only four years to bring Wisconsin back to the top of the Big Ten outdoor track standings. In his first return to Evanston since leaving Northwestern in 1960 to become Wisconsin's coach, Walter guided the 1964 Badgers to the Conference title, the UW's fourth ever. It was Wisconsin's first Big Ten outdoor crown since a Tom Jones-coached team won in 1931, also in Evanston.ttt

The Badgers scored 64 points to beat Michigan by 12 points. The UW scored in 13 of the 15 events and had four individual champions: Barry Ackerman in the long jump (23'1"), Don Henrickson in the discus (166'4"), Mike Manley in the mile (4:12.0) and Gene Dix in the 120-yard high hurdles (14.5). The win climaxed a great turnaround for Wisconsin under Walter.

His first team, in 1961, finished last in the Big Ten as had two of the four teams prior to his arrival, but by 1962 the Badgers had won the indoor crown and climbed to second outdoors. They repeated that runner-up outdoor finish in '63. Wisconsin finished the season with a string of 17 consecutive victories in indoor and outdoor dual and triangular meets.

WISCONSIN TIMELINE

1964:   Cassius Clay (later to become Muhammad Ali) defeated Sonny Liston to become world heavyweight boxing champion.

Big Ten sports information directors established the Robert C. Woodworth Award to honor the long-time Purdue SID, who had died, and to be presented to members of the press, radio or TV who had made meritorious contributions to the Big Ten.

Ken Barnes scored a then-school-record 42 points as the Badgers lost 92–73 to Indiana at the Field House.

WISCONSIN HEADLINER

RICK REICHARDT
BASEBALL, FOOTBALL

Rick Reichardt was one of Wisconsin's greatest two-sport stars, excelling in both football and basketball in the early 1960s. The Stevens Point native earned all-America honors in 1964, finishing second in national batting statistics with a .443 average on 47 hits in 106 at-bats. With a .472 average in Big Ten play, he repeated as Conference batting champion, becoming only the second player since 1939 to repeat as the league's top hitter. He also led the Badgers in home runs and stolen bases. Reichardt had hitting streaks of 15 games (from the '63 season) and 17 games. In football, the Badgers also counted on him. He was also the Big Ten's leading pass receiver in 1963, with 26 receptions for 383 yards and one touchdown. His TD came on a 50-yard pass play from quarterback Hal Brandt for a 17–14 UW victory. Reichardt signed a baseball contract with the Los Angeles Angels after his junior season.

LEADING THE WAY

Oscar C. Damman
National "W" Club

Oscar C. Damman has been a familiar name to Wisconsin athletes for more than three generations. A 1931 UW graduate, the Madison native has enjoyed a 60-year-plus association with the university, serving since 1958 as National "W" Club coordinator. Damman began his university service in 1936 at the Wisconsin Union, where he held a variety of positions, including Theater Ticket Sales Manager, for the next 14 years. From 1950-55, Damman managed student loans and supervised non-federal gift accounts. He became Athletic Ticket Sales Manager in 1956 and two years later was named by athletic director Ivan Williamson as the department's coordinator to the National "W" Club. He was named assistant to the athletic director in 1964 and served in various administrative roles until his 1991 retirement from the Division of Intercollegiate Athletics. Damman received the "Know Your Madisonian" Distinguished Person Award in 1965 and was National "W" Club "Man of the Year" for 1986. Damman was inducted into the UW Athletics Hall of Fame in 1996.

LEADING THE WAY

Archie Simonson
Fencing Coach

Archie Simonson spent 22 seasons as Wisconsin's fencing coach, compiling a 195–121 record (.617 winning percentage) against national and Midwest competition. Succeeding the "father" of Wisconsin fencing, Arpad Masley, in 1951, Simonson guided the Badgers to Big Ten championships in 1955, 1957 and 1959. Twelve of his fencers won Conference titles, with foilists Bruce Taubman (1967–68) and Neal Cohen (1970, 1972) repeat winners. And 13 Badger fencers earned all-America honors under his tutelage. Rick Baumann and Dick Odders earned back-to-back-to-back-to-back all-America honors in epee from 1966–69.

A W FIRST

Paul Bunyan Axe symbolizes rivalry

The Paul Bunyan Axe is not as old as the story of the mythical giant of lumber camps in the Midwest, but it's only appropriate that it's the primary symbol of the Wisconsin-Minnesota football rivalry, the longest running in the nation. Each year the winner of game between the UW and UM-heading into its 90th straight contest and 106th in the last 107 seasons-is presented with the axe, complete with scores inscribed on the handle. The tradition began after a 16-0 Badger loss to the Gophers in 1948 when the National "W" Club presented Minnesota an axe "wielded by Bunyan" and another tradition was born.

BADGER BIG TEN FINISHES...

Football: 7th (tie)
coached by Milt Bruhn

Cross Country: 3rd
coached by Tom Bennett

Basketball: 8th
coached by John Erickson

Indoor Track: 1st
coached by Charles Water

Swimming: 6th
coached by John Hickman

Wrestling: 9th
coached by George Martin,
(tie for 10th in NCAA)

Baseball: 9th
coached by John Jamieson

Tennis: 8th
coached by John Powless

Gymnastics: 4th
coached by George Bauer

Outdoor Track: 3rd
coached by Charles Walter

The Big Event

Wisconsin wins Big Ten indoor track title

Wisconsin's track fortunes continued on the upswing in 1965, with the UW winning its second Big Ten indoor track championship in three seasons. Coach Charles "Rut" Walter's Badgers scored 46 points in the meet at Champaign, Illinois, to hold off Michigan State by a half-point in what remains the tightest margin between the first- and second-place teams in Big Ten indoor track history.

Wisconsin had three individual champions: Ken Latigo-Olal in the 880-yard run (1:53.3); Gerry Beatty in the 70-yard high hurdles (8.5 seconds); and Bill Holden, who cleared 6'6" to win the high jump. A couple weeks later, Wisconsin finished in a 25th place tie in the inaugural NCAA indoor championships at Cobo Arena in Detroit. Holden was third in the high jump and Al Montalbano fourth in the 600-yard run to become Wisconsin's first indoor track all-Americans.

WISCONSIN TIMELINE

1965: President Lyndon Johnson signed the Voting Rights Act into law.

The Conference provided team championship trophies in football, basketball, baseball and hockey.

Wisconsin beat Minnesota 5–4 in overtime for its first win against as Western Collegiate Hockey Association team after 13 straight losses; six weeks later, Bob Johnson was named head coach.

BADGER BIG TEN FINISHES...

Football: 7th (tie)
coached by Milt Bruhn

Cross Country: 4th
coached by Charles Walter

Basketball: 7th
coached by John Erickson

Indoor Track: 2nd
coached by Charles Walter

Swimming: 5th
coached by John Hickman

Wrestling: 4th
coached by George Martin

Baseball: 7th
coached by Art Mansfield

Golf: 3rd
coached by John Powless

Outdoor Track: 5th
coached by Charles Walter

The Big Event

Coatta, Johnson take over football hockey duties

Coaching change was the order of the day at Wisconsin in 1965, with high profile football and hockey programs undergoing changes in leadership.

Veteran football coach Milt Bruhn resigned and John Coatta, a former Badger who had lettered in 1949, 1950 and 1951 for Ivy Williamson-coached teams that went 18–7–2, was hired.

In his 11 years as Wisconsin's head man, Bruhn compiled a 52–45–6 mark, second only to turn-of-the-century coach Phil King on the all-time UW victory list. He guided the Badgers to Rose Bowl appearances in 1960 and 1963 and posted six winning seasons.

Coatta, in three seasons, couldn't find the winning touch. His first team was 0–9–1 and tied for ninth in the Big Ten followed by a winless campaign and last place finish in 1968. Though his 1969 team improved to 3–7 overall and 3–4 in the Big Ten for a fifth–place tie, he was replaced by John Jardine.

In hockey, Wisconsin's reborn varsity program was on the verge of becoming nationally prominent. On April 1, 1966, Bob Johnson was hired as head coach following John Riley's retirement.

Johnson resigned June 1, 1982, after 15 years as head coach with a 267–175–23 record. His Badgers won three NCAA titles, made seven national tournament appearances and attracted the largest crowds in the nation.

WISCONSIN TIMELINE

1966: The National and American football leagues announced that they would merge in 1970.

The Conference authorized freshman competition in sports other than football for a two-year trial period.

The Badgers mounted the greatest comeback in the school's basketball history, coming from a 22–point deficit to beat Ohio State 82–81 in overtime.

1966–67

BADGER BIG TEN FINISHES...

Football: 7th
coached by Milt Bruhn

Cross Country: 3rd
coached by Charles Walter

Basketball: 4th,
coached by John Erickson

Indoor Track: 1st
coached by Charles Walter,
(5th-tie, NCAA)

Swimming: 5th
coached by John Hickman

Wresting: 6th
coached by George Martin

Baseball: 4th
coached by Art Mansfield

Golf: 9th
coached by John Jamieson

Gymnastics: 6th
coached by George Bauer

Tennis: 5th
coached by John Powless

Outdoor Track: 4th
coached by Charles Walter

The Big Event

Wisconsin wins first of five straight Big Ten track crowns

Coach Charles "Rut" Walter and assistants Bob Brennan and Tom Bennett had established a Big Ten track juggernaut at Wisconsin by the mid-1960s. The Badgers reclaimed the indoor Big Ten title in 1967 after relinquishing the honors to Michigan State the year earlier. Wisconsin would not lose an indoor championship until 1972.

Ironically, the front and back ends of the five–year win skein would take place in Madison. In 1967, the Badgers piled up 56 points at home to edge the Spartans by 3 points for the title, Coach Charles "Rut" Walter's third indoor win (and fourth overall) since coming to Wisconsin from Northwestern in 1960. Badgers winners in that 1967 meet were Ray Arrington in the 880–yard run (1:51.8) and Mike Butler in both the 70-yard high hurdles (8.2 seconds) and low hurdles (7.6 seconds).

Both would become all-time UW track greats, with Arrington that year winning the first of his three straight Big Ten and NCAA indoor 880 titles and Butler due to win five more indoor hurdles championships. Brennan succeeded Walter after the 1969 season and in his two years as Badger coach guided teams to firsts indoors and seconds outdoors.

WISCONSIN TIMELINE

1965: Dr. Christian Barnard and a team of surgeons performed the first human heart transplant in Cape Town, South Africa.

The Conference liberalized the recruiting regulation, including an increase to two home visitations.

Wisconsin set a single-game men's basketball scoring team record with a 120–82 win over Southern Methodist.

1967–68

BADGER BIG TEN FINISHES...

Football: 9th (tie)
coached by John Coatta

Cross Country: 5th
coached by Charles Walter

Basketball: 5th
coached by John Erickson

Indoor Track: 1st
coached by Charles Walter

Swimming: 4th
coached by John Hickman

Wrestling: 6th
coached by George Martin

Baseball: 3rd
coached by Art Mansfield

Golf: 5th (tie)
coached by John Jamieson

Gymnastics: 5th (tie)
coached by George Bauer

Tennis: 7th
coached by John Powless

Outdoor Track: 3rd
coached by Charles Walter

The Big Event

Badgers win 20 hockey games for first time

It took only three seasons for Wisconsin hockey coach Bob Johnson to guide the Badgers to their first 20-victory season. Wisconsin's 21–10 record would begin a string of six straight 20-plus win seasons.

In fact, since that breakthrough season, only four UW teams have failed to win 20. The UW's previous season high was the 16-win total posted in 1966–67 but the '68 campaign showed the college hockey world that Wisconsin hockey had not only come of age but was on the rise.

Only in 1973–74 and 1979–80 would a team coached by "Badger Bob" fail to win 20 games. The Badgers were led by two-time UW scoring leader Bert DeHate, who scored 15 hat tricks from 1967–69, including 12 in the '67–68 season, and is one of only three UW players to have scored five goals in a game. With 108 career goals, DeHate is second only to Mark Johnson (125 goals) on the all-time UW goal-scoring list.

WISCONSIN TIMELINE

1968: Civil rights leader Martin Luther King, Jr., was assassinated in Memphis.

Herman F. Rohrig became the Big Ten's first full-time supervisor of Conference football and basketball officials.

Wisconsin joined the Western Collegiate Hockey Association, joining Big Ten rivals Michigan, MSU, and Minnesota.

BADGER BIG TEN FINISHES...

Football: 10th
coached by John Coatta

Cross Country: 3rd
coached by Robert Brennan

Basketball: 8th (tie)
coached by John Powless

Indoor Track: 1st
coached by Charles Walter

Swimming: 5th
coached by John Hickman

Wrestling: 6th
coached by George Martin

Baseball: 5th (tie)
coached by Art Mansfield

Golf: 9th
coached by John Jamieson

Gymnastics: 5th
coached by George Bauer

Tennis: 7th
coached by John Desmond

Outdoor Track: 1st
coached by Charles Walter

The Big Event

Badgers sweep track titles for retiring coach

The best gift Wisconsin could come up with for retiring track coach Charles "Rut" Walter was something every coach likes: a winner. In fact, the Badgers doubled that pleasure for the veteran coach in 1969, winning the Big Ten indoor and outdoor titles. The Badgers had come close before Walter, taking a first in one meet and a second in the other in the same year, but it was the first time they had pulled off the indoor-outdoor double.

Led by veterans Ray Arrington and Mike Butler, Wisconsin won its third straight indoor title, scoring 65 points at Champaign to easily outpace runner-up Indiana (42). Arrington, who would win his third straight NCAA indoor championship in the 1,000–yard run two weeks later, was a double winner in the 880–yard run and in the mile.

The Badgers' third individual win came from Mike Butler, whose 70–yard high hurdles victory was his third straight. In the outdoor affair at West Lafayette, Indiana, the Badgers' 80 points was more than enough to replicate their indoor victory over Indiana (64). Nine individual titlists, a UW record, carried Wisconsin to its first outdoor championship in five years.

Winners included Arrington in the 880 and mile; Mark Winzenreid in the 660; Dean Martell in the three-mile run; Fred Lands in the steeplechase; Butler in the 120–yard high hurdles; Pat Murphy in the intermediate hurdles; Tom Thies in the pole vault; and Mike Bond in the triple jump. The mile relay team of Dick Hewlett, Larry Floyd, Winzenreid and Mark Kartman capped the Wisconsin triumph with a win in the meet's last event. Assistant Coach Bob Brennan succeeded Walter and guided the UW to Conference indoor titles in his two years at the helm.

WISCONSIN TIMELINE

1969: Apollo 11 astronauts Neil Armstrong and Edwin "Buzzi" Aldrin became the first men to set foot on the moon.

The Conference authorized freshman competition in sports other than football and basketball effective with the 1969–70 academic year.

Senior Ray Arrington won the third of his three straight NCAA indoor 1,000–yard run titles for the Badger track team.

RAY ARRINGTON
TRACK, CROSS COUNTRY

Ray Arrington epitomized the excellence of the middle distance runner on stellar Wisconsin track teams of the late 60s. The smooth-striding native of Clairton, Pennsylvania, won eight Big Ten Conference titles in the 880 and mile during his three years of varsity competition from 1967–69. But it was in the recently–established NCAA indoor championships at Detroit's Cobo Arena that Arrington really made his mark. He won three consecutive NCAA titles and all-American honors at 1000 yards from 1967–69, setting an NCAA record of 2:07.8 in his first NCAA meet effort. In 1969, Arrington set Big Ten indoor marks in both the 880 (1:49.9) and mile (4:02.2). He captained the Wisconsin team that won indoor and outdoor titles his senior season and was named Wisconsin Athlete of the Year for both 1967 and 1969. Arrington was inducted into the UW Athletic Hall Fame in 1993.

JOE FRANKLIN
BASKETBALL

A unanimous first-team all-Big Ten selection in 1968 who set a UW career scoring record, Joe Franklin was a fifth-round draft choice of the Milwaukee Bucks in that year's NBA draft. Franklin, a Madison native who prepped at Central High School, scored 1,215 points in three seasons from 1965–68. He averaged 22.7 points per game as a senior and had a career rebounding average of 11.9 per game, including a single-game high of 27 vs. Purdue. Franklin scored 30 or more points a game on seven occasions. He was team captain for 1967–68 and the Badgers' MVP for both his junior and senior seasons. Franklin was inducted into the UW Athletic Hall of Fame in 1997.

RUSS HELLICKSON
WRESTLING, FOOTBALL

The name of Stoughton native Russ Hellickson is synonymous with wrestling excellence at Wisconsin, with his career running the gamut from athlete to head coach. Holder of both a bachelor's and a master's degree from the UW, Hellickson was a three-time "W" award–winner in wrestling and a 1967 football letterman. Holder of 10 national freestyle wrestling titles, Hellickson was a three-time Pan American Games gold-medal winner and a member of the 1976 and 1980 U.S. Olympic teams, winning a silver at 220 lbs. in Montreal in '76 and serving as captain of the Olympic-boycotting U.S. squad of 1980. Inducted into the National Wrestling Hall of Fame in 1989 and a charter member of the Midlands Wrestling Hall of Fame in 1993, Hellickson has served as a TV commentator for wrestling at the Olympics and at the Goodwill Games. After 14 years as the assistant or head coach at his alma mater, Hellickson became Ohio State's head coach in 1987. He was named to the UW Athletic Hall of Fame in 1995.

LEADING THE WAY

Charles "Rut" Walter
Track and Field Coach

Charles "Rut" Walter's life was track and field, and he spent it all at two Big Ten schools, Northwestern and Wisconsin. In 1960, the Badgers lured the 31-year NU coach to Madison, where he coached Wisconsin for 10 seasons and enjoyed his greatest successes. The Kokomo, Indiana, native guided Wisconsin to Big Ten indoor titles in 1962, 1965, 1967, 1968 and 1969 and to Conference outdoor championships in 1964 and 1969. That double win by the Badgers in '69 would stand alone in UW track history for 26 years until equaled by the 1995 team. Walter posted a 50–9 career dual meet mark, 17–3 in triangulars, and coached 57 individual Big Ten champions. Rut was no slouch himself as an undergraduate at Northwestern in the late 1920s, winning Big Ten 440–yard dash titles from 1927–29 and the NCAA crown in 1929. A member of the Drake Relays Hall of Fame, Walter was inducted into the UW Athletic Hall of Fame in 1993.

BADGER BIG TEN FINISHES...

Football: 5th (tie)
coached by John Coatta

Cross Country: 3rd
coached by Robert Brennan

Basketball: 6th (tie)
coached by John Powless

Indoor Track: 1st
coached by Bob Brennan,
(5th-tie, NCAA)

Swimming: 5th
coached by Jack Pettinger

Wrestling: 7th
coached by George Martin

Baseball: 4th
coached by Art Mansfield

Golf: 9th
coached by Tom Bennett

Gymnastics: 7th
coached by George Bauer

Tennis: 8th
coached by John Desmond

Ice Hockey: 4th
(WCHA) coached by Bob Johnson,
(3rd, NCAA)

Outdoor Track: 2nd
coached by Robert Brennan

The Big Event

Alan Thompson runs for 220 yards in debut

Wisconsin's season-opening football game in 1969 against No. 6-ranked Oklahoma was supposed to be a stage on which Sooners' running back and Heisman Trophy-hopeful Steve Owens could showcase his considerable talents. Owens didn't disappoint. But neither did Badger Alan "A-Train" Thompson.

Owens, who went on to win the '69 Heisman, rushed 40 times for 189 yards and scored on four short touchdown plunges to lead the Sooners to a 48–21 victory at Camp Randall Stadium in Madison.

Owens, however, was outgained by Thompson, the Badgers' sophomore fullback making his collegiate debut. Thompson, a native of Dallas, set an all-time Wisconsin record by rushing for 220 yards on 33 carries, breaking the old mark of 200 yards set by Alan "The Horse" Ameche in 1951 against Minnesota.

Only one other back (Jerry Thompson, 37 times vs. Iowa in 1944) in Wisconsin history had carried the ball more times in a game than Alan Thompson did against the Sooners. The "A-Train" scored on touchdown runs of 13 and 14 yards against Oklahoma.

Alan Thompson went on to rush for 907 yards in 1969, a total second only to Ameche's 946-yard season in Wisconsin annals. Thompson also scored nine touchdowns. His performance against the Sooners was the only time during his career that he rushed for 200 yards in a game.

WISCONSIN TIMELINE

1970: Legendary football coach Vince Lombardi died of cancer in Washington.

The Big Ten approved 11 football games in 1971, providing the additional game be with a Conference opponent to assure a minimum of eight Big Ten games.

Clarence Sherrod finished the year with 570 points to become the third Wisconsin basketball player in five years to set a single-season scoring mark.

MARK WINZENREID
TRACK

Five-time all-American Mark Winzenreid was one of the dominant American middle distance runners in the late 1960s and early 1970s for Wisconsin coaches "Rut" Walter and Bob Brennan. The Monroe native won three NCAA titles, including the indoor 880-yard crowns in 1969 and 1971 and the outdoor 800 in his senior season of 1971. He also won five Big Ten titles and was the indoor U.S. Track and Field Federation 880 champ in 1968. Winzenreid represented the United States in international competition numerous times over his career and once held the world indoor record in the 1,000-yard run. He's a member of the Wisconsin track and field "Hall of Honor."

ALAN THOMPSON
FOOTBALL

Alan "A-Train" Thompson electrified Wisconsin fans from 1969–71. He led the Badgers in scoring in 1969 with nine touchdowns and throughout his career was a dependable back for John Coatta's last team and John Jardine's first two. Thompson, a native of Dallas, set an all-time Wisconsin record by rushing for 220 yards on 33 carries, scoring on TD runs of 13 and 14 yards against Oklahoma. Thompson had five more 100-yard-plus rushing games in his career but never again approached the totals of his first game. His career total of 2,005 rushing yards ranks him ninth on the all-time Wisconsin list. The Dallas Cowboys selected Thompson in the 14th round of the 1972 NFL draft.

LEADING THE WAY

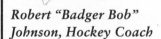

Robert "Badger Bob" Johnson, Hockey Coach

As long as hockey is played at Wisconsin, the legacy of Robert "Badger Bob" Johnson will last. The late Wisconsin coach (1966–82) guided the Badger hockey teams to NCAA titles in 1973, 1977 and 1981 before turning his coaching magic to the National Hockey League and winning the 1991 Stanley Cup with the Pittsburgh Penguins. Johnson remains the only coach to ever guide teams to both NCAA and Stanley Cup victories. His record at Wisconsin was 367–125–23 over 15 seasons. A Minneapolis native who played collegiate hockey at North Dakota and Minnesota, Johnson graduated from Minnesota in 1954 and coached at the high school level for seven years before moving to Colorado College as hockey and baseball coach in 1963. Johnson served as executive director of USA Hockey from 1987–90 before returning to the bench with the Penguins. He also coached the 1976 U.S. Olympic team that took fourth in the Olympic Winter Games. His son Mark, a former Badger and NHL star who is now a UW assistant coach, was a 1991 inductee into the UW Athletic Hall of Fame that his father was named to a year later.

THE LIST

WISCONSIN'S MEN'S CONFERENCE MEDAL OF HONOR WINNERS

1960	1965
Dale L. Hackbart	Gary V. Kirk
1961	**1966**
Gerald L. Kulcinski	David N. Fronek
1962	**1967**
Thomas M. Hughbanks	Dennis J. Sweeney
1963	**1968**
Hugh V. (Pat) Richter	Michael Gluck
1964	**1969**
William R. Smith	Karl Rudat

BADGER BIG TEN FINISHES...

Football: 5th (tie)
coached by John Jardine

Cross Country: 5th
coached by Robert Brennan

Basketball: 7th (tie)
coached by John Powless

Indoor Track: 1st
coached by Robert Brennan, (3rd, NCAA)

Swimming: 6th
coached by Jack Pettinger

Wrestling: 5th
coached by Duane Kleven

Baseball: 6th
coached by Tom Meyer

Golf: 9th
coached by Tom Bennett

Gymnastics: 8th
coached by George Bauer

Tennis: 6th
coached by John Desmond

Ice Hockey: 3rd
(WCHA) coached by Bob Johnson

Outdoor Track: 2nd
coached by Robert Brennan

The Big Event

New coaches change "look" of Wisconsin teams

Five new head coaches changed the look of Wisconsin teams during and after the 1970–71 school year.

Most notably, John Jardine had taken over the football reins from John Coatta for the 1970 season. The veteran prep coach and long-time college assistant guided the Badgers to a 4–5–1 season and with victories in three of the last five games offered hope of better days ahead.

Duane Kleven took over the wrestling program following the drowning death of 32-year veteran coach and hall-of-famer George Martin in a boating accident.

Tom Meyer succeeded another Wisconsin legend, Art "Dynie" Mansfield as baseball coach and took the Badgers to a 9–9 Big Ten season and sixth in the standings.

Following two Big Ten indoor titles and a pair of seconds outdoors, Bob Brennan resigned as track and cross country coach just two years after succeeding Charles "Rut" Walter. Long-time Indiana assistant Bill Perrin was named head track coach while Dan McClimon became the Badgers' head cross country coach.

WISCONSIN TIMELINE

1971:   The 26th amendment to the Constitution, lowering the voting age to 18, was ratified.

Commissioner William R. Reed died; Wayne Duke became the Conference's fourth commissioner.

Wisconsin high jumper Pat Matzdorf cleared 7'6 3/4" to set a world record in the U.S./U.S.S.R. meet at Berkeley, California.

BADGER BIG TEN FINISHES...

Football: 6th (tie)
coached by John Jardine

Cross Country: 4th
coached by Dan McClimon

Basketball: 5th (tie)
coached by John Powless

Indoor Track: 3rd
coached by Bill Perrin

Swimming: 5th
coached by Jack Pettinger

Wrestling: 9th
coached by Duane Kleven

Baseball: 6th
coached by Tom Meyer

Golf: 9th
coached by Tom Bennett

Gymnastics: 8th
coached by Raymond Bauer

Tennis: 5th
coached by John Desmond

Ice Hockey: 2nd (WCHA)
coached by Bob Johnson,
(3rd, NCAA)

Outdoor Track: 5th
coached by Bill Perrin

The Big Event

Badgers win Big Ten hockey, take 3rd nationally

Wisconsin got off to a quick start in the 1971–72 hockey season, winning 14 of its first 15 games, including pairs of victories at home against Michigan and Michigan State. Those victories, coupled with a split of the games at Michigan and two more wins at MSU, allowed the Badgers to win the four-team "race" for the Big Ten championship despite losing three of four to Minnesota.

It was a strange year for Coach Bob Johnson's club, which lost three of its last five regular season contests but then rebounded to win the Western Collegiate Hockey Association playoff. The Badgers advanced to the NCAA and lost 4–1 to Boston University in the national semifinals.

The UW defeated Denver 5–2 in the third-place game, setting the stage for its NCAA championship run of the next season. Jeff Rotsch was a first-team all-American on defense for Wisconsin.

WISCONSIN TIMELINE

1972: Eleven Israeli athletes taken captive by Arab guerrillas at the Munich Olympics were killed in an abortive rescue attempt.

Approval was given by the Big Ten for freshman competition in football and basketball in the fall of 1972.

PAT MATZDORF
TRACK AND FIELD

High jumper Pat Matzdorf, one of the last great straddle jumpers, starred for UW track teams in the early 1970s, winning a pair each of Big Ten and NCAA titles. But the Sheboygan native leaped into track and field history in 1971 when he cleared 7'6 1/4" in the U.S.-U.S.S.R. meet in San Francisco to set a world record. Matzdorf won Conference indoor titles in 1970 and 1971, setting a league mark of 7'3" in the latter. He also won NCAA championships indoors (1971, with a meet record 7'2" jump) and outdoors (1970, at 7'1"). Matzdorf twice won Drake Relays high jump titles and has been named to that prestigious meet's hall of fame. He was named Wisconsin's "Sports Personality" for 1971 and in 1972 received the UW Big Ten Conference medal of honor. Matzdorf was one of 35 charter members inducted into the UW Athletic Hall of Fame in 1991.

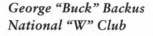

George "Buck" Backus
National "W" Club

Racine native George "Buck" Backus was a fixture with the National "W" Club for more than 20 years, serving as executive director from 1965–83. Backus quietly and soundly built the club into a powerful arm of Wisconsin's athletic program. He first joined it as director of concessions in 1962 and moved into the executive director's role three years later. Thanks to his efforts, monies generated by the club have helped build the athletic ticket office, the club's Kubly and Culver Rooms in Camp Randall Stadium, the football and hockey offices, the Dan McClimon Memorial Track and the Dave McClain indoor practice facility. Backus was honored by the Madison Pen and Mike Club with the Pat O'Dea Award in 1980.

THE LIST

WISCONSIN'S MEN'S BIG TEN CROSS COUNTRY CHAMPIONS

1907	William Bertles	1983	John Easker
1910	Irvin Dohman	1984	Tim Hacker
1911	C.R. Cleveland	1985	Tim Hacker
1912	Irvin White	1991	Donovan Bergstrom
1918	Bernardo Elsom	1998	Matt Downin
1921	George Finkle	1999	Matt Downin
1925	Victor Chapman	2000	Jason Vanderhoof
1926	John Zola	2002	Matt Tegenkamp
1939	Walter Mehl	2003	Simon Bairu
1947	Don Gehrmann	2004	Simon Bairu
1948	Don Gehrmann	2005	Simon Bairu
1951	Walter Dieke	2007	Matt Withrow
1972	Glenn Herold	2010	Landon Peacock
1978	Steve Lacy	2011	Mohammed Ahmed
1981	Tim Hacker		

THE LIST

UW ROWING COACHES

MEN'S

1894-Amos W. Marston	1941–42-Allen Walz
1895–98-Andrew O'Dea	1943-George Rea
1899-C.C. McConville	1946-Allen Walz
1900–06-Andrew O'Dea	1947–68-Norm Sonju
1907–10-Edward Ten Eyck	1969–96-Randy Jablonic
1911–28-Harry "Dad" Vail	1996–2003-Chris Clark
1929–34-George "Mike" Vail	2004–present-Bebe Bryans
1935–40-Ralph Hunn	

WOMEN'S

1973–79-Jay Mimier	1980–present-Sue Ela

BADGER BIG TEN FINISHES...

Football: 9th
coached by John Jardine

Cross Country: 3rd
coached by Dan McClimon

Basketball: 9th
coached by John Powless

Indoor Track: 4th
coached by Bill Perrin, (8th-tie, NCAA)

Swimming: 3rd
coached by Jack Pettinger

Wrestling: 3rd
coached by Duane Kleven

Baseball: 4th (tie)
coached by Tom Mayer

Golf: 9th
coached by Tom Bennett

Gymnastics: 8th
coached by Raymond Bauer

Tennis: 4th (tie)
coached by Denny Schackter

Ice Hockey: 3rd(WCHA)
coached by Bob Johnson,
(1st, NCAA)

Outdoor Track: 6th
coached by Bill Perrin

The Big Event

Wisconsin wins first NCAA hockey title

In the 10th season since the hockey program at Wisconsin was resuscitated, the Badgers reached the promised land, winning their first NCAA championship with a 4–2 win over Denver on March 17, 1973. The win at fabled Boston Garden, on St. Patrick's Day, no less, culminated a 29–9–2 campaign for the Badgers and seventh-year Coach Bob Johnson.

The UW won 11 of its first 12 games, lost two games at Michigan Tech in early February and slumped a bit as the season wound down, but gained momentum in the playoffs. Wisconsin knocked off Minnesota, a 2–1–1 regular season series winner over the Badgers, by 8–6 and 6–4 scores in first round of the Western Collegiate Hockey Association playoffs. The Badgers then edged Notre Dame, 4–4 and 4–3 in a total goals series, to move into the NCAA tourney.

Freshman Dean Talafous was the hero of the NCAA semis against Cornell, scoring with five seconds left in regulation to tie the game 5–5 and force overtime. He then scored again with 33 seconds remaining in the OT to give Wisconsin a 6–5 win. It gave the Badgers momentum for the final, where the UW's pressure defense stopped Denver.

WISCONSIN TIMELINE

1973: The Conference allowed graduate students to compete under certain specific conditions.

Accords ending the Vietnam War were signed in Paris.

Wisconsin's men's cross country team finished fifth in the inaugural NCAA district qualifying meet and advances to the NCAA nationals. The UW has qualified for the national meet every year since, the only university in the nation to do so.

WISCONSIN HEADLINER

RUFUS FERGUSON
FOOTBALL

Rufus "Roadrunner" Ferguson still stands seventh on the all-time Badger career rushing list with 2,814 yards, more than a generation after ending his Wisconsin career. The Miami native, who prepped at Killian High School, was a first-team all-Big Ten pick at running back in 1971 and in 1972. The first UW back to exceed 1,000 yards in a season (1,222 in 1971), Ferguson also set a single-season scoring mark that year with 80 points. Ferguson ran for 100 yards or more 12 times in his career, reaching a single-game high of 211 yards against Minnesota in 1971. A standout student as well, Ferguson was a second-team academic All-American in 1971 and a first-team all-academic pick as a senior. He was the MVP of the 1972 North-South Shrine Game. Ferguson was inducted into the UW Athletic Hall of Fame in 1993.

WISCONSIN HEADLINER

D'LYNN DAMRON
DIVING

D'Lynn Damron, one of the pioneering women athletes at Wisconsin, became the UW's first women's national diving Champion in 1970, winning national one- and three-meter diving events. The Madison West product went on to win the one-meter crown again in 1973 and earn runner-up honors in the three-meter event that same year. The women's program was not phased in to the Division of Intercollegiate Athletics until 1974 so Damron, like some other UW women's athletes, was forced to compete with little support and minimal publicity. Recognition of her accomplishments and of the role that she played in paving the way for a generation of athletes to follow came in 1992, when she was inducted into the UW Athletic Hall of Fame.

THE LIST

UW'S MEN'S
BASKETBALL COACHES

Coach	Seasons	Years	Record
James Elsom	1899–1904	6	25–14
Emmett Angell	1904–08	4	43–15
Haskell Noyes	1908–11	3	26–15
Walter Meanwell	1911–17, 1920–34	20	246–99
Guy Lowman	1917–20	3	34–19
Harold Foster	1934–59	25	265–267
John Erickson	1959–68	9	100–114
John Powless	1968–76	8	88–108
Bill Cofield	1976–82	6	63–101
Steve Yoder	1982–92	10	128–165
Stu Jackson	1992–94	2	32–25
Stan Van Gundy	1994–95	1	3–14
Dick Bennett	1995–2000	5	93–69
Brad Soderberg	2000–01	1	16–10
Bo Ryan	2001–present	12	291–113

THE LIST

UW'S MEN'S
BASKETBALL

1,000 point scorers (1900s)

Michael Finley (1991–95)	2,147
Danny Jones (1986–90)	1,854
Claude Gregory (1977–81)	1,745
Rick Olson (1982–86)	1,736
Trent Jackson (1985–89)	1,545
Clarence Sherrod (1968–71)	1,408
Cory Blackwell (1981–84)	1,405
Tracy Webster (1991–94)	1,264
Wes Mathews (1977–80)	1,251
Joe Franklin (1965–68)	1,215
Dale Koehler (1972–76)	1,200
Dick Cable (1951–55)	1,180
Joe Chrnelich (1976–80)	1,171
Don Rehfeldt (1944–45, 1946–50)	1,169
Leon Howard (1970–73)	1,165
Scott Roth (1981–85)	1,156
James Johnson (1966–69)	1,147
Ken Siebel (1960–63)	1,084
Tim Locum (1987–91)	1,077
Larry Petty (1977–81)	1,066
Chuck Nagle (1966–69)	1,064
J.J. Weber (1983–87)	1,021
Willie Simms (1987–91)	1,015

BADGER BIG TEN FINISHES...

Football: 8th
coached by John Jardine

Cross Country: 2nd
coached by Dan McClimon

Basketball: 4th (tie)
coached by John Powless

Indoor Track: 4th
coached by Bill Perrin

Swimming: 2nd
coached by Jack Pettinger

Wrestling: 4th
coached by Duane Kleven

Baseball: 8th
coached by Tom Meyer

Golf: 9th
coached by Tom Bennett

Gymnastics: 8th
coached by Raymond Buer

Tennis: 6th (tie)
coached by Denny Schackter

Ice Hockey: 5th
(WCHA) coached by Bob Johnson

Outdoor Track: 3rd
coached by Bill Perrin

The Big Event

UW cagers' 16 wins most in 12 years

Wisconsin started out like a house afire in the 1973–74 basketball season, winning nine of its first 10 game. The sole loss was a 49–48 overtime heartbreaker on the road to rising national power Marquette. Coach John Powless's squad trounced Northwestern 87–53 in the Big Ten opener at the Wisconsin Fieldhouse, won a non-conference game at Ohio and the lost a 52–51 nail-biter at Indiana, where the Badgers had won only three times in 25 years.

Wins at the Fieldhouse over Illinois and Ohio State gave the UW a 3–1 Big Ten slate but a string of five losses in six games—three of them close and two blowouts—punctured Wisconsin's hopes of contending for the title. An 87–80 home win over Michigan State and road wins at Iowa and Northwestern gave Wisconsin a 16–8 overall mark and 8–6 Big Ten record, good for a fourth-place tie in the Conference.

The wins were the most for Wisconsin since a 17–7 campaign in 1961–62. And until 1997, Powless's 1974 Badgers were the last to post a winning Big Ten season. Three of his players that year earned Big Ten recognition, with Gary Anderson named to the Associated Press all-Big Ten second team, Kim Hughes to United Press International's third unit and Dale Koehler to UPI honorable mention. Hughes was a three-time UW rebounding leader and with twin brother Kerry was featured on the February 9, 1974, cover of The *Sporting News* as "Wisconsin's Twin Terrors."

WISCONSIN TIMELINE

1974: Richard Nixon became the first U.S. president to resign from office.

Charles D. Henry II and John D. Dewey were named assistant commissioners of the Big Ten; Conference offices were moved to Schaumburg, Illinois.

Billy Marek scored five touchdowns and runs for 304 yards as Wisconsin beats Minnesota 49–14.

WISCONSIN HEADLINER

CINDY BREMSER
TRACK AND FIELD

Cindy Bremser was one of the pioneers in women's sports at Wisconsin and the first track and field athlete to make a national impact for Coach Peter Tegen's fledgling women's track program in 1974. In fact, her career is filled with firsts. Bremser, a Mishicot, Wisconsin, native, didn't begin her UW track career until her junior year, a year prior to its becoming a varsity sport. She became UW's first track all–American with her third place finish in the AIAW mile in 1975. Bremser went on to compete on 15 national teams from 1975–88, including the 1984 Olympics in Los Angeles, where she became the first UW female track Olympian, placing fourth in the 3000–meter run. She is the only woman to have won six Drake Relays 1,500 meter titles and was inducted into the Drake Relays Hall of Fame in 1985. A 1974 nursing graduate, she added a masters in pediatric nursing in 1985. She was the first woman member of the National "W" Club Board of Directors and was a charter inductee in the UW Athletic Hall of Fame in 1991.

WISCONSIN HEADLINER

BILLY MAREK
FOOTBALL

Tailback Billy Marek paced the Badgers in scoring and all-purpose yardage during his last three seasons of varsity competition at Wisconsin, putting together three straight 1,200-yard seasons. The Chicago native had been recruited at Wisconsin along with by Badger mentor (and former Chicago Catholic League coach) John Jardine. The 5'8" Marek had 17 100-yard rushing games in his Wisconsin career and stands first on the all-time UW rushing list, 143 yards ahead of Ron Dayne, prior to the 1998 season. Marek led the nation in scoring in 1974 with 114 points, a 12.7 average. With 278 career points off 46 touchdowns and one PAT, Marek is tied with kicker Todd Gregoire at the top of the UW scoring list. His biggest day came in 1974 against Minnesota, when he scored a Badger record five touchdowns and rushed for 304 yards in a 49–14 UW win. He was named *Sports Illustrated's* national offensive back of the week.

WISCONSIN HEADLINER

MIKE WEBSTER
FOOTBALL

Rhinelander native Mike Webster starred at center for Badger football teams of the early 1970s before starting a 17-year National Football League career. Webster won "W" awards in 1971, 1972, and 1973 and earned all-Big Ten honors the latter seasons. He was also the Badgers' tri-captain and MVP his senior season before seeing post-season action in the East-West SI Game, the Hula Bowl, the Senior Bowl and the College All-Game. Selected by the Pittsburgh Steelers in the fifth round o 1974 NFL draft, Webster played 15 years with them—including four Super Bowl championship teams—before ending his career with the Kansas City Chiefs. Webster was selected to and played; in nine all-Pro football games. He was inducted into the UW Athletic Hall of Fame in 1995.

THE LIST

WISCONSIN'S NATIONAL COLLEGIATE ROWING CHAMPIONSHIPS IN THE 1970S

Men's national collegiate titles
(all at 2000 meters) 1972—Freshman 8
1973—Varsity 8
1973—Junior Varsity 8
1973—Freshman 8
1974—Varsity 8
1974—Junior Varsity 8
1975—Varsity 8
1975—Varsity 4 w/o Coxswain
1976—Varsity 4 w/o Coxswain
1979—Freshman 8

Women's national collegiate titles
(both at 1000 meters)
1975—Varsity 8
1979—Novice 8

BADGER BIG TEN FINISHES...

MEN'S

Football: 4th
coached by John Jardine

Cross Country: 2nd
coached by Dan Mcclimon

Basketball: 8th
coached by John Powless

Indoor track: 3rd
coached by Bill Perrin

Swimming: 2nd
coached by Jack Pettinger

Wrestling: 2nd
coached by Duane Kleven,
(6th, NCAA)

Baseball: 5th
coached by Tom Meyer

Golf: 8th
coached by Tom Bennet

Gymnastics: 6th
coached by Raymond Bauer

Tennis: 2nd
coached by Denny Schackter

Ice Hockey: 4th
(WCHA) coached by Bob Johnson

Outdoor Track: 5th
coached by Bill Perrin

WOMEN'S

Swimming: 5th
coached by Roger Ridenour

The Big Event

Women's athletics debuts at UW

The first year of women's intercollegiate athletics at Wisconsin was highly successful. Despite having a budget of only $118,000, the Badger women's teams won one national championship and competed on the national level in cross country, swimming and diving and track.

Twelve women's sports began practice and competition during the fall of 1974—badminton, basketball, cross country, fencing, field hockey, golf, gymnastics, rowing, swimming and diving, tennis, track and field and volleyball.

In women's rowing, the varsity eight boat won the National Women's Rowing Association national championship. The Badgers covered the 1,000-meter course in 3:07.3, winning by over three seconds over Vesper Rowing Club.

In cross country, Cindy Bremser finished sixth in a national invitational. She also earned all-American honors in track with a third-place finish in the mile. As a team, Wisconsin finished 19th at the Association of Intercollegiate Athletics for Women (AIAW) Championship.

The women's swimming and diving team finished 30th at the AIAW Championship and fifth in the Big Ten meet. Peggy Anderson finished second on the one-meter board and sixth on the three-meter board to earn all-American honors.

Several other teams posted winning records or competed in unofficial Big Ten or regional competition during their initial seasons. The volleyball team was 28–4 and finished fifth in the AIAW regional. Fencing was 10–5 overall and tied for fifth in the Great Lakes Tournament.

The gymnastics team was 20–15, including a fifth–place finish in unofficial Big Ten competition and 10th in the region. The tennis team finished third in the Big Ten while the basketball team finished with an 11–7 mark.

WISCONSIN TIMELINE

1975: Work began on the Alaska oil pipeline.

Big Ten athletic directors voted to use three-man crews in basketball effective with the 1975–76 season.

Wisconsin erased a 22-point deficit for its greatest men's basketball comeback ever in an 82–81 overtime win over Ohio State at the Field House.

LEADING THE WAY

John Jardine
Football Coach

John Jardine served as Wisconsin's football coach from 1970–77 during an era of revitalization of the Badger program. The Chicago native compiled a 25–38–1 record in eight seasons as the UW coach, including a 7–4 mark in 1974, Wisconsin's first winning season since 1963. Starring for that squad were tackle Dennis Lick and tailback Billy Marek, both of whom shared Jardine's Chicago Catholic League roots. Jardine was a coaching prodigy and was actually helping coach at St. George High School in Evanston before he had even graduated. At Purdue, Jardine played both ways at guard and linebacker. A year after graduation, he became head coach at Fenwick High School in Oak Park, Illinois, and posted a 51–6–1 record in five years. He then assisted at Purdue and UCLA before coming to Madison. Jardine remained in Madison and was active in the insurance business and Badger football broadcasts. He died in Madison at age 54 in 1990.

A W FIRST

Marek scores five touchdoums against Gophers

Billy Marek, the Badgers' dependable running back from 1973–75, was never so reliable as on November 23, 1974, at home against Minnesota. No Badger had ever scored five touchdowns in a game before the junior from Chicago turned the trick while running for 304 yards. Coach John Jardine's best Wisconsin team crushed the Gophers 49–14 en route to a 7–4 season. Marek's five touchdowns and 30 points are still Wisconsin single game marks. He led the Badgers in all–purpose yardage in each of his three seasons and ranks second to Terrell Fletcher on the all-time UW list.

A W FIRST

Badgers star on TV

Wisconsin looked good on television in 1974. Coach John Jardine's Badgers played two regional, non-conference foes in ;ed games for the first time. Playing in Madison, the UW he measure of two Big Eight opponents, beating fourth-ranked Nebraska 21–20 on September 21 and Missouri 59–20 two weeks later in games broadcast by ABC. Wisconsin, behind running back Billy Marek, finished 7–4 for Jardine's only winning n in Madison.

A W FIRST

First women's basketball season produces good results

The first women's intercollegiate basketball practices were held at the Wisconsin Field House in October, 1974, under the direction of Coach Marilyn Harris. The Badger women played their first home game on January 11, 1975, beating UW-Green Bay 45–38. Wisconsin finished 11–7 overall and 6–2 at home in its first season.

1975—76

BADGER BIG TEN FINISHES...

MEN'S

Football: 6th
coached by John Jardine

Cross Country: 2nd
coached by Dan Mcclimon

Basketball: 9th
coached by John Powless

Indoor track: 2nd
coached by Bill Perrin

Swimming: 2nd
coached by Jack Pettinger

Wrestling: 3rd
coached by Duane Kleven,
(4th, NCAA)

Baseball: 7th
coached by Tom Meyer

Golf: 9th
coached by Tom Bennet

Gymnastics: 4th
coached by Raymond Bauer

Tennis: 3rd
coached by Denny Schackter

Ice Hockey: 7th
(WCHA) coached by Bill Rothwell

Outdoor Track: 2nd
coached by Bill Perrin

WOMEN'S

Swimming: 5th
coached by Roger Ridenour

Volleyball: 6th
coached by Pat Hielscher

Golf: 8th
coached by Jane Eastham

Outdoor Track: 1st
coached by Peter Tegen

The Big Event

Wrestlers win three NCAA titles

Wisconsin wrestling served notice it was to be taken very seriously as one of the nation's top programs in 1976 when the Badgers had a school-record three national champions and earned their highest finish ever (fourth) at the NCAA Championships in Tucson, Arizona.

The Badgers entered the national meet having finished third at the Big Ten championships after a compiling a 13–3 dual record. Lee Kemp (158) and Gary Sommer (Hwt.) won conference titles. The UW won regular-season duals with Michigan, Michigan State and Oklahoma, with the three losses coming to Iowa, Iowa State and Oklahoma State.

It was in Tucson, however, that Coach Duane Kleven's Badgers showed their depth as a team. Kemp, a native of Chardon, Ohio, was the only undefeated wrestler (39–0) in the nation in '75–76 and went on to defeat Washington's Tom Brown in the NCAA title match. Kemp won two more NCAA crowns at 158 and compiled a 143–6–1 record during his Wisconsin career.

Jack Reinwand, wrestling at 126 pounds, defeated Harold Wiley of UC-Santa Barbara for his national title. Reinwand had finished fourth at the NCAA the year before. Pat Christensen won his '76 NCAA title at 167 pounds with a win over Iowa's Dan Wagemann.

The Badgers finished the tournament with 64 points, just one-half point behind third-place Oklahoma State.

WISCONSIN TIMELINE

1976: The supersonic Concorde jetliner was put into service by England and France.

Athletic directors voted to establish a minimum price of $8 for football tickets, effective in the fall of 1977.

Edwina Qualls took over for what would become a 10–year stint as UW's women's basketball coach.

WISCONSIN HEADLINER

CRAIG NORWICH
HOCKEY

Two-time all-American defenseman Craig Norwich lettered three times for Badger hockey teams from 1974–77. The Edina, Minnesota, native was the first Badger to twice earn all-America honors. For his career, Norwich scored 42 goals and had 126 assists for 168 points, second to Theran Walsh on the all–time defensemen's point list. Norwich's 42 career goals are still the most by a Badger defenseman. His 18 goals during the Badgers' 1976–77 NCAA championship season rank him in a second-place tie on the all-time list while his 83 points that same season are the most by a defenseman. Norwich was picked by the Montreal Canadiens in the 1975 National Hockey League draft and saw action from 1979–81 with Winnipeg, St. Louis and Colorado.

WISCONSIN HEADLINER

DENNIS LICK
FOOTBALL

Four–time letterwinner (1972–75) Dennis Lick earned consensus all-America honors for Coach John Jardine's Badgers in 1975 despite missing the last three games because of an injury. Lick, a native of Chicago, was one of Wisconsin's most punishing offensive linemen as he blocked for Billy Marek, Wisconsin's all-time leading rusher. Lick also received first-team all-America honors in 1974 from The Sporting News to become Wisconsin's first all-American since Pat Richter in 1962. Lick was selected in the first round of the 1976 National Football League draft by his hometown Bears. He played with Chicago until his retirement in 1981.

BADGER MOMENT

Russ Hellickson's most memorable wrestling moment

Former Wisconsin wrestling star (and coach) Russ Hellickson had many great memories from his career as a competitor, including a silver medal in the 1976 Olympic Games. But no single moment in his own career stood out for Hellickson as much as the 1976 NCAA wresltling finals in Tucson. Three Badgers—Jack Reinwand, Lee Kemp and Pat Christenson—won national championships and provided Hellickson his greatest memory. "No feeling generated through my own competition has ever matched the extreme satisfaction and pride I felt," he remembers. "On that Saturday evening I had made no personal sacrifices, yet I achieved a level of emotional elation higher than any other wrestling has ever provided me. It was gratifying to have been able to share probably their most memorable moment and to have felt at least a part of their accomplishment."

THE LIST

WISCONSIN'S NCAA WRESTLING CHAMPIONS

1974	Rick Lawinger, 142 lbs.
1976	Jack Reinwand, 126 lbs. Lee Kemp, 158 lbs. Pat Christensen, 167 lbs.
1977	Jim Haines, 118 lbs. Lee Kemp, 158 lbs.
1978	Lee Kemp, 158 lbs. Ron Jeidy, 190 lbs.
1980	Andy Rein, 150 lbs.
1985	Jim Jordan, 134 lbs.
1986	Jim Jordan, 134 lbs.
1989	Dave Lee, 167 lbs.
1991	Matt Demaray, 150 lbs.
1992	Matt Demaray, 150 lbs.
1996	Jeff Walter, Hwt.
2000	Donny Pritzlaff, 165 lbs.
2001	Donny Pritzlaff, 165 lbs.
2010	Andrew Howe, 165 lbs.

1976–77

BADGER BIG TEN FINISHES...

MEN'S

Football: 7th (tie)
coached by John Jardinc

Cross Country: 4th (tie)
coached by Dan McClimon

Basketball: 7th (tie)
coached by Bill Cofield

Indoor Track: 4th
coached by Bill Perrin

Swimming: 2nd
coached by Jack Pettinger

Wrestling: 3rd
coached by Duane Kleven,
(6th, NCAA)

Baseball: 8th
coached by Tom Meyer

Golf: 8th (tie)
coached by Tom Bennett

Gymnastics: 6th
coached by Raymond Bauer

Tennis: 3rd (tie)
coached by Denny Schackter

Ice Hockey: 1st
(WCHA) coached by Bob Johnson,
(1st, NCAA)

Outdoor Track: 4th
coached by Bill Perrin

WOMEN'S

Basketball: 8th (tie)
coached by Edwina Qualls

Swimming: 3rd
coached by Roger Ridenour

Volleyball: 6th
coached by Pat Hielscher

Golf: 8th
coached by Jackie Hayes

Outdoor Track: 2nd
coached by Peter Tegen

The Big Event

Badgers take Big Ten, WCHA and NCAA hockey titles

Wisconsin's finest hockey season ever culminated on March 26, 1977, when the Badgers defeated Michigan 6–5 on a Steve Alley goal 23 seconds into overtime for their second NCAA title. It was a bit of delicious irony for Wisconsin, which had lost 7–6 to Michigan at home in its season opener.

Coach Bob Johnson's team finished the season with a 37–7–1 record, a UW record for wins in a season, and became the first team to win Big Ten, Western Collegiate Hockey Association and NCAA championships in the same season. The UW never lost two games in a row and ended the season on a roll, going 22–1–1 in its last 24 contests. And the Badgers' seven losses—to Michigan, Michigan State, Notre Dame, Harvard, Minnesota and Denver and the Spartak Club of Russia in an exhibition game—were all, except Spartak, avenged by UW victories.

In post-season action, Wisconsin swept through the WCHA play-offs, beating Colorado College twice by 3–1 scores and then mowing down Minnesota (9–5, 8–3) and Michigan (4–0, 5–4). It took an overtime goal by Mike Eaves to give the Badgers a 4–3 NCAA semifinal win over New Hampshire and berth in the title game against Michigan. Wisconsin won six of the seven games it played against Michigan, especially the one that really counted.

Honors aplenty came to the Badgers, as well. Johnson was named national coach of the year while his son Mark, a forward who had a UW rookie record 36 goals, was named freshman of the year. Defenseman Craig Norwich, goaltender Julian Baretta and center Mike Eaves were named to the all-American team. Baretta was named NCAA tournament MVP and Norwich and defenseman John Taft were picked for the all-tournament team.

WISCONSIN TIMELINE

1977: Treaties granting eventual control of the Panama Canal to Panama were signed by President Jimmy Carter and Gen. Omar Torrijos Herrera.

Big Ten athletic directors voted that there must be at least six varsity teams in a sport, with the exception of fencing, to hold a Conference championship.

The UW women's basketball team won its first WWIAC state large school championship, beating cross-state rival UW-La Crosse for the first time.

MIKE EAVES
HOCKEY

Two-time all-American forward Mike Eaves was a stalwart of four Badger hockey teams. One of them, the 1976–77 unit, won the NCAA title as Eaves earned the first of his all-America honors. Eaves, a native of Kanata, Ontario, became the first Badger to eclipse 200 career points, totaling 267 points— still a school record. He still owns the longest scoring streak in Wisconsin history at 21 straight games, set during the 1977–78 season, and totaled 89 points that season. He was the Western Collegiate Hockey Association's most valuable player as a senior in 1978 and twice was named the Badgers' MVP. The three-time Wisconsin captain shared WCHA scoring honors with teammate Mark Johnson in 1977–78 and was the Wisconsin recipient of the Big Ten Conference Medal of Honor. Eaves went on to a career in the National Hockey League, playing with the Minnesota North Stars from 1978–83 and the Calgary Flames from 1983–86. He's now an assistant coach with the Philadelphia Flyers. He was inducted into the UW Athletic Hall of Fame in 1992.

CARIE GRAVES
CREW

Spring Green native Carie Graves is Wisconsin's only three-time Olympian, making the U.S. crew team in 1976, 1980 and 1984. Graves earned a bronze in 1976 a year after leading the UW to its first national championship in crew. She also made the 1980 American team which boycotted the Moscow Olympics but came back four years later in Los Angeles to win the gold as a member of the U.S. eight. Graves, a three-time silver medalist in women's eight at the 1975, 1981 and 1983 world championships, was the first inductee into the UW Women's Athletics Hall of Fame in 1984 and also has been named to the U.S. Rowing Association's Hall of Fame. She was named the U.S. Olympic Committee's Athlete of the Year in 1984 and received the Southland Corporation's "Olympia Award" that year for excellence and achievement. She graduated with an English degree in 1976 and earned a master's in educational administration from Harvard in 1985. She was one of 35 charter inductees into the UW Athletics Hall of Fame in 1991.

THE BUD SONG

When you say Wis-con-sin

The playing of the Bud song is an integral part of any performance by the Wisconsin band. The tune, a spinoff of the song "You've Said It All," a jingle originally written by Steve Karmen for Budweiser beer commercials and copyrighted by Sandlee Publishing Co. in 1970, has become legendary at the UW.

Band director Michael Leckrone said its popularity began at a 1975 hockey game when the crowd wanted a polka and had the beer commercial in the tunes it played. Leckrone told the band that substituting "Wisconsin" for "Budweiser" would work.

It did. And after a come-from-behind football win over Oregon in 1978 during which the song got the crowd revved up and the Badgers scored right after, Leckrone said, "from then band could never play enough 'Bud.'"

THE LIST

WISCONSIN'S WOMEN'S VOLLEYBALL COACHES

Coach	Record	Years
Kay Von Guten	25–4	1974–75
Pat Hielscher	85–42–7	1975–78
Kristi Conklin	89–45–6	1978–81
Niels Pedersen	5–29	1981–82
Russ Carney	38–80	1982–86
Steve Lowe	106–63	1986–91
Margie Fitzpatrick	22–10	1991–92
John Cook	101–65	1992-98
Pete Waite	305–147	1999–2012
Kelly Sheffield		2013

BADGER BIG TEN FINISHES...

MEN'S

Football: 8th
coached by John Jardine
Cross Country: 1st
coached by Dan McClimon
Basketball: 9th (tie)
coached by Bill Cofield
Indoor Track: 3rd
coached by Dan McClimon
Swimming: 3rd
coached by Jack Pettinger
Wrestling: 2nd
coached by Duane Kleven
(4th, NCAA)
Baseball: 3rd
coached by Tom Meyer
Golf: 8th
coached by Dennis Tiziani
Gymnastics: 7th
coached by Raymond Bauer
Tennis: 2nd
coached by Denny Schackter
Ice Hockey: 2nd (WCHA)
coached by Bob Johnson
Outdoor Track: 3rd
coached by Dan McClimon

WOMEN'S

Basketball: 7th (tie)
coached by Edwina Quails
Indoor Track: 1st
coached by Peter Tegen
Swimming: 2nd
coached by Carl Johansson
Volleyball: 2nd
coached by Pat Hielscher
Golf: 7th
coached by Jackie Hayes
Outdoor Track: 1st

The Big Event

Cross country, fencing, hockey take Big Ten titles

Wisconsin, behind Jim Stintzi's second-place finish, won its first Big Ten cross country championship in 27 years in the fall of 1977. Coach Dan McClimon's team scored a low of 52 points to defeat Illinois and Ohio State, which each scored 75 points. Stintzi earned all-America honors as Wisconsin took sixth in the NCAA meet in its highest national finish since 1951. The UW had won 15 Big Ten hill-and-dale titles since the meet's inception in 1910 and had 20 first-division finishes from 1950–76, including three straight runner-up slots from 1973–75 under McClimon. The victory would kick start a remarkable string of 17 Big Ten championships over the next 20 years for the UW harriers.

Coach Bob Johnson's hockey team also took the Big Ten crown, posting an 8–3–1 mark against Conference rivals Michigan, Michigan State and Minnesota. The Badgers, led by Mark Johnson's 48 goal, 86 point season and Mike Eaves's 43 goal, 89 point campaign chalked up a 28–12–3 season en route to the Western Collegiate Hockey Association playoff championship and a fourth-place finish in the NCAA tournament. Eaves, the UW's Big Ten Conference Medal of Honor winner in 1978, was named a first-team all-American for the second straight season while Johnson earned identical honors for the first time.

Coach Tony Gillham's fencers took Wisconsin's third Big Ten championship in the '77–78 campaign. It was the UW's sixth fencing title. Leading the Badgers were Dean Rose and Steve Vandenberg. Rose won the first of his two Big Ten championships in foil while Vandenberg took the second of his two epee titles. Wisconsin successfully defended its championship in 1979 and also won Conference titles in 1982, 1984 and 1985 before fencing was discontinued as a Big Ten–sponsored sport after the 1986 season.

WISCONSIN TIMELINE

1978: Elvis Presley died in Memphis at age 42.

The Conference eliminated the rule requiring, in football, that only Conference opponents be scheduled in November.

The Badgers beat eventual NCAA basketball champion Michigan State 83–81 at the Field House.

MARK JOHNSON
HOCKEY

Mark Johnson, a two-time UW hockey All-American in the late 1970s for his father, legendary coach "Badger Bob" Johnson, has come full circle to Madison, where as a prep in 1976 he led Madison Memorial High School to the state title. Following an 11–year professsional career with five National Hockey League teams, Johnson returned to campus in 1996 as an assistant to Jeff Sauer. Prior to joining the UW staff, Johnson earned coach of the year honors for guiding the Madison Monsters to a winning record and Colonial Hockey League playoff berth in their inaugural season. Johnson still holds UW record for most goals in a career (125) and season (48) and was a member of the UW's 1977 NCAA champs. One of only three Badgers to twice be named a first-team all-American, Johnson was the leading scorer (5 goals, 6 assists) for the 1980 U.S. Olympic hockey team, which stunned the world with its "Miracle on Ice" at Lake Placid. Holder of a degree in kinesiology, Johnson was named a charter member of the UW Athletics Hall of Fame in 1991.

LEE KEMP
WRESTLING

Lee Kemp, one of the pre-eminent names in Wisconsin wrestling history, did a lot of good things in threes. Kemp, a native of Cardon, Ohio, won three NCAA wrestling titles at 158 lbs. from 1976–78. He also won a like number of Big Ten championships and Midlands Tournament titles over the same span. And three times Kemp parcipated in the East-West College All-Star dual meet. Kemp was undefeated and untied at 39–0–0 in 1975–76 for the Badgers and compiled a career mark of 143–6–1. He was the world freestyle champion in 1978 and then followed that with a spectacular 1979, winning the world freestyle again, the Pan American Games title and the National AAU title. He was awarded the Sun Cup in 1978 as the outstanding amateur wrestler of the year. In 1984, Kemp received the "*Olympia Award*" from the Southland Corporation for outstanding amateur athletic participation.

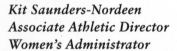
LEADING THE WAY

Kit Saunders-Nordeen
Associate Athletic Director
Women's Administrator

A pioneer in the organization and development of women's sports both in Wisconsin and nationally, Kit Saunders Nordeen was named the UW's first athletic director for women in 1974. She guided the transition of women's sports in Madison from the recreational level to interollegiate status. In 1983, she was named an associate athletic director supervising 22 men's and women's non-revenue sports; she resumed her role as primary women's administrator in 1986 until her retirement in 1989. She earned master's and doctoral degrees from Wisconsin. Nordeen, the first inductee into the UW Women's Athletics Hall of Fame in 1984, was one of the founders of the Wisconsin Women's Intercollegiate Athletic Conference in 1971 and later served as its president. She also was first vice president of the Association of Intercollegiate Athletics for Women from 1979–82 and was inducted into the UW Athletic Hall of Fame in 1998.

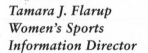
LEADING THE WAY

Tamara J. Flarup
Women's Sports
Information Director

One of the leaders for women in the field of sports information, Tam Flarup was the women's sports information director at Wisconsin for almost 25 years. Since becoming women's SID in 1977, Flarup was instrumental in a number of successful Big Ten and NCAA Championships and worked at several NCAA Women's Final Fours. As a member of the College Sports Information Directors of America, Flarup served on a number of committees including chair of the Publicists for Women's Sports. Through CoSIDA, a number of her media guides have been honored with national awards including several "Best in the Nation" honorees. The native of Eagle Grove, Iowa, came to Wisconsin after one year as the first women's SID at the University of Kansas. The 1975 Iowa State graduate earned a double major in journalism and physical education while playing on the women's golf team.

1978-79

BADGER BIG TEN FINISHES...

MEN'S
Football: 6th
coached by Dave McClain
Cross Country: 1st
coached by Dan McClimon,
(3rd, NCAA)
Basketball: 8th (tie)
coached by Bill Cofield
Indoor Track: 5th
coached by Dan McClimon,
(8th-tie, NCAA)
Swimming: 6th
coached by Jack Pettinger
Wrestling: 2nd
coached by Duane Kleven,
(5th, NCAA)
Baseball: 2nd
coached by Tom Meyer
Golf: 8th, coached by Dennis Tiziani
Gymnastics: 7th
coached by Mark Pflughoeft
Tennis: 5th
coached by Denny Schackter
Ice Hockey: 3rd(tie) (WCHA)
coached by Bob Johnson,
(4th, NCAA)
Outdoor Track: 3rd
coached by Dan McClimon

WOMEN'S
Cross Country: 1st
coached by Peter Tegen
Basketball: 7th (tie)
coached by Edwina Qualls
Indoor Track: 1st
coached by Peter Tegen
Swimming: 6th
coached by Carl Johansson
Volleyball: 5th (tie)
coached by Kristi Conklin
Golf: 6th, coached by Jackie Hayes
Outdoor Track: 1st
coached by Peter Tegen

The Big Event

Matthews beats "Magic," Spartans

Coach Bill Cofield's Wisconsin men's basketball team won 12 games in 1978–79–the most at the UW in five years–but none was bigger than the season finale.

Riding a modest three-game winning streak, the Badgers, led by guards Wes Matthews, Arnold Gaines and Dan Hastings, center Larry Petty and forwards Claude Gregory and Joe Chrnelich, played host to a fourth-ranked Michigan State squad that featured the legendary Earvin "Magic" Johnson and all-America forward Greg Kelser in the last game of the regular season for both teams.

Michigan State, which brought a 10–game winning streak of its own to the UW Field House, was as advertised–but the Badgers played a fine first half and led 44–43 at the intermission behind 12 points from Gregory and 11 from Chrnelich. Johnson and Kelser each had 12 points for the Spartans, who shot .548 from the field.

Neither team led by more than four points in the second half until the Badgers took a 78–73 lead with 3:12 remaining. But Michigan State came back and eventually tied it at 81 on a pair of Johnson free throws with 0:03 left.

Matthews put an exclamation point on the tense game with a historic 50–foot buzzer–beater that gave the Badgers a two–point win.

Gregory finished with 25 points and 16 rebounds to pace the Badgers, while Johnson put up 26 points, 13 rebounds and eight assists in his last Big Ten game. MSU went on to win its first NCAA title in the sport.

WISCONSIN TIMELINE

1979: Thousands fled their homes near the Three Mile Island nuclear plant in Pennsylvania when officials warned of the risk of a core meltdown.

Wisconsin connected on 32 of 43 field goal attempts for a single–game men's school record in a 78–54 win over Army.

Mark Johnson closed out his Wisconsin hockey career as the top goal scorer (125) in UW history.

WISCONSIN HEADLINER

STEVE LACY
TRACK, CROSS COUNTRY

Two-time Olympian Steve Lacy was the first Wisconsin runner to break 4 minutes in the mile, running 3:59.64 in 1977. A native of nearby McFarland, Wis., "Lace" didn't have far to go when recruited by Coach Dan McClimon. Staying close to home paid off. Lacy won six Big Ten titles, including three consecutive indoor mile crowns. A four–time "W" award winner in both track and cross country, he was also a three-time indoor track all-American and ran the second leg on the Badgers' 1976 NCAA indoor champion two–mile relay unit. Lacy and discus thrower Arlie Mucks, Sr., are the only two–time track and field Olympians from Wisconsin. Lacy earned a spot at 1,500 meters on the ill-fated U.S. team that boycotted the 1980 Moscow Olympics. He also competed in Los Angeles in 1984 in the 5,000–meter run. He's a member of the Wisconsin track and field "Hall of Honor."

LEADING THE WAY

Jim Mott
Sports Information
Director

Jim Mott spent his entire adult life in Madison, serving as men's sports information director for the Badgers from 1966 until his retirement in 1990. A Wisconsin graduate with bachelor's degrees in zoology (1954) and journalism (1956), Mott served as assistant SID for 12 years until taking the top post. Well-respected by his peers, Mott was named to the College Sports Information Directors of America (CoSIDA) Hall of Fame in 1979 and received the organization's Arch Ward Award, the highest bestowed by CoSIDA on one of its own, in 1986. Mott served on the U.S. Olympic team's press liaison staff for the 1976 Olympic Winter Games in Lake Placid, N.Y., handling media relations duties for the gold medal-winning U.S. hockey team. Jim was inducted into the UW Athletic Hall of Fame in 1990. He passed away in Madison in 2009.

McClain wins in debut as football coach

It may not have been pretty, but football Coach Dave McClain's debut at Wisconsin got the Badgers started on a winning note.

The Badgers hosted the University of Richmond to open the '78 gridiron campaign and, despite entering Spider territory only twice all afternoon, registered a 7–6 victory before a crowd of 60,877 at Camp Randall Stadium. The win allowed McClain to become the first Wisconsin football coach to win his debut since Milt Bruhn in 1956.

Richmond's Steve Adams kicked field goals in each of the consin, however, responded with a school record-tying 80-yard touchdown pass from freshman quarterback John Josten to split end David Charles with 10:13 left in the first half. Steve Veith booted the extra point o conclude the scoring for the day.

Matthews leads nation in punt returns

Ira Matthews had 16 punt returns, three for touchdowns, to lead the nation in 1978. Matthews had return yardage of 270 for an average of 16.9 yards per return, still a UW season record. His longest was a 78-yard return against Minnesota. The four-time letterwinner returned one punt as a freshman but never fell out of double figures after that. He had 15 in 1976 and 13 in 1977. Matthews' career total of 45 still ranks third on the all-time Wisconsin list, as does his yardage total of 443.

1979-80

BADGER BIG TEN FINISHES...

MEN'S
Football: 7th (tie)
coached by Dave McClain
Cross Country: 1st
coached by Dan McClimon
Basketball: 8th
coached by Bill Cofield
Indoor Track: 6th
coached by Dan McClimon
Swimming: 6th
coached by Jack Pettinger
Wrestling: 2nd
coached by Duane Kleven,
(7th, NCAA)
Baseball: 4th
coached by Tom Meyer
Golf: 6th
coached by Dennis Tiziani
Gymnastics: 8th
coached by Mark Pflughoeft
Tennis: 3rd (tie)
coached by Denny Schackter
Ice Hockey: 9th (WCHA)
coached by Bob Johnson
Outdoor Track: 6th
coached by Dan McClimon

WOMEN'S
Cross Country: 1st
coached by Peter Tegen
Basketball: 5th (tie)
coached by Edwina Qualls
Indoor Track: 1st
coached by Peter Tegen
Swimming: 5th
coached by Carl Johansson
Volleyball: 5th (tie)
coached by Kristi Conklin
Golf: 7th,
coached by Jackie Hayes
Outdoor Track: 1st
coached by Peter Tegen

The Big Event

UW women claim Big Ten indoor and outdoor track titles

The Wisconsin women's track teams had its most successful season on record in 1979–80, winning unofficial Big Ten indoor and outdoor championships and finishing second in the AIAW Indoor Championship.

The Badgers remained undefeated in Big Ten indoor meets, winning their third title in as many years. Wisconsin scored 128 points to easily outdistance second place Ohio State (79). The UW won seven events and set six Big Ten records.

Wisconsin also continued its dominance at the Big Ten outdoor meet winning its third consecutive title. The Badgers outscored Michigan State, 157–90, and won six events, setting three Big Ten and two UW records.

Wisconsin qualified 16 athletes for the 1980 Association of Intercollegiate Athletics for Women (AIAW) indoor championship and finished second in the team race. Texas-El Paso won the meet with 40 points while the Badgers scored 25 points behind national champion Pat Johnson, who won the long jump on her last attempt of the meet, leaping 20'10". Suzie Houston also earned all–American honors with a third-place finish in the 2,000-meter run.

The Badgers also finished ninth in the AIAW outdoor championship.

WISCONSIN TIMELINE

1980: The U.S. announced it would boycott the Moscow Olympic Games to protest the Soviet Union's invasion of Afghanistan.

The Council of Ten adopted a resolution to establish a task force to prepare a plan for incorporating women's athletics into the Conference.

Claude Gregory scored 29 points and pulled down 17 rebounds in his last game for Wisconsin.

KRIS THORSNESS
ROWING

A two-time Olympian, Kris Thorsness was a gold medalist in 1984 as a member of the sweep eight. She also participated in the 1988 Olympics in the four with coxswain. Thorsness, a native of Anchorage, Alaska, was a member of five U.S. national teams competing in the world championship. During her Wisconsin career, from 1977–82, she led the Badgers to a second–place finish in the varsity eight at the 1980 national championship and fourth–place finish in 1982.

RAY SNELL
FOOTBALL

Ray Snell, a native of Baltimore, Maryland, was a first-team all-America selection by *The Sporting News* in 1979. The 295–lb. lineman, known for his speed and agility, blocked for Ira Matthews and Dave Mohapp on Coach Dave McClain's second Badger squad. Snell was the 22nd overall pick by the Tampa Bay Buccaneers in the first round of the 1980 National Football League draft.

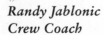

LEADING THE WAY

Randy Jablonic
Crew Coach

Randy Jablonic's career as a Badger rower from 1957–60 began a 40-year association with the sport at the University of Wisconsin. A member of the 1959 national champion varsity eight crew, he competed in the 1960 Olympic Trials in the four-person event. Jablonic went on to serve as frosh coach in the program's history at the conclusion of the 1968 season. His crews won the Ten Eyck Trophy–awarded to the school that scores the most points in the National Intercollegiate Rowing Championship–10 times. Jablonic's varsity eight crew won its fifth national collegiate title in 1990 and earned a trip to the Royal Henley Re-gatta in London. He was named the Eastern Association of Rowing Colleges Coach of the Year for his achievements.

THE LIST

MEN'S CONFERENCE MEDAL OF HONOR WINNERS [THE 1970s]

1970	1975
Douglas R. McFadyen	James R. Dyreby, Jr.
1971	**1976**
Don Vandrey	Patrick J. Christenson
1972	**1977**
Pat Matzdorf	Peter W. Brey
1973	**1978**
Keith D. Nosbusch	Michael Eaves
1974	**1979**
Gary D. Anderson	Steve Lacy

1980-81

BADGER BIG TEN FINISHES...

MEN'S

Football: 6th (tie)
coached by Dave McClain
Cross Country: 4th
coached by Dan McClimon
Basketball: 9th
coached by Bill Cofield
Indoor Track: 4th
coached by Dan McClimon
Swimming: 3rd
coached by Jack Pettinger
Wrestling: 3rd
coached by Duane Kleven
Baseball: 4th (tie)
coached by Tom Meyer
Golf: 9th, coached by Dennis Tiziani
Gymnastics: 6th
coached by Mark Pflughoeft
Tennis: 8th
coached by Denny Schackter
Ice Hockey: 2nd (WCHA)
coached by Bob Johnson,
(1st, NCAA)
Outdoor Track: 6th
coached by Dan McClimon

WOMEN'S

Cross Country: 2nd
coached by Peter Tegen
Basketball: 5th (tie)
coached by Edwina Qualls
Indoor Track: 1st
coached by Peter Tegen
Swimming: 4th
coached by Carl Johansson
Volleyball: 7th
coached by Kristi Conklin
Golf: 8th, coached by Jackie Hayes
Outdoor Track: 1st
coached by Peter Tegen

The Big Event

Badgers win third NCAA hockey title

Wisconsin won its third NCAA hockey title on March 28, 1981, in its sixth trip to the national collegiate tournament. The Badgers had posted a 23–13 regular season record and a 17–11 second-place showing in the Western Collegiate" Hockey Association. In fact, they had dropped three of their last five regular season games and had been eliminated by Colorado College in the WCHA playoffs.

Picked for the NCAA tourney as an at–large entry, the Badgers re-sponded, beating Clarkson College 9–8 in a total goal series in the NCAA quarterfinals. In the national semis, at Duluth, Minnesota, Wisconsin defeated Northern Michigan 5–1, setting up a rematch with a Minnesota team that had beaten the UW in three of four regular season games. They stunned the heavily favored Gophers 6–3 for their most improbable championship, thus earning the nick-name, the "Back Door Badgers."

Goaltender Marc Behrend was named the tournament MVP. It was Coach Bob Johnson's last NCAA title. The veteran coach resigned following Wisconsin's second–place NCAA finish in 1982.

WISCONSIN TIMELINE

1981: Walter Cronkite signed off for the last time as the anchor of the *CBS Evening News*.

Nine of the 10 conference universities (with Minnesota as the exception) voted to affiliate their women's athletic programs with the Conference; the first official women's championship was held, in field hockey, in the fall of 1981.

Wisconsin defeated No. 1–ranked Michigan 21–14 in football, and eventually went to the Garden State Bowl, its first bowl appearance in 28 years.

137

MARC BEHREND
HOCKEY

Marc Behrend, a native of Madison (LaFollette H.S.), stayed home to play college hockey and it turned out well for both him and the Badgers. Behrend was in goal for Wisconsin's NCAA championship seasons of 1981 and 1983. He recorded 30 saves in the UW's 6–3 NCAA finals win over Minnesota in the surprising 1981 campaign. In the 1983 NCAA title game, the 6–2 win over Harvard was largely credited to Behrend. The veteran goalie had nine and 10 saves in the first and second periods, respectively, as the Badgers nursed 1–0 and 2–0 leads before blowing the game open in the third period. For his efforts in both of those championship runs, Behrend was named the NCAA tournament MVP as well as the Badgers' most valuable for the '83 season. He finished his Wisconsin career with a 49–8–3 mark for a UW record winning percentage of .842. Behrend had a career 2.64 goals-against average, a .912 save percentage and four shutouts. He was the goaltender for the U.S. Olympic hockey team in 1984 and played three seasons for the NHL's Winnipeg Jets.

ANN FRENCH &
CLAIRE ALLISON
BADMINTON

The 1979 Broderick Award winner for badminton, Ann French was a four-year all-American while competing from 1978–82. She and doubles partner Claire Allison, who competed for the UW from 1980–83, won the 1981 and 1982 Association of Intercollegiate Athletics for Women (AIAW) national title. French also finished among the top eight players in singles competition all four years and earned six all-American honors. French, a native of Elmhurst, Ill., was the UW's inaugural Medal of Honor winner for women in 1982. In addition to winning two AIAW doubles titles, Allison, a native of Montreal, was the runner–up in singles at the 1982 AIAW Championship and won the singles title at the 1983 National Intercollegiate Badminton Championship. She and Sandra Colby won the 1983 NIBC doubles title.

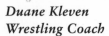

LEADING THE WAY

Duane Kleven
Wrestling Coach

Duane Kleven more than lived up to expectations after he succeeded George Martin as Wisconsin wrestling coach in 1970. In a dozen seasons as the Badgers' mentor, Kleven directed the UW matmen to a 132–48–5 record, guided 26 wrestlers to all-America honors and finished among the Big Ten's top three teams on nine occasions. His teams had six top-10 NCAA finishes, including a school-best fourth place in 1976. In his first season, Kleven led Wisconsin to a 13–4 record, tying the school record for most wins in a season. The National Wrestling Coaches Association named him NCAA coach of the year in 1976–77, a year after the U.S. Wrestling Federation had accorded him similar honors. An outstanding prep wrestler at Stoughton High School, Kleven also competed for the Badgers. He began his coaching career in 1962 with Wisconsin High School in Madison, served in the military and guided Racine Park High School to two state titles. Kleven then coached UW–Oshkosh to a 10–7 mark in 1969 before coming to Madison.

THE LIST

WISCONSIN'S OLYMPIC ROWERS

Women

Men

Mark Berkner, 1992
Bob Espeseth, 1980, 1984, 1988
Neil Haleen, 1976
Dave Krmpotich, 1988
Stewart MacDonald, 1968, 1976
Tim Michelsen, 1972
Eric Mueller, 1996
Matt Smith, 2004

Chris Cruz, 1980
Cindy Eckert, 1988, 1992
Yasmin Farooq, 1992, 1996
Carol Feeney, 1992
Sarah Gengler, 1988, 1992
Carie Graves, 1976, 1980, 1984
Melissa Iverson, 1996
Mara Keggi, 1988
Peggy McCarthy, 1976, 1980
Kim Santiago, 1998, 1992 (alt.)
Kris Thorsness, 1984, 1988
Chari Towne, 1984
Jackie Zach, 1976
Torrey Folk, 2000
Kristia Hedstrom, 2012

BADGER BIG TEN FINISHES...

MEN'S
Football: 3rd (tie)
coached by Dave McClain
Cross Country: 1st
coached by Dan McClimon
Basketball: 10th
coached by Bill Cofield
Indoor Track: 3rd
coached by Dan McClimon
Swimming: 5th
coached by Jack Pettinger
Wrestling: 3rd
coached by Duane Kleven
Baseball: 4th
coached by Tom Meyer
Golf: 6th
coached by Dennis Tiziani
Gymnastics: 6th
coached by Mark Pflughoeft
Tennis: 3rd
coached by Dave Pelisek
Ice Hockey: 2nd (WCHA)
coached by Bob Johnson,
(2nd, NCAA) Outdoor Track: 3rd
coached by Dan McClimon

WOMEN'S
Cross Country: 2nd
coached by Peter Tegen
Basketball: 5th (tie)
coached by Edwina Quails
Indoor Track: 1st
coached by Peter Tegen
Swimming: 4th
coached by Carl Johansson
Volleyball: 10th
coached by Niels Pedersen
Golf: 5th
coached by Jackie Hayes
Gymnastics: 8th
coached by Jenny Hoffman–Convisor
Tennis: 6th
coached by Kelly Ferguson
Outdoor Track: 3rd
coached by Peter Tegen

The Big Event

Women begin official Big Ten competition

Women's athletics became an official part of the Big Ten Conference during the 1981–82 season. Teams had been competing in unofficial league championships prior to 1981, but these championships are not officially recognized.

In 1981–82, the Big Ten Conference sponsored women's championships in 11 sports–basketball, cross country, field hockey, golf, gymnastics, swimming, softball, tennis, indoor track, outdoor track, and volleyball. Wisconsin won the 1982 Big Ten indoor track championship for its first official league title.

1981–82 also marked a change in the women's athletic program at Wisconsin. Field hockey was dropped after the 1980–81 season with soccer picked as its replacement. Craig Webb was hired as the first women's soccer coach at Wisconsin and he led his team to a 12th-place finish in the AIAW national championship.

Soccer also had its first all-American that year as Karen Lunda earned third-team honors.

1981–82 would also be the last year that Wisconsin women's athletics would compete on the national level under the AIAW banner. The NCAA began offering women's championships in 1981–82 resulting in two national champions in many sports that season. Without the support of a number of larger universities, the AIAW was forced to disband.

WISCONSIN TIMELINE

1982: The space shuttle Columbia was launched on its first commercial mission.

The Big Ten approved an increase in the number of permissible basketball games to 28.

Wisconsin scored 6–0 football win at Ohio State, its first victory in Columbus since 1918.

WISCONSIN HEADLINER

TIM KRUMRIE
FOOTBALL

Noseguard Tim Krumrie's play was a primary reason Wisconsin returned to post-season bowl action (in 1981 and 1982) after a 19-year absence. Krumrie, a Mondovi, Wis., native, was a three-time, first-team all-Big Ten performer and helped lead the Badgers to the 1981 Garden State and 1982 Independence bowls (he was voted the game MVP). Krumrie was a consensus all-America choice in 1981 and earned first–team acclaim a year later, as well. He set a then-Wisconsin record for career tackles with 444 and still ranks third all–time at the UW. Krumrie was a Lombardi Award semifinalist twice (1981 and 1982) at Wisconsin and was a 10th-round draft choice of the NFL's Cincinnati Bengals. A two-time Pro Bowl participant, he played 12 years for Cincinnati, including Super Bowl XXIII in 1989.

WISCONSIN HEADLINER

PAT JOHNSON
TRACK AND FIELD

Pat Johnson starred at Wisconsin from 1978–82 as one of the mainstays of the Coach Peter Tegen's burgeoning Badger women's track and field program. Johnson, a 20"2 1/4" high school long jumper out of Chicago (DuSable High School), became a three-time national long jump champion and seven-time all-American for the Badgers. Remarkably, she qualified in the long jump for every national meet during her career. She won Association of Intercollegiate Athletics for Women (AIAW) indoor long jump titles in 1980 and 1982 and the AIAW outdoor championship in a record 21'4 3/4" in '82. Johnson won 12 Big Ten titles, including seven of a possible eight in the long jump. She was inducted into the UW Athletic Hall of Fame in 1997.

VandenBoom intercepts three Michigan passes

Matt VandenBoom, a three-year letterwinner for the Badgers from 1980–82, never had a more memorable game than in Wisconsin's season opener September 12, 1981, in Madison. Vanden-Boom, a junior and former walk–on from Kimberly, Wis., intercepted three passes to key the Badgers' 21–14 upset of top–ranked Michigan. Coach Dave McClain's team won four of its first five games and finished 7–5 after losing to Tennessee in the Garden State Bowl, its first bowl appearance outside the Rose Bowl. VandenBoom, who had six interceptions for the season, is in a 10-way tie for second on the Wisconsin record board for most interceptions in a game. Clarence Bratt had four against Minnesota in 1954.

State's top four distance runners come to UW

Wisconsin track coach Dan McClimon had a coach's dream come true in 1981, when the top four distance runners in the state–and four of the best in the nation–all signed letters of intent to compete at Wisconsin. John Easker of Wittenberg–Birnamwood, Tim Hacker and Joe Stintzi of Menomonee Falls (North) and Scott Jenkins of Kenosha (Bradford) all had credentials aplenty, with Easker, Hacker and Jenkins with state prep titles under their belts. All went on to stellar careers at Wisconsin, with each earning multiple all-America honors. All were key to the Badgers' 1982 NCAA cross country title, with Hacker and Jenkins finishing fourth and fifth in the race. Hacker, Jenkins and Stinzti also ran on the UW's NCAA title–winning 1985 team, with Hacker taking Wisconsin's second-ever NCAA individual crown.

BADGER BIG TEN FINISHES...

MEN'S

Football: 4th
coached by Dave McClain
Cross Country: 1st
coached by Dan McClimon,
(1st, NCAA)
Basketball: 10th
coached by Steve Yoder
Indoor Track: 3rd
coached by Dan McClimon
Swimming: 5th
coached by Jack Pettinger
Wrestling: 6th
coached by Russ Hellickson
Baseball: 5th
coached by Tom Meyer
Golf: 3rd
coached by Dennis Tiziani
Gymnastics: 6th
coached by Mark Pflughoeft
Tennis: 4th
coached by Dave Pelisek
Ice Hockey: 3rd (WCHA)
coached by Jeff Sauer, (1st, NCAA)
Outdoor Track: 4th
coached by Ed Nuttycombe

WOMEN'S

Cross Country: 2nd
coached by Peter Tegen
Basketball: 5th
coached by Edwina Qualls
Indoor Track: 2nd
coached by Peter Tegen
Swimming: 7th
coached by Carl Johansson
Volleyball: 6th (tie)
coached by Russ Carney
Golf: 7th,
coached by Jackie Hayes
Gymnastics: 7th
coached by Jenny Hoffman-Convisor
Tennis: 4th
coached by Kelly Ferguson
Outdoor Track: 1st
coached by Peter Tegen

The Big Event

Badgers win NCAA titles in cross country and hockey

Wisconsin won its first ever title in men's cross country and its fourth national collegiate hockey title in the 1982–83 season. Coach Dan McClimon's harriers earned their first hill-and-dale win in November, 1982, at Bloomington, Indiana, scoring 59 points to defeat runner-up Providence, which had 138. Wisconsin became the first champ from the Big Ten since Michigan State in 1959.

Pacing the Badgers were sophomores Tim Hacker and Scott Jenkins, who finished fourth and fifth, respectively, in the 10,000-meter race. The three other Wisconsin scorers also earned all-American honors. John Easker placed 16th, Joe Stintzi 23rd and Jim Brice 26th. Randy Berndt (47th) and Don Volkey (84th) rounded out the Badger finishers. It was, unfortunately, Coach McClimon's only national title with his prize recruits of 1981. He was killed in a plane crash the following spring.

It was another success on ice in March 1983 as the Badgers claimed their fourth NCAA championship with a 6–2 win over Harvard. It was the first NCAA title for Coach Jeff Sauer, who had been named to succeed Bob Johnson just nine months earlier.

Wisconsin's tournament advance wasn't easy at first. Chris Chelios and Paul Houck scored the tying and game-winning goals as the Badgers beat North Dakota 6–5 in triple overtime–the longest game in school history–to advance to the WCHA championships. Two wins over Minnesota gave the UW the WCHA win and top West seed in the NCAA. A win over St. Lawrence moved the Badgers into the NCAA semifinals against Providence which they beat 2–0 to move into the title game. Senior goaltender Marc Behrend was named NCAA tournament MVP for the second time in his career.

WISCONSIN TIMELINE

1983: The OPEC oil cartel cut its per-barrel price from $34 to $29, the first price cut in its 23-year history.

The first *Big Ten Women's Records Book* was published.

Al Toon set a Big Ten record with 252 yards receiving in Badgers' 42–38 win at Purdue.

ROSE CHEPYATOR-THOMSON
CROSS COUNTRY, TRACK

Rose Chepyator-Thomson, who began running at Wisconsin as a 25-year-old mother with two children, became one of the best distance runners in Wisconsin's illustrious women's track and cross country history. An 11-time all-American from 1979–83, Chepyator-Thomson was a two-time NCAA champ at 1,500 meters and six times won Big Ten track titles. She also won three Big Ten cross country crowns and in 1983 won the UW Big Ten Medal of Honor and was named an NCAA post–graduate scholarship winner. In 1987, Chepyator-Thomson won the 800-meter run at the National Indoor Masters' Championships. She completed her master's degree in physical education in 1986, added a second in educational and policy studies in 1988 and in 1990 earned a doctorate in physical education from the UW. Inducted into the UW Athletic Hall of Fame in 1994, Chepyator-Thomson is currently a professsor of education and men's and women's cross country coach at SUNY–Brockport.

CINDY ECKERT &
CAROL FEENEY
ROWING

Cindy Eckert (1983–87) and Carol Feeney (1984–86) were silver medal winners in the 1992 Olympics. The duo were members of the women's four without coxswain that finished second. Eckert, a native of Brookfield, Wisconsin, was a seven–year member of the U.S. national team. She also participated in the 1988 Olympics in the women's four with coxswain that finished fifth. At Wisconsin, Eckert was a member of the varsity eight boat that won the 1986 national title. She also won two Eastern Sprint titles and the 1986 San Diego Crew Classic championship. Feeney, from Oak Park, Illinois, was a four-year member of the U.S. national team. At Wisconsin, she was a member of the varsity eight boat that won the 1986 national title.

THERESA HUFF
BASKETBALL

The only UW woman to have her jersey (No.21) retired, Theresa Huff was a four-time MVP for the Badgerwomeni's basketball team from 1979–83. Huff, who led Milwaukee Riverside High School to the 1978 and 1979 WIAA state tournaments, at one time held 30 Wisconsin records. A finalist for the 1983 Wade Trophy, Huff amassed 62 double–doubles (double figures in points and reounds) in 118 career games. Huff led Wisconsin to its first post-season appearance to end the 1981–82 season as the Badgers reached the quarter-finals of the Association of Intercollegiate Athletics for Women national tournament. Huff became Wisconsin's first professional women's player and the first American woman to play on a Spanish professional league in 1983–84. She was named to Wisconsin's all–decade team in 1991 in conjunction with the Big Ten Conference's observance of 10 years of women's sports competition. Huff was inducted into the UW Athletic Hall of Fame in 1998.

MEGAN SCOTT
VOLLEYBALL,
BASKETBALL, TRACK

The only three-sport letter-winner in Wisconsin women's athletics history, Megan Scott lettered in volleyball, basketball and track in just two seasons in Madison. The Platteville, Wisconsin, native transferred to the UW after playing basketball at the University of Kansas for two years. She played volleyball at Wisconsin for two years, earning all-Big Ten honors as a senior. Scott led the Badgers in kills and blocks per game. Scott turned to basketball at the UW for one year and earned second-team all-Big Ten honors. She led the teams in rebounding and ranked third in scoring as the Badgers finished second in the Big Ten. Scott wrapped up her UW career in track by finishing fifth in the discus at the 1984 Big Ten outdoor championship.

WISCONSIN HEADLINER

TIM GILLHAM
FENCING

Tim Gillham wasted no time in establishing himself on the Big Ten and national fencing scene. The son of Wisconsin coach Tony Gillham won the Big Ten epee title in his first season and went on to place third in the NCAA championships. He was the Badgers' most valuable fencer on a team that finished second in the Big Ten and 10th nationally. Gillham repeated his victories in the 1984 and 1985 Big Ten meets–becoming the first fencer to win more than two titles in 61 years of Conference fencing competition–and again earned all-America honors in both of those seasons. He never got a chance to try for a fourth Big Ten title and all-America honors; fencing was discontinued as a Big Ten sport prior to the 1985–86 season.

LEADING THE WAY

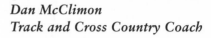

Dan McClimon
Track and Cross Country Coach

Dan McClimon, who guided Wisconsin to its first NCAA men's cross country title in 1982, guided Badger teams for 12 seasons before his death in a plane crash in 1983. "Mac" was named NCAA cross country coach of the year three times and began a Still-ongoing streak in 1972 that has seen Wisconsin qualify for every NCAA championship meet. McClimon coached 51 NCAA track and cross country all-Americans and three NCAA individual champions. He posted a 52–6 dual meet record in cross country, including a 30-meet winning streak. His teams won Big Ten titles from 1977–79 and again in 1981 and 1982 as well as five NCAA District IV championships. Seven of his teams recorded top-10 NCAA finishes, including a third in 1978 and a fourth in 1981 in addition to the UW's first NCAA title a year later.

THE LIST

UW SWIMMING NCAA PARTICIPATION

* Wisconsin's men's team has appeared in the event 44 times

* The men's team has had 3 individual/relay champions

* Men's coach Jerry Darda was voted Big Ten Diving Coach of the Year in 1991

* The women's team has had 21 relay champions and 46 individual swimming champions

* In 1999, Ellen Stonebraker was voted Swimmer of the Championships

* In 2002 and 2003, Carly Piper was voted Swimmer of the Championships

THE LIST

BADGERS VS. BIG TEN FOOTBALL OPPONENTS

Opponent	UW record	Last UW win
Chicago	19-16-5	1937, 27-0
Illinois	36-36-7	2012, 31-14
Indiana	39-18-2	2012, 62-14
Iowa	42-42-2	2010, 31-30
Michigan	14-49-1	2010, 48-28
Michigan State	22-30	2011, 42-39
Minnesota	56-58-8	2012, 38-13
Nebraska	4-4	2012, 70-31
Northwestern	56-33-5	2010, 70-23
Ohio State	18-55-5	2010, 31-18
Penn State	9-7	2011, 45-7
Purdue	43-29-8	2012, 38-14

1983-84

BADGER BIG TEN FINISHES...

MEN'S

Football: 4th
coached by Dave McClain
Cross Country: 1st
coached by Martin Smith
Basketball: 10th
coached by Steve Yoder
Indoor Track: 3rd
coached by Ed Nuttycombe
Swimming: 5th
coached by Jack Pettinger
Wrestling: 4th
coached by Russ Helickson
(4th, NCAA)
Baseball: 4th, coached by Steve Land
Golf: 7th, coached by Dennis Tiziani
Gymnastics: 7th
coached by Mark Pflughoeft
Tennis: 3rd
coached by Pat Klingelhoets
Ice Hockey: 4th (WCHA)
coached by Jeff Sauer
Outdoor Track: 1st
coached by Ed Nuttycombe

WOMEN'S

Cross Country: 1st
coached by Peter Tegen
Basketball: 2nd
coached by Edwina Qualls
Indoor Track: 1st
coached by Peter Tegen
Swimming: 6th
coached by Carl Johansson
Volleyball: 7th (tie)
coached by Russ Carney
Golf: 8th, coached by Jackie Hayes
Gymnastics: 6th
coached by Jenny Hoffman-Convisor
Tennis: 5th
coached by Kelly Ferguson
Outdoor Track: 1st
coached by Peter Tegen

The Big Event

Badger women win Big Ten "triple crown" in cross country, indoor and outdoor track

Wisconsin won its first Big Ten Conference "triple crown"– conference titles in cross country, indoor track and outdoor track during the same season–for women's sports in 1983–84.

The cross country team started it out by winning its first conference title in four years. Wisconsin scored 52 points to easily outdistance Purdue, which finished second with 71 points. Cathy Branta won her second consecutive Big Ten individual championship covering the 5,000-meter course in Champaign, Illinois, in 16:26.2.

The Badgers continued their winning ways during the 1984 indoor track season, winning the Big Ten indoor title with 104 points. Indiana finished a close second with 99.5 points. Branta was again the star of the meet, winning the mile in 4:38.31 and the two mile in 9:52.77. She set Big Ten meet records in both events and was named the Athlete of the Championship. Other event winners were Katie Ishmael in the three-mile run in a meet record of 15:19.70; Sharon Dollins with a meet record 40'0" triple jump; and Dorothea Brown with a 20'3 1/2" long jump.

Wisconsin completed its Triple Crown sweep at the Big Ten outdoor meet, scoring 124 points to win by 10 points over Indiana. ranta and Ishmael both won two events to lead the team. Branta set meet records of 4:16.47 in the 1,500 meters and 9:15.30 in the 3000 meters. Ishmael won the 5000 meters in a meet record of 16:23.57 and the 10,000 meters in 34:24.1.

Dollins and Brown again claimed the horizontal jumps with Dollins winning in a meet record of 41'1 / 4" and Brown taking the long jump at 20'10 1/2".

WISCONSIN TIMELINE

1984: The Games of the XXIIIrd Olympiad opened in Los Angeles, minus a Soviet-led bloc of 15 nations.

Athletic directors approved a 10–week double round–robin volleyball schedule for 1985.

The UW's fourth straight seven–win football season ended with 20–19 loss to Kentucky in the Hall of Fame Bowl.

WISCONSIN HEADLINER

AL TOON
FOOTBALL, TRACK

Al Toon's speed and agility made him a major force on Wisconsin football and track teams of the early 1980s. He was twice named an all-Big Ten first-team selection in football and twice won Big Ten triple jump titles in track. Toon, who came to Madison from Newport News, Virginia. (Menchville High School), earned six "W" awards in his two sports. Toon still holds Badger records for top receiving yard-age in a game (252 vs. Purdue) and in a career (2,103 yards). And he still tops the UW list for career receptions (131) and is second in receiving touchdowns (19). Toon was twice the Badgers' MVP and played in the post–season in the Hall of Fame Bowl, the Japan Bowl and the Hula Bowl; in the latter, he was the offensive MVP with 10 receptions for 124 yards and 2 touchdowns. An all-American in the triple jump in 1982, Toon set a Big Ten record of 54'7 1/4". Following his Badger days, Toon went on to a distinguished NFL career with the New York Jets from 1985–92. He was inducted into the UW Athletic Hall of Fame in 1995.

WISCONSIN HEADLINER

ISABELLE HAMORI
FENCING

Isabelle Hamori recorded the best finish ever for a UW woman fencer at the NCAA championship. The New Orleans native finished second at the 1987 championship, leading the Badgers to a ninth-place team finish. Hamori also finished 12th as a sophomore and as a junior. Hamori was a three-time Big Ten champion, leading the Badgers to the team title as a sophomore, junior and senior. She was named a four-time team MVP for Wisconsin.

THE LIST

LEARNING ABOUT CAMP RANDALL

* After 84 years, the stadium received a new renovation beginning in 2001.

* In 2005, the renovated stadium was opened. The new capacity was 80,321, over 4,000 higher than the pre-renovation.

* On November 6, 2004, 83,069 were in attendance for a game against Minnesota.

* The song "Jump Around" has become part of a popular tradition at UW home games.

A  FIRST

Badgers post best record at home

Wisconsin's women's basketball team chalked up a 12–1 home record and had its best-ever Big Ten Conference finish at 13–5 under Coach Edwina Qualls. Season highlights included a 79–70 win at home over eventual Conference champion Ohio State and a three-game winning streak to end the season and ensure a runner-up finish.

LEADING THE WAY

Peter Tegen Track and Cross Country Coach

After 30 seasons as women's track and cross country coach at Wisconsin, it's safe to say that Peter Tegen has become a legend. The native of Hanover, Germany, a fixture on the UW and national track scene since 1974, left UW in 2004 and was inducted into the UW Athletic Hall of Fame in 2013. Tegen coached more than 40 national champions in cross country and track and his athletes garnered all-America honors 249 times. Tegen coached the Badgers to two NCAA cross country titles, and 39 times the Badgers won Big Ten team titles under his direction. Included in that list are an unprecedented three straight "triple triples"—wins in Conference cross country, indoor and outdoor track—from 1983–86. Most noted among Tegen's athletes are the three Olympians he's coached: Cindy Bremser (1984), Suzy Favor Hamilton (1992 and 1996) and Kathy Butler (1996).

LEADING THE WAY

Dave McClain Football Coach

Dave McClain's sudden death by heart attack in April, 1986, shocked and saddened those who had witnessed the fine job he did in reviving the Badger football program, as well as those who knew him as a good family man and an enthusiastic, committed coach. McClain came to Wisconsin in December, 1977, and guided the Badgers to a 46–42–3 record that included three bowl appearances. The first coach to take Wisconsin to back–to–back bowl games (1981 Garden State Bowl and 1982 Independence Bowl), he also coached the UW to the '84 Hall of Fame Bowl. McClain, a native of Upper Sandusky, Ohio, came to Wisconsin from Ball State and, four years into his tenure in Madison, had the Badgers, consistent losers for more than a decade, in a bowl game. The UW's indoor practice facility is named after McClain.

THE LIST

MEN'S CONFERENCE MEDAL OF HONOR WINNERS [1980s]

1980	Thomas G. Stauss
1981	David C. Goodspeed
1982	David Mohapp
1983	David Farley
1984	John Johannson
1985	John Easker
1986	Tim Hacker
1987	J.J. Weber
1988	Paul Gruber
1989	Dave Lee

A  FIRST

Badger harriers finish 1–2–3 in Big Ten

John Easker led a 1–2–3 sweep finish for Wisconsin in the 1983 Big Ten men's cross country championship, the first time a UW harrier squad had accomplished the feat. With Scott Jenkins placing second and Joe Stintzi third, Coach Martin Smith's Badgers led to a 19-point victory, their third straight Conference title, total was the second-lowest in the meet's history, trailing a 1959 Michigan State that also went 1–2–3, and its 52-point margin of victory over Michigan was the second-greatest in meet annals. The 1991 UW team would equal its predecessor's feat.

BADGER BIG TEN FINISHES...

MEN'S
Football: 4th
coached by Dave McClain
Cross Country: 3rd
coached by Martin Smith
Basketball: 9th
coached by Steve Yoder
Indoor Track: 3rd
coached by Ed Nuttycombe
Swimming: 5th
coached by Jack Pettinger
Wrestling: 2nd
coached by Russ Hellickson
Baseball: 5th
coached by Steve Land
Golf: 6th (tie)
coached by Dennis Tiziani
Gymnastics: 6th
coached by Mark Pflughoeft
Tennis: 7th
coached by Pat Klingelhoets
Ice Hockey: 3rd (WCHA)
coached by Jeff Sauer
Outdoor Track: 2nd
coached by Ed Nuttycombe

WOMEN'S
Cross Country: 1st
coached by Peter Tegen, (1st, NCAA)
Basketball: 7th (tic)
coached by Edwina Qualls
Indoor Track: 1st
coached by Peter Tegen
Swimming: 6th
coached by Carl Johansson
Volleyball: 9th (tie)
coached by Russ Carney
Golf: 7th
coached by Chris Regenberg
Gymnastics: 6th
coached by Terry Bryson
Tennis: 3rd
coached by Kelly Ferguson
Outdoor Track: 1st
coached by Peter Tegen

The Big Event

Badger harriers win UW's first women's NCAA title

Wisconsin's first NCAA title for women came in 1984 when the Badgers won the NCAA Cross Country Championship.

Led by individual champion Cathy Branta, top-ranked Wisconsin scored 63 points to run by Stanford, which totalled 89 points. Branta covered the 5,000 meters on the Penn State University campus in a course record of 16:15.6. The senior from Slinger, Wisconsin, finished almost seven seconds ahead of second–place Shelly Steeley of Florida, who crossed in 16:22.3.

Junior Katie Ishmael finished sixth overall in 16:37.7 to earn her second all-American honor. Also gaining all-America status were sophomore Kelly McKillen, who finished 17th in 16:56.3; and sophomore Birgit Christiansen, who was 28th in 17:05. All five Badger scorers finished among the top 45 runners with freshman Stephanie Herbst crossing in 17:17.6 as the fifth scorer. Other finishers were sophomore Stephanie Bassett, who was 58th in 17:28.5; and junior Holly Hering, who finished 67th in 17:34.6.

"Can you imagine four all–Americans and a national championship?" said UW coach Peter Tegen, who was named the NCAA Coach of the Year. "I don't know what to think yet. Everything has happened so fast. It just hasn't sunk in yet, but I can say, it's the finest thing that's ever happened to Wisconsin women's cross country."

Wisconsin had finished among the top 10 teams in seven AIAW championships and two NCAA championships prior to winning its first national title.

WISCONSIN TIMELINE

1985: Patty Cookset became the first female jockey to ride in the Preakness.

Athletic directors approved an increase in the football travel squad from 60 to 70.

Mary Ellen Murphy was named the third coach in Wisconsin's women's basketball history.

WISCONSIN HEADLINER

CATHY BRANTA–EASKER
CROSS COUNTRY, TRACK

Five-time NCAA and 11-time Big Ten champion Cathy Branta-Easker won just about every track honor possible in 1984 and 1985, her last two years at Wisconsin. The Slinger, Wisconsin, native in 1985 won the Jumbo Elliott Award, the Jesse Owens Award, the Broderick Award and the Big Ten Medal of Honor. A three-time winner of the Wisconsin Athlete of the Year award from 1983–85, Branta–Easker won NCAA championships in cross country (1984), in the 3,000-meter run indoors (1984), the 3K outdoors (1984) and both the 1,500 and 3,000 in the 1985 outdoor meet. She was also a three-time U.S. national champ. In 1985, she also won the 3,000 at the World University Games and at the U.S. Olympic Festival. She was runner-up in the 1984 World Cross Country Championships and an alternate for the 3K for the 1984 U.S. Olympic team. She was named to the UW Athletic Hall of Fame in 1993. Married to former Wisconsin men's distance all-American John Easker, they live outside Wausau.

WISCONSIN HEADLINER

JOHN EASKER
CROSS COUNTRY, TRACK

A key member of Wisconsin's first men's cross country national championship team in 1982, John Easker was a four-time cross country and three-time all-America distance runner in track. A native of Birnamwood, Wisconsin, Easker was a five-time Big Ten track champion. He was the Big Ten cross country champion in 1983 and won the District IV cross country title in 1983 and 1984. He finished 16th overall during the Badgers' 1982 NCAA championship performance and came back the next two years to finish fourth and third, respectively, at the NCAA meet. Easker went on to become a runner-up in the 1984 USA Senior Men's International Cross Country Trials and helped lead the U.S. to a second-lace finish in the World Cross Country Championships. He and is wife, former five-time UW national women's distance champ Cathy Branta, live outside Wausau.

WISCONSIN HEADLINER

RICHARD JOHNSON
FOOTBALL

Three-time "W" award winner Richard Johnson was named to numerous all-America teams following the 1984 season. A speedy defensive back, he was named *Sports Illustrated's* national defensive player of the week following Wisconsin's 35–34 win on the road over Missouri in 1984. In that game, Johnson blocked two kicks, intercepted a pass and recovered a blocked punt for a touchdown. He also set the UW career mark for blocked kicks (9). The Houston Oilers picked him in the first round of the 1985 National Football League draft.

THE LIST

WOMEN'S CONFERENCE MEDAL OF HONOR WINNERS [1980s]

1982	Ann French
1983	Rose Thomson
1984	Janet Huff
1985	Cathy Branta
1986	Lisa Fortman
1987	Amy Justeson
1988	Chris Gilles
1989	Maureen Hartzheim

1985-86

BADGER BIG TEN FINISHES...

MEN'S

Football: 8th
coached by Dave McClain
Cross Country: 1st
coached by Martin Smith
Basketball: 9th
coached by Steve Yoder
Indoor Track: 1st
coached by Ed Nuttycombe
Swimming: 7th
coached by Jack Pettinger
Wrestling: 2nd
coached by Russ Helickson
Baseball: 2nd, coached by Steve Land
Golf: 6th, coached by Dennis Tiziani
Gymnastics: 5th
coached by Mark Pflughoeft
Tennis: 7th
coached by Pat Klingelhoets
Ice Hockey: 3rd (WCHA)
coached by Jeff Sauer
Outdoor Track: 1st
coached by Ed Nuttycombe

WOMEN'S

Cross Country: 1st
coached by Peter Tegen, (1st NCAA)
Basketball: 10th
coached by Edwina Qualls
Indoor Track: 1st
coached by Peter Tegen
Swimming: 7th
coached by Carl Johansson
Volleyball: 9th
coached by Russ Carney
Golf: 7th
coached by Chris Regenberg
Gymnastics: 4th
coached by Terry Bryson
Tennis: 2nd
coached by Kelly Ferguson
Outdoor Track: 1st
coached by Peter Tegen

The Big Event

Wisconsin wins men's, women's NCAA cross country titles

The UW men's and women's cross country teams made history in the NCAA championships in November, 1985, at Dretzka Park in Milwaukee. Coach Martin Smith's men and Coach Peter Tegen's women notched wins in the NCAA cross country meet, the first time men's and women's teams from one school had won in the same year.

Leading Wisconsin was senior Tim Hacker, from nearby Menomonee Falls, who won his first NCAA title by sprinting away from Iowa State's Yobes Ondieke and Marquette's Keith Hanson in the final 1 1/2 miles to become the UW's second NCAA champ in the sport. The Badgers, unbeaten and ranked first all year, placed five runners among the top 43 finishers to score 67 points and upend defending champion Arkansas (104). Joe Stintzi (11th), Scott Jenkins (24th), Kelly Delaney (26th) and Rusty Korhonen (43rd) were the other UW scorers. Hacker, Stintzi, Jenkins, and Delaney earned all-America honors.

The women's victory–the second straight by Tegen's team–was almost as impressive. Led by Big Ten and NCAA District IV champion Stephanie Herbst's seventh-place finish, the Badgers scored 58 points to Iowa State's 98. Joining Herbst as all-Americans were Katie Ismael in 15th and Lori Walter in 22nd. Other members of the squad were Michelle Lumley, Holly Hering, Stephanie Bassett, Kelly McKillen, and Birgit Christiansen.

WISCONSIN TIMELINE

1986: Kodak lost a patent suit to Polaroid and abandoned the instant-photo market.

The Big Ten and the Pac-10 entered into an agreement with ABC-TV for the televising of college football games through the 1990 season.

Wisconsin took eventual NCAA champ Indiana to three overtimes before losing 86–85 at the Field House.

Suzy Favor won the first of her nine NCAA track and field championships, running 4:41.69 in the mile at the NCAA indoor meet at Oklahoma City.

JIM JORDAN
WRESTLING

One of the winningest wrestlers In Wisconsin history, Jim Jordan compiled a 156–28–1 (.846) record during his four-year career. Jordan, one of only three multiple NCAA wrestling champions in Badger annals, won national titles at 134 pounds in 1985 and 1986. A native of St. Paris, Ohio, Jordan compiled a 47–4–0 mark in 1984–85, including a 7–4 win over Oklahoma State's John Smith in the national title match. He followed that with a 49–3–1 slate (still the winningest season in UW history) in 1985–86 that included his second NCAA crown. Jordan was a three-time all-American, two-time Big Ten champion and National Wrestling Coaches Association All-Star in 1985. Jordan was named to the Amateur Wrestling News Freshman All-American team a year after completing a stellar high school career during which he registered a 154–1 record and four state titles.

RODDY KIRSCHENMAN
SWIMMING

Roddy Kirschenman is one of just six men's swimmers in Wisconsin history to earn at least four all-America honors. The Omaha, Nebraska, native swam for the Badgers from 1986–89. In 1987, he finished eighth in the 1650 freestyle to earn his first all-America distinction. His second all-America honor came a year later when he was 16th with the 800 freestyle relay team. Kirschenman took home a pair of all-America accolades his senior year ('89), finishing 15th in the 500 freestyle and 16th with the 800 freestyle relay team. He earned all-Big Ten mention in 1987. Kirschenman set the school record in the 1650 freestyle in '87, as well. He also set two UW Natatorium/SERF pool records in the 1650 freestyle and with the 800-yard freestyle relay team. Kirschenman was on the U.S. National Team that placed third in the 1,500 at the 1987 World University Games.

TONY GRANATO
HOCKEY

Tony Granato was the first of the three hockey-playing Granato brothers to play at Wisconsin. A veteran of the National Hockey League, Granato played at the UW from 1983–87. He is the school's fourth all-time leading scorer with 100 goals and 120 assists for 220 points in 152 games. He is third in career goals at Wisconsin. A native of Downers Grove, Illinois, Granato was a 1987 Hobey Baker Award finalist as college hockey's player of the year and was a second team all-American that season. He played for the 1988 U.S. Olympic Team. A two–time all-Western Collegiate Hockey Association selection, Granato was an inspiration to the entire NHL when he came back to play the 1996–97 season after under going brain surgery in February, 1996. He earned the NHL's prestigious Bill Masterton Trophy for "perseverance, sportsmanship and dedication to hockey."

TIM HACKER
CROSS COUNTRY, TRACK

Wisconsin has won five NCAA team men's cross country titles and Tim Hacker, a native of Menomonie Falls, Wisconsin, was an integral part of two of them. A nine-time all-American in cross country and track, he finished fourth nationally to lead the Badgers to the 1982 NCAA cross country crown and came back three years later to win the individual NCAA title as the Badgers again grabbed the team championship in '85. Hacker, who later was an assistant coach for the Badgers from 1987–92, won Big Ten titles in 1981, '84 and '85. Hacker anchored the UW's distance medley relay NCAA champion at the indoor championships in 1985. He was a three-time winner of Wisconsin's Tom Jones Most Valuable Runner award and won both the Don Gehrmann Leadership Award and Dan McClimon Memorial Award in 1985.

WISCONSIN HEADLINER

STEPHANIE HERBST
CROSS COUNTRY, TRACK & FIELD

Stephanie Herbst made her mark in the UW record books as one of the nation's top distance runners. A former collegiate record holder in the 10,000 meters, Herbst won three NCAA titles. She won the 3000 meters at the 1986 indoor championship and was a double winner at the 1986 outdoor championship taking the 5000 and the 10,000 meter titles.

Herbst was a six-time all-American and a seven-time Big Ten champion including two cross country titles. She led the Badgers to the 1985 NCAA cross country title and nine Big Ten championships. Herbst was named the 1986 Suzy Favor-Big Ten Female Athlete of the Year and was also nominated for the Brodenck Award in track and cross country. The Chaska, Minnesota, native was a two-time Academic all-American and two-time Academic all-Big Ten honoree majoring in business.

WISCONSIN HEADLINER

YASMIN FAROOQ
ROWING

Yasmin Farooq has the distinction of being named to the U.S. National Rowing Team eight years. The coxswain from Waupun, Wisconsin, was named to the 1992 and 1996 U.S. Olympic teams and has competed in six World Championships. Her crew won the gold medal at the 1995 World Championship. She medaled nine times in international competition.

At Wisconsin, Farooq coxed two national championship crews—the freshman eight in 1985 and the junior varsity eight in 1986. She earned Academic all-Big Ten honors as a senior.

WISCONSIN HEADLINER

TIM MADDEN
TENNIS

One of the winningest men's tennis players in Wisconsin history with 112 victories, Tim Madden earned all-Big Ten honors three times during his four-year career under Coach Pat Klingelhoets. A product of Lewiston, Illinois, Madden put together a career record 12–43 (.723) and led the Badgers in wins three times (23–5 in 1985–86, 17–7 in 1986–87 and 30–15 in 1987–88). Madden, who teamed with Jack Waite to compile a 1–1 record in doubles at the 1988 NCAA Championships, twice served as team captain for the Badgers and earned the team's Sportsmanship Award each of his four years. He was also named Big Ten Sportsman of the Year in 1987–88 and again in 1988–89. Madden was named Wisconsin's MVP in 1986–87 and 1987–88.

WISCONSIN HEADLINER

ANDY RECTENWAL
SOCCER

The career scoring leader in Wisconsin men's soccer history, forward Andy Rectenwal completed his four years as a Badger with a school-record 46 goals and 28 assists for 120 points. He is among all-time leaders in assists and game-winning goals (11) for the Badgers. Rectenwal, a native of Bloomington, Minnesota, was a two-time all-Mideast selection (1986 and 1987) and a first-team all-Big Ten choice in 1987. Rectenwal, who captained the Badgers that year, still holds the UW single-season record for points with 45 in 1986. He also holds school records for goals in a game (four vs. Michigan in 1986) and points in a game (eight vs. Michigan in 1986).

RICK OLSON
BASKETBALL

Madison native Rick Olson stayed home to play his college ball and became one of the best players in school history. Olson, who fell just 10 points of becoming Wisconsin's all-time scoring leader when his four–year earner ended in 1986 (he scored 1,736 points), is third all-time in minutes played (3,962) and is tied with Michael Finley for third in career starts (112). Olson, in fact, started every game during his four years at Wisconsin. He is the UW's career free throw percentage leader (.870) and set a then-Big Ten record for consecutive free throws made when he connected on 36 straight during 1984 and 1985. A third-team all-Big Ten selection in 1985–86, he was an honorable mention all-league choice in 1984–85. He was selected in the seventh round of the 1986 NBA draft by the Houston Rockets.

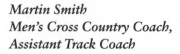

Martin Smith
Men's Cross Country Coach,
Assistant Track Coach

Martin Smith's 15-year run as head coach of the Wisconsin men's cross country program was marked by nothing but success. Smith, who also was an assistant track coach for the Badgers, guided the Badgers to two (1985 and 1988) NCAA cross country titles, 12 Big Ten team championships and 10 District IV crowns. His Wisconsin squads finished in the top five at the NCAA meet nine times. Among the student-athletes he coached, four have won Big Ten individual championships, 33 have earned all-America accolades, 38 have been named all-Big Ten and another 51 have been academic all-Big Ten honorees. The Badgers' eight straight Big Ten cross country titles from 1985–92 tied for the sixth-longest dynasty in Big Ten history in any sport. Smith is now head track coach and cross country coach at Iowa State University.

THE LIST

RETIRED FOOTBALL
NUMBERS

33

Ron Dayne was the winner of the 1999 Heisman Trophy. He broke the NCAA's career rushing mark and several Big Ten records.

35

Alan Ameche, two-time all-American and 1954 Heisman Trophy Winner.

40

Elroy Hirsch, nicknamed "Crazylegs," ran for 786 yards in Wisconsin's 8–1–1 season in 1942.

80

Dave Schreiner, two–time all-American named Big Ten player of the year in 1942.

83

Allan Shafer, a quarterback who was fatally injured in the 1944 Wisconsin-Iowa game and in whose memory the "Living Memorial" scholarship is awarded.

88

Pat Richter was a leader on the 1962 Big Ten championship team and the former Director of Athletics.

THE LIST

BIG TEN ATHLETE OF
THE YEAR WISCONSIN
WOMEN'S NOMINEES

1983
Cathy Branta, track and cross country
1984
Cathy Branta, track and cross country
1985
*Cathy Branta, track and cross country
1986
*Stephanie Herbst, track and cross country
1987
Suzy Favor, track and cross country
1988
*Suzy Favor, track and cross country
1989
*Suzy Favor, track and cross country
* won award

BADGER BIG TEN FINISHES...

MEN'S
Football: 8th (tie)
coached by Jim Hilles
Cross Country: 1st
coached by Martin Smith
Basketball: 8th
coached by Steve Yoder
Indoor Track: 3rd
coached by Ed Nuttycombe
Swimming: 4th
coached by Jack Pettinger
Wrestling: 2nd,
coached by Andy Rein
Baseball: 4th (tie)
coached by Steve
Land Golf: 8th,
coached by Dennis Tiziani
Gymnastics: 7th
coached by Mark Pflughoeft
Tennis: 8th
coached by Pat Klingelhoets
Ice Hockey: 3rd (tie)
(WCHA) coached by Jeff Sauer
Outdoor Track: 3rd
coached by Ed Nuttycombe

WOMEN'S
Cross Country: 1st
coached by Peter Tegen
Basketball: 8th (tie)
coached by Mary Murphy
Indoor Track: 1st
coached by Peter Tegen
Swimming: 4th
coached by Carl Johansson
Volleyball: 8th (tie)
coached by Steve Lowe
Golf: 8th
coached by Chris Regenberg
Gymnastics: 6th
coached by Terry Bryson
Tennis: 3rd coached
by Kelly Ferguson
Outdoor Track: 4th
coached by Peter Tegen

The Big Event

Suzy Favor becomes youngest NCAA track champ

Suzy Favor, less than a year removed from Stevens Point High School, became Wisconsin's youngest national collegiate champion when she won the mile in the NCAA indoor track and field championships in March, 1986, at Oklahoma City.

Favor, already touted as one of the nation's premier women distance runners as a freshman, won the mile in 4:41.69. She also won the 1,500-meter run in a meet record 4:09.85 that spring in the NCAA outdoor meet that at Baton Rouge, Louisiana.

Favor won at least one title in seven of the eight NCAA meets in which she competed from 1987–90 and amassed nine NCAA crowns. She also won 21 Big Ten Conference track championships and ran on two winning relay teams.

WISCONSIN TIMELINE

1987: Chrysler Corp. announced it would buy financially ailing American Motors Corp.

Athletic directors approved a move from baseball divisional play to a 28–game schedule, with the top four teams advancing to the Conference tournament.

Suzy Favor was named Big Ten Female Athlete of the Year-the first of three times she won the award which eventually bore her name.

WISCONSIN HEADLINER

SUZY FAVOR HAMILTON
CROSS COUNTRY, TRACK

Suzy Favor Hamilton's career at Wisconsin epitomizes excellence in athletics. That she has been paired with no less a track legend than Jesse Owens speaks volumes for her. Competing as Suzy Favor, not only was she one of the most accomplished athletes in Wisconsin history, but also in the annals of the NCAA. The Stevens Point native six times earnea atniete oт the meet honors at Big Ten Conference track or cross country meets and five times was named by coaches as Athlete of the Year for one of her two sports. Her championship numbers are nothing short of staggering–9 NCAA individual track titles, 23 Big Ten track titles, 14 all-America honors in track and cross country, 7 UW records, 40 straight wins in finals races and only 2 losses in 56 collegiate finals. She won an unprecedented three straight Jesse Owens-Big Ten Female Athlete of the Year awards and other national and collegiate honors too numerous to mention. Twice a U.S. Olympian (1992, 1996), Hamilton still is a nationally ranked distance runner. Three times (1992, 1996, 2000), Hamilton was inducted into the UW Athletics Hall of Fame in 1996.

WISCONSIN HEADLINER

PAUL GRUBER
FOOTBALL

One of the best offensive linemen in Wisconsin history, Paul Gruber earned first-team all-America honors from The *Sporting News* in 1987. A player with tremendous size, strength and speed, he was regarded by some as the top offensive lineman in college football in 1987. A native of Prairie du Sac, Wisconsin, Gruber was a first-team all-Big Ten selection and team captain that year. He started 32 of 33 games during his four-year (1984–87) Badger career. Gruber was a first-round draft choice of the Tampa Bay Buccaneers in 1988 and went on to become a first-team all-rookie selection. An all-league player several times during his 10-year career with the Buccaneers, he missed only four games due to injury and holds Tampa Bay records for most games played (151) and started (151).

THE LIST

UW HOCKEY
COACHES' RECORDS

Coach (Seasons)	Record
Robert Blodgett (1923–24)	3–9–1
W.R. Brandow (1926–27)	1–9–0
Spike Carlson (1930–31)	4–6–1
Mike Eaves (2002–present)	209–156–44
John Farquhar (1927–30)	21–20–7
Kay Iverson (1924–26)	9–10–5
Bob Johnson (1966–82)	267–175–23
John Riley* (1963–66)	34–19–3
Bill Rothwell** (1975–76)	12–24–2
Jeff Sauer (1982–2002)	489–306–46
Art Thomsen* (1931–35, 1963–64)	17–24–4
A.C. Viner (1921–23)	3–13–3

*co-coaches during 1963–64
**coached while Bob Johnson was on leave to coach Olympic team

THE LIST

BIG TEN CHAMPIONSHIPS
WON BY WISCONSIN
WOMEN'S TEAMS

Cross Country	1983, 1984, 1985 1986, 1987, 1988, 1991, 1995, 1997
Fencing	1986, 1987
Golf	1994
Hockey	2006–07, 2009–12
Lightweight Rowing	2004–09
Rowing	2009
Soccer	2005
Tennis	1996
Indoor Track	1982, 1984, 1985, 1986, 1987, 1990, 1996
Outdoor Track	1983, 1984, 1985, 1986, 1990, 1991, 1996
Volleyball	1990, 1997, 2001

1987-88

BADGER BIG TEN FINISHES...

MEN'S
Football: 10th
coached by Don Morton
Cross Country: 1st
coached by Martin Smith,
(1st, NCAA)
Basketball: 7th
coached by Steve Yoder
Indoor Track: 5th
coached by Ed Nuttycombe
Swimming: 5th
coached by Jack Pettinger
Wrestling: 4th
coached by Andy Rein
Baseball: 5th
coached by Steve Land
Golf: 6th (tie)
coached by Dennis Tiziani
Gymnastics: 5th
coached by Mark Pflughoeft
Tennis: 3rd
coached by Pat Klingelhoets
Ice Hockey: 2nd (WCHA)
coached by Jeff Saucr
Outdoor Track: 4th
coached by Ed Nuttycombe

WOMEN'S
Cross Country: 1st
coached by Peter Tegen
Basketball: 10th
coached by Mary Murphy
Indoor Track: 5th
coached by Peter Tegen
Swimming: 10th
coached by Carl Johansson
Volleyball: 5th (tie)
coached by Steve Lowe
Golf: 6th
coached by Chris Regenberg
Gymnastics: 5th
coached by Terry Bryson
Tennis: 2nd
coached by Kelly Ferguson
Outdoor Track: 2nd
coached by Peter Tegen

The Big Event

Tegen wins 25th Big Ten title as UW coach

Coach Peter Tegen earned his 25th Big Ten Conference championship in women's track or cross country when his harriers won the 1987 Big Ten Conference cross country title.

The Badgers placed all five scorers among the top 11 finishers to score 42 points, half the number of points of second-place finisher Iowa. And the team did it without all-Americans Stephanie Herbst and Lori Wolter who quit the team prior to the start of the season.

Sophomore Suzy Favor paced the Badgers with a third-place finish in 17:03. Minnesota's Eileen Donaghy won the individual title in 16:58. Freshman Kim Kauls earned all-Big Ten honors with a sixth-place finish in 17:29. Senior Carole Harris finished ninth in 17:43, Tammy Breighner was 10th in 17:45 and Mary Hartzheim finished 11th in 17:46.

The Wisconsin women earned a berth in the NCAA Championship by winning the NCAA IV meet with 56 points. Harris was the top UW finisher coming in sixth in 17:11.2.

The Badgers wrapped up their season with a sixth-place finish in the NCAA championship. Oregon won the team title with 98 points while Wisconsin scored 155 points. For the second year in a row, Favor led the individual effort for the Badgers, earning all-American honors with a 21st-place finish. Favor covered the 5,000-meter course in 16:47.6. Harris also earned all-American honors crossing in 16:49.1, good for 24th place. Other scorers were Gordy Hartzheim, 49th in 17:13.4; Mary Hartzheim, 52nd in 17:15.2; and Breighner, 76th in 17:37.5.

WISCONSIN TIMELINE

1988: The 15th Olympic Winter Games opened in Calgary, Alberta, Canada.

Athletic directors approved a move from baseball divisional play to a 28–game schedule, with the top four teams advancing to the Conference tournament.

Suzy Favor was named Big Ten Female Athlete of the Year—the first of three times she won the award which eventually bore her name.

155

1988—89

BADGER BIG TEN FINISHES...

MEN'S

Football: 9th (tie)
coached by Don Morton
Cross Country: 1st
coached by Martin Smith
Basketball: 6th (tie)
coached by Steve Yoder
Indoor Track: 5th
coached by Ed Nuttycombe
Swimming: 5th
coached by Jack Prttinscr
Wrestling: 7th
coached by Andy Rein
Baseball: 9th
coached by Steve Land
Golf: 4th (tie)
coached by Dennis Tiziani
Gymnastics: 5th
coached by Mark Pflughoeft
Tennis: 5th
coached by Pat Klingelhoets
Ice Hockey: 3rd (WCHA)
coached by Jeff Sauer
Outdoor Track: 3rd
coached by Ed Nuttycombe

WOMEN'S

Cross Country: 1st
coached by Peter Tegen
Basketball: 8th (tie)
coached by Mary Murphy
Indoor Track: 3rd
coached by Peter Tegen
Swimming: 8th
coached by Carl Johansson
Volleyball: 8th
coached by Steve Lowe
Golf: 7th
coached by Chris Regenberg
Gymnastics: 6th
coached by Terry Bryson
Tennis: 2nd
coached by Kelly Ferguson
Outdoor Track: 2nd
coached by Peter Tegen

The Big Event

Men's basketball makes NIT

It had been awhile–42 years, to be exact. Coach Steve Yoder's 1988–89 UW men's basketball team returned to post-season play for the first time since 1947 when the Badgers compiled a 17–11 regular-season record to qualify for the National Invitation Tournament.

The 1988–89 Badgers got an early jump on the season with an 8–0 mark on a two-week summer tour of Denmark, Finland and Sweden. Wisconsin returned from overseas and proceeded to register an 8–2 mark in non-conference play, capturing the First Bank Classic in Milwaukee with a 70–55 win over state-rival Marquette in the title game. UW senior Danny Jones earned tournament MVP honors. The Badgers later defeated Marquette, 61–59, to complete a season sweep of the Warriors.

Wisconsin opened Conference play with a come-from-behind win over Minnesota at the UW Field House. Four straight losses followed before the Badgers played themselves back into post-season contention by winning six of their next eight for a 7–6 record with five league games left to play. The UW, however, dropped four of its last five to finish the league campaign in a sixth-place tie with Purdue at 8–10.

Though bypassed by the NCAA, the Badgers gained entry to the NIT and defeated New Orleans in a first-round game at the Field House, 63–61, before being eliminated by St. Louis in the second round.

The Badgers' 18 victories were the most at Wisconsin since 1940–41. Yoder was named District XI and Midwest Coach of the Year. Jones and Trent Jackson earned second-team all-Big Ten mention.

WISCONSIN TIMELINE

1989: The Supreme Court ruled that burning the American flag as a form of political protest is protected by the 1st Amendment.

James E. Delany became the Big Ten's fifth commissioner.

Danny Jones snapped Wisconsin's career scoring mark with his first basket in a game against Ohio State; he ended his career with 1,854 points.

BADGER BIG TEN FINISHES...

MEN'S
Football: 9th
coached by Don Morton
Cross Country: 1st
coached by Martin Smith
Basketball: 8th (tie)
coached by Steve Yoder
Indoor Track: 5th
coached by Ed Nuttycombe
Swimming: 9th
coached by Jack Pettinger
Wrestling: 7th, coached by Andy Rein
Baseball: 9th, coached by Steve Land
Golf: 3rd coached by Dennis Tiziani
Gymnastics: 6th
coached by Mark Pflughoeft
Tennis: 3rd
coached by Pat Klingelhoets
Ice Hockey: 1st (WCHA)
coached by Jeff Sauer
Outdoor Track: 4th
coached by Ed Nuttycombe

WOMEN'S
Cross Country: 6th
coached by Peter Tegen
Basketball: 9th (tie)
coached by Mary Murphy
Indoor Track: 1st
coached by Peter Tegen
Swimming: 6th
coached by Carl Johansson
Volleyball: 5th (tie)
coached by Steve Lowe
Golf: 4th
coached by Dennis Tiziani
Gymnastics: 4th
coached by Terry Bryson
Tennis: 3rd
coached by Kelly Ferguson
Outdoor Track: 1st
coached by Peter Tegen

The Big Event

Hockey wins WCAA title

Led by a strong core of seven seniors, Coach Jeff Sauer's eighth Wisconsin hockey team rolled to the WCHA regular-season and playoff titles before capping a 36–9–1 season with the school's fifth NCAA championship.

Sauer's squad was fortunate to have all the ingredients necessary for a championship team–talent and leadership being two of the most noticeable. The Badgers, with a senior class that included Tom Sagissor, John Byce, Chris Tancill, Gary Shuchuk, Rob Mendel, Mark Osiecki and captain Steve Rohlik, finished the campaign by going 18–1–1.

Wisconsin jumped out to a 9–1 mark to start the season, but was just 9–8 over its next 17 games, including a 4–3 loss at Northern Michigan on January 19. The Badgers, however, bounced back the next night against the Wildcats–winning 10–1–and went on to sandwich two nine–game winning streaks around just one loss at Minnesota and one tie with North Dakota.

The Badgers clinched the league title with a 5–4 OT win over North Dakota on February 24 and notched the WCHA playoff crown on March 12 with a 7–1 win over arch-rival Minnesota. The UW swept an NCAA Tournament quarterfinal series from Maine, defeated Boston College 5–4 in the semifinals and Colgate 7–3 in the title game at Detroit's Joe Louis Arena behind a Byce hat trick.

Shuchuk earned first-team all-America honors, while Tancill was named the NCAA Tournament MVP.

WISCONSIN TIMELINE

1990: The Dow Jones Industrial Average ended the day above 2800 for the first time, at 2810.15.

Pennsylvania State University was admitted to the Big Ten.

Don Davey became first four-time first-team academic all-American in NCAA Division I football history.

WISCONSIN HEADLINER

GARY SHUCHUK
HOCKEY

Wisconsin's Big Ten Athlete of the Year nominee in 1990, forward Gary Shuchuk helped lead the Badger hockey team to a 36–9–1 overall record and a 7–3 win over Colgate in the '90 NCAA title game at Detroit's Joe Louis Arena. Shuchuk, a native of Edmonton, Alberta, earned first-team all-America honors that season after leading the Badgers in scoring with 41 goals and 39 assists for 80 points. Named the Badgers' MVP, Shuchuk served the team as an assistant captain. He finished his Wisconsin career with 85 goals (seventh on the all-time UW list) and 91 assists for 176 points in 177 games. Shuchuk went on to play three seasons apiece for the National Hockey League's Detroit Red Wings and Los Angeles Kings.

WISCONSIN HEADLINER

DANNY JONES
BASKETBALL

Wisconsin's career scoring leader for five years from 1990–95, Danny Jones is now the UW's second-leading scorer with 1,854 career points. Jones, a forward from Rockford, Illinois, was an Associated Press honorable mention all-American in 1989 after helping lead the Badgers to the NIT (the school's first post-season appearance since 1947). Jones, a two-time, second-team all-Big Ten choice, was also a two-time Badger team captain. He led the Badgers in scoring in 1988–89 and '89–90 and in rebounding in '87–88 and '88–89. Jones set a then school-record for points in a season when he scored 611 in 1988–89. He scored in double figures in 91 games for the Badgers, including a stretch of 33 straight.

WISCONSIN HEADLINER

LISA BOYD
VOLLEYBALL

Lisa Boyd became Wisconsin's first volleyball all-American in 1990 after leading the Badgers to their first-ever Big Ten Conference title and NCAA tournament appearance. She was named the Big Ten Player of the Year and also earned all-region selection that year. The 6–2 middle blocker led the Big Ten in blocks per game and ranked among the conference leaders in a number of other categories. The Dolton, Illinois, native earned honorable mention all-Big Ten honors as a sophomore and as a junior. She led the volleyball team to its first post-season appearance ever when the Badgers won the inaugural National Invitational Volleyball Championship in 1989.

LEADING THE WAY

Andy Rein
Wrestling, Wrestling Coach

Andy Rein contributed to the Wisconsin wrestling program as both an athlete and coach. Rein wrestled for the Badgers from 1977–80, serving as team captain in each of his last two seasons. A three-time all-American, he capped his career by going undefeated (40–0) as a senior and winning the NCAA title at 150 pounds with a 4–2 win over Oregon's Scott Bliss in the finals. Rein posted a 115–19–1 career mark and won Big Ten titles in 1978 and 1980. A gold medal-winner at the 1979 Pan American games, he won a silver medal at 149.5 pounds as a member of the 1984 U.S. Olympic team. Rein coached the Badgers from 1987–1993 and compiled a 69–35–3 record that included honors as 1987 Rookie Coach of the Year by *Amateur Wrestling News* and 1992 Big Ten Coach of the Year. Rein coached 14 all-Americans and three national champions at Wisconsin.

1990—91

BADGER BIG TEN FINISHES...

MEN'S
Football: 10th
coached by Barry Alvarez
Cross Country: 1st
coached by Martin Smith
Basketball: 7th
coached by Steve Yoder
Indoor Track: 5th
coached by Ed Nuttycombe
Swimming: 7th
coached by Jack Pettinger
Wrestling: 4th
coached by Andy Rein
Golf: 5th
coached by Dennis Tiziani
Gymnastics: 6th
coached by Mark Pflughoeft
Soccer: 1st
coached by Jim Launder
Tennis: 5th
coached by Pat Klingelhoets
Ice Hockey: 3rd (WCHA)
coached by Jeff Sauer
Outdoor Track: 5th
coached by Ed Nuttycombe

WOMEN'S
Cross Country: 2nd
coached by Peter Tegen
Basketball: 7th
coached by Mary Murphy
Indoor Track: 4th
coached by Peter Tegen
Swimming: 7th
coached by Carl Johansson
Volleyball: 1st
coached by Steve Lowe
Golf: 3rd
coached by Dennis Tiziani
Gymnastics: 6th
coached by Terry Bryson
Tennis: 2nd
coached by Kelly Ferguson
Outdoor Track: 1st
coached by Peter Tegen

The Big Event

Badgers win women's Big Ten volleyball crown

Nineteen-ninety was a year of firsts for the Wisconsin volleyball team. The Badgers won their first Big Ten Conference title, made their first NCAA tournament appearance, earned their first Big Ten Player of the Year honor, named their first all-American and had their first Big Ten Coach of the Year.

Wisconsin wrapped up its first Conference title on the road with a win at Michigan State to finish with a 16–2 league record. Senior Lisa Boyd was named the Big Ten Player of the Year with juniors Arlisa Hagan and Liz Tortorello also being named to the first team. Steve Lowe was named the Big Ten Coach of the Year.

The Badgers defeated Illinois in the first round of the NCAA tournament in front of a record crowd of 10,935 in the UW Field House. The record crowd made Wisconsin one of the nation's leaders in attendance as the Badgers averaged 2,199 spectators per match to lead the Big Ten.

Wisconsin lost to Penn State in the semifinals of the NCAA Mideast Regional to end its season 29–8. Boyd and Hagan earned all-region honors with Boyd being named Wisconsin's first all-American, earning second-team honors.

The Badgers also suffered a greater loss in August, 1991, when Lowe passed away from complications due to lung cancer.

WISCONSIN TIMELINE

1991: The U.S. and allies launched an assault against Iraqi troops in Kuwait.

The BigTen-SEC Challenge in women's basketball was held at Iowa, with Iowa, Purdue, Auburn and Georgia the participating teams.

Wisconsin women partcipated in their first NCAA basketball tournament, losing 85–74 to Montana in a first-round game.

DON DAVEY
FOOTBALL

Defensive end Don Davey typified the term "student-athlete" during his four-year (1987–90) career as a football player at Wisconsin. Davey was the first four-time academic all-American (university division) in history. A native of Manitowoc, Wisconsin, Davey was also a four-time academic all-Big Ten choice. He set a then-school record for career tackles for loss with 49 and completed his Badger career with 267 total tackles. He led the Big Ten in sacks with seven to earn first-team all-league honors in 1990. A team captain in 1990, Davey earned bachelor's and master's degrees in mechanical engineering. Davey was a third-round choice of the Green Bay Packers in 1991 and played in Green Bay from 1991–94. He spent the 1995–97 campaigns with the Jacksonville Jaguars.

WISCONSIN HEADLINER

JACK WAITE
TENNIS

Waukesha, Wisconsin, native Jack Waite is the winningest men's tennis player in Wisconsin history. Waite, who played for Coach Pat Klingelhoets from 1988–91, racked up a 131–47 (.736) mark during his four-year career. He was 31–14 in 1988–89, 40–5 in 1989–90 and 38–17 in 1990–91. Wisconsin's Big Ten Medal of Honor winner for 1990–91, Waite was a two-time all-Big Ten player and was named Big Ten Player of the Year in 1991. He played singles in the 1991 NCAA Championships and came away with a 1–1 mark. Waite was a three-time academic all-Big Ten selection, three-time Badger MVP and three-time winner of Wisconsin's Sportsmanship Award. He was named Big Ten Sportsman of the Year in1989–90.

WISCONSIN HEADLINER

TROY VINCENT
FOOTBALL

Although he played just one year of high school football, Troy Vincent became one of the nation's top cornerbacks and punt returners for Barry Alvarez's first two Wisconsin teams. A 1991 all-America selection, Vincent was also honored that year as the Big Ten's co-Defensive Player of the Year. He was runner-up for the Jim Thorpe Award, given to the nation's top defensive back. Vincent was selected by the Miami Dolphins as the seventh overall choice in the 1992 National Football League draft.

WISCONSIN HEADLINER

PATRICK TOMPKINS
BASKETBALL

Patrick Tompkins was Wisconsin's top rebounder in 1990 and 1991, earning first-team all-Big Ten honors as a senior. He also was the Badgers' most valuable player. In 1990, Tompkins pulled down an average 6.4 rebounds per game, a stat that improved to 8.8 per game in 1991. He had 14 "double–doubles" (double figures in points and rebounds in a game) in his career. Tompkins was a key player for Coach Steve Yoder on two National Invitation Tournament teams.

HEATHER TAGGART
SOCCER

The only two-time first-team all-American in women's soccer, goalkeeper Heather Taggart led the Badgers to a 17–3 record and a second-place finish at the 1991 NCAA Championship. Wisconsin appeared in four consecutive NCAA tournaments during Taggart's years. The four-time all-region selection was named the 1991 Adidas Goalkeeper of the Year and was a finalist for the Adidas Soccer Player of the Year award. Taggart set UW career records for shutouts (52.5), fewest goals allowed (37) and saves (310). A Chancellor's Scholar and Golden Key National Honor Society member, Taggart majored in biochemistry and molecular biology at Wisconsin. She was a 1992 first-team academic all-American and three-time Academic All-Big Ten selection. Taggart, a native of Omaha, Nebraska, was named Wisconsin's Female Athlete of the Year and UW Big Ten Medal of Honor recipient in 1992. She received an NCAA Post-graduate Scholarship in 1992 which she used to attend medical school at the University of Nebraska.

Steve Lowe
Volleyball Coach

With Steve Lowe at the helm, the Badger volleyball program burst onto the national scene. Unfortunately, that dream burst when Lowe unexpectedly passed away in 1991 from complications due to cancer. Lowe was named the UW volleyball coach in 1986 and built the program into a national power. In 1989, he directed the Badgers to the title in the inaugural National Invitational Volleyball Championship, their first postseason appearance ever. The following year he steered Wisconsin to its first Big Ten title and guided the Badgers to their first NCAA tournament appearance and first national ranking, finishing 10th in the final 1990 NCAA poll. Lowe also produced Wisconsin's first volleyball all-American with Lisa Boyd earning second-team honors in 1990. Lowe, who had a 108–64 career record in five years at Wisconsin, earned 1990 Big Ten and AVCA Mideast Coach of the Year honors.

Cheryl Marra
Associate Athletic Director

In her fifteen years as an associate athletic director, Cheryl Marra was the catalyst in bringing three NCAA Championships to the University of Wisconsin. In 1993, the NCAA Division I women's volleyball championship was held in Madison and garnered the highest attendance in the history of women's collegiate volleyball. One of the most successful NCAA women's golf tournaments was held in Madison in 1998. Marra was instrumental in hosting a number of successful Big Ten and NCAA tournaments at Wisconsin. Marra, who came to Wisconsin from Denison University where she served as the women's athletic director from 1983–90, supervised men's and women's basketball, men's and women's golf, men's and women's swimming and diving, volleyball, and other teams. She also served as the primary women's athletic administrator to the Big Ten Conference and the NCAA. Marra has a bachelor's degree in physical education and health and a master's degree in physical education from Ohio State. She resigned in 2005.

First Big Ten volleyball title

The 1990 season was one of firsts for the Wisconsin volleyball team. The Badgers won their first Big Ten Conference title, made their first NCAA tournament appearance, earned their first Big Ten Player of the Year honor, named their first all-American and had their first Big Ten Coach of the Year. Wisconsin won its first league crown with a 16–2 league record. Senior Lisa Boyd was named the Big Ten Player of the Year and Arlisa Hagan and Liz Tortorello also were named to the first team. Steve Lowe was named the Big Ten Coach of the Year. The Badgers defeated Illinois in the first round of the NCAA tournament before a record crowd of 10,935 in the UW Fieldhouse. Wisconsin lost to Penn State in the semifinals of the NCAA Mic east Regional to end its season 29–8. Boyd was named Wisconsin' first all-American, earning second-team honors. The Badgers also suffered a loss in August of 1991 when Lowe passed away from complications due to lung cancer.

BADGER BIG TEN FINISHES...

MEN'S
Football: 9th (tie)
coached by Don Morton
Cross Country: 1st
coached by Martin Smith
Basketball: 6th (tie)
coached by Steve Yoder
Indoor Track: 5th
coached by Ed Nuttycombe
Swimming: 5th
coached by Jack Pettinger
Wrestling: 7th
coached by Andy Rein
Baseball: 9th
coached by Steve Land
Golf: 4th (tie)
coached by Dennis Tiziani
Gymnastics: 5th
coached by Mark Pflughoeft
Tennis: 5th
coached by Pat Klingelhoets
Ice Hockey: 3rd (WCHA)
coached by Jeff Sauer
Outdoor Track: 3rd
coached by Ed Nuttycombe

WOMEN'S
Cross Country: 1st
coached by Peter Tegen
Basketball: 8th (tie)
coached by Mary Murphy
Indoor Track: 3rd
coached by Peter Tegen
Swimming: 8th
coached by Carl Johansson
Volleyball: 8th
coached by Steve Lowe
Golf: 7th
coached by Chris Regenberg
Gymnastics: 6th
coached by Terry Bryson
Tennis: 2nd
coached by Kelly Ferguson
Outdoor Track: 2nd
coached by Peter Tegen

The Big Event

UW women 2nd in NCAA soccer tournament

The Wisconsin women's soccer team made its fourth consecutive appearance in the NCAA tournament in 1991 and advanced to the championship game.

The Badgers lost to nine-time champion North Carolina, 3–1, to finish second in the nation, the highest finish ever in the 11-year history of the program.

Wisconsin received a first-round bye and defeated seventh-ranked Hartford 1–0 in the quarterfinals. At the NCAA Championship, the Badgers defeated second-ranked Colorado College 1–0 before losing to the Tar Heels to finish 17–3.

Senior Heather Taggart became Wisconsin's only two-time first-team all-American and was also named the adidas Goalkeeper of the Year. The Omaha, Nebraska, native was nominated for the Hermann Trophy, honoring the women's soccer player of the year. Senior Kari Maijala also earned first-team all-American honors.

WISCONSIN TIMELINE

1992: Democrat Bill Clinton won the presidency over incumbent President George Bush.

The Conference approved a cross–licensing merchandising program.

Wisconsin reached the NIT basketball tournament for the third time in five years, but lost 77–73 to Rice in a first-round game at the Field House.

MATT DEMARAY
WRESTLING

Matt Demaray is one of just four multiple NCAA champions in Wisconsin wrestling history. A 150-pound native of Apple Valley, Minnesota, Demaray won back-to-back NCAA titles in 1991 and 1992. One of the winningest wrestlers in Wisconsin history with 150 victories, Demaray went 42–0 en route to his first title win, 4–3, over Iowa State's Steve Hamilton in 1991. A year later Demaray defeated Penn State's Troy Sunderland 5–2 for his second national crown. Demaray's record during his last two seasons was 80–3. A two-time Big Ten champion, he competed in two National Wrestling Coaches Assciation All-Star meets. Demaray was Big Ten Wrestler of the year in 1991. He also earned first-team academic all-America honors from the National Wrestling Coaches Association in 1991–92. Demaray was Wisconsin's Big Ten Medal of Honor recipient as a senior.

DUANE DERKSEN
HOCKEY

The second winningest goaltender in Wisconsin hockey history with an 80–40–6 career record, Duane Derksen helped lead the Badgers to four straight NCAA Tournaments (1989–92), including two championship game appearances and one title (1990). Derksen was the all-NCAA Tournament goalie in 1990. A product of Morden, Manitoba, Derksen was a second-team all-American and finalist for the Hobey Baker Award as college hockey's player of the year in 1991–92. He is first in career games (126) and minutes (7,444) played at Wisconsin and second in career saves (3,222). Derksen was named Western Collegiate Hockey Association Player of the Year in 1992 and earned selection to the all-WCHA second-team twice and first-team once. Derksen was a 1988 draft choice of the National Hockey League's Washington Capitals.

LEADING THE WAY

Paula Bonner
Assistant Athletic Director

Paula Bonner was always an advocate of women's sports. In 1983, she was appointed assistant athletic director in charge of women's athletics. Bonner administered the complete operation of the sport program until leaving in 1989 for a position with the UW Alumni Association. Under Bonner, the women's athletic program was ranked among the top 20 in the nation. The program included several nationally ranked teams which won four national championships. Her research on gender equity issues helped get additional funding for women's athletics with a budget increase from $780,000 to $1.2 million. Bonner, a native of South Carolina, was the chair of the UW Athletic Board's Women's Sports Committee. She was a charter member of the Wisconsin Task Force on Women's athletics and served as a co-host of the Badger Women's Sports Show.

THE LIST

MEN'S HOCKEY ALL-AMERICANS (FIRST TEAM)

Forwards

Mike Eaves (1977, 1978)
Mark Johnson (1978, 1979)
John Newberry (1982)
Patrick Flatley (1983)
Paul Ranheim (1988)
Gary Shuchuk (1990)
Steve Reinprecht (2000)
Dany Heatley (2000, 01)
Blake Geoffrion (2010)

Defensemen

John Jagger (1970)
Jeff Rotsch (1972)
Brian Engblom (1975)
Craig Norwich (1976, 1977)

Theran Welsh (1980)
Bruce Driver (1982)
Paul Stanton (1988)
Barry Richter (1993)
Brian Rafalski (1995)
Jeff Dessner (2000)
Jamie McBain (2009)
Brendan Smith (2010)
Justin Schultz (2011, 12)

Goaltenders

Julian Baretta (1977)
Roy Schultz (1980)
Bernd Bruckler (2004)
Brian Elliott (2006)

BADGER BIG TEN FINISHES...

MEN'S
Football: 6th (tie)
coached by Barry Alvarez
Cross Country: 1st
coached by Martin Smith
Basketball: 8th (tie)
coached by Stu Jackson
Indoor Track: 3rd
coached by Ed Nuttycombe
Swimming: 6th
coached by Jack Pettinger
Wrestling: 6th
coached by Andy Rein
Golf: 1st
coached by Dennis Tiziani
Soccer: 2nd
coached by Jim Launder
Tennis: 9th
coached by Pat Klingelhoets
Ice Hockey: 2nd
coached by Jeff Sauer
Outdoor Track: 4th
coached by Ed Nuttycombe

WOMEN'S
Cross Country: 4th
coached by Peter Tegen
Basketball: 10th
coached by Mary Murphy
Indoor Track: 2nd
coached by Peter Tegen
Swimming: 9th
coached by Nick Hansen
Volleyball: 7th
coached by John Cook
Golf: 5th
coached by Dennis Tiziani
Tennis: 2nd
coached by Kelly Ferguson
Outdoor Track: 3rd
coached by peter Tegen

The Big Event

Wisconsin men win Big Ten golf tournament

Wisconsin won its second Big Ten golf championship—and first since 1957—with a seven-stroke victory over Ohio State on Indiana's course in Bloomington. Coach Dennis Tiziani's team totaled 1,159 strokes for the 72-hole tournament. The score equaled the sixth-best in Big Ten golf history.

Leading the Badgers was Jason Fitchett, who carded a 287 off rounds of 70, 76, 74, and 67 to finish second by five strokes to Iowa's Brad Klapprott. Finishing among the top five in the Conference in a fifth-place tie at 288 were Jim Pejka (71–75–74–68) and Ben Walter (70–75–70–73). Also scoring for Wisconsin was Joe Ring, with a 302, while Mark Scheibach carded a 303.

The Badgers had been building toward a title, having placed in the Big Ten's first division the four previous seasons. The tee-to-green success continued for the Badgers in 1994 as they again topped the Big Ten standings with a 1,151 stroke total and three-stroke margin over Northwestern in the tournament at Ann Arbor.

Walter shot a 274 to become Wisconsin's fourth Big Ten medalist. He set Big Ten records for lowest 36-hole score (65–65–130) and lowest 54-hole score (65–65–70–200) en route to the win. Tiziani was named Big Ten Coach of the Year for both 1993 and 1994.

WISCONSIN TIMELINE

1993: Tennis Hall-of-Famer and rights advocate Arthur Ashe died at age 49 of complications from the AIDS virus.

The Conference extended Commissioner James E. Delany's contract through 1998.

Wisconsin shared the Big Ten football title and beat UCLA 21–16 in the 1994 Rose Bowl.

WISCONSIN HEADLINER

WISCONSIN HEADLINER

DONOVAN BERGSTROM
CROSS COUNTRY,
TRACK

A two-time cross country and three-time track all-American, Donovan Bergstrom was another in a long line of great Wisconsin runners. A native of Elgin, Minnesota, Bergstrom won the 1993 NCAA 3,000-meter stee-plechase title after finishing fourth in 1990 and second in 1992. Bergstrom won the Big Ten steeple-chase in 1992 and 1993. Wisconsin won the 1990, '91 and '92 Big Ten cross country titles with Bergstrom. A cross country all-American in 1991 and 1992, he was named the UW's Most Valuable Runner in 1990 and 1991 and served as the Wisconsin team captain in 1992. Bergstrom was Wisconsin's 1993 Conference Medal of Honor winner as well as its nominee for Big Ten Athlete of the Year. A psychology major, Bergstrom was a three-time academic all-Big Ten selection in track and cross country and the first student-athlete named three times to the U.S. Cross Country Coaches Association all-academic team.

CLARE EICHNER
TRACK

Four-time NCAA champion Clare Eicher starred for Coach Peter Te-gen's women's track teams from 1988–93. A seven-time all-Ameri-can, Eichner made 1993 her special season, winning both the mile and the 3,000-meter run at the NCAA indoor championships. She repeat-ed the double at the outdoor meet, taking wins in both the 1,500 and 3000. After her senior season, Eichner won the 3K at the World University Games. She first earned all-America honors at the 1991 NCAA outdoor meet with a sixth in the 3,000. By the next season, Eichner improved to second in the indoor 3K and fifth in the outdoor race. A 10-time Big Ten champion, she won three consecutive 1,500–3000 doubles at the outdoor meet and two straight mile-3000 doubles indoors. Eichner was named 1993 Wisconsin Fe-male Athlete of the Year and was nominated for the 1993 Honda Award in track and field.

THE LIST

MEN'S AND WOMEN'S CONFERENCE MEDAL OF HONOR WINNERS [1990s]

1990
John Byce and Susan Temple

1991
Jack Waite and Elaine Demetroulis

1992
Matt Demaray and Heather Taggart

1993
Donavan Bergstrom and Kim Sherman

1994
Louis Hinshaw and Susie Holt

1995
Jeff Gold and Dana Tzakis

1996
Scott Lamphear and Lauren Gavaris

1997
Alastir Steel and Kathy Butler

1998
Eric Raygor and Katie Voigt

1999
Brian Doherty and Shannon Brown

A  FIRST

Record crowd for NCAA volleyball at Field House

Wisconsin hosted the NCAA Division I volleyball championship at the Field House. Madison quickly gained a reputation as a hotbed for collegiate vol-leyball when 11,155 fans attended the finals ses-sion. More than 21,000 attended all the sessions.

1993—94

BADGER BIG TEN FINISHES...

MEN'S
Football: 1st (tie)
coached by Barry Alvarez
Cross Country: 2nd
coached by Martin Smith
Basketball: 7th
coached by Stu Jackson
Indoor Track: 5th
coached by Ed Nuttycombe
Swimming: 8th
coached by John Davey
Golf: 1st,
coached by Dennis Tiziani
Soccer: 3rd (tie)
coached by Jim Launder
Tennis: 4th
coached by Pat Klingelhoets
Ice Hockey: 3rd
coached by Jeff Sauer
Outdoor Track: 3rd
coached by Ed Nuttycombe

WOMEN'S
Cross country: 4th
coached by Peter Tegen
Basketball: 9th
coached by Mary Murphy
Indoor Track: 3rd
coached by Peter Tegen
Swimming: 5th
coached by Nick Hansen
Volleyball: 5th
coached by John Cook
Golf: 1st
coached by Dennis Tiziani
Soccer: 2nd (tie)
coached by Dean Duerst
Tennis: 4th
coached by Kelly Ferguson
Outdoor Track: 3rd
coached by Peter Tegen

The Big Event

Badgers share Big Ten football title, Win Rose Bowl

After eight straight losing season, the Badgers were back in a big way in 1993 ... back to the top of the Big Ten and back to Pasadena for the first time since 1963. Picked to finish in the middle of the Big Ten pack, Coach Barry Alvarez's football team posted a school record 10–1–1 mark and a 6–1–1 Big Ten record en route to a share of the Conference championship with Oho State (which tied the Badgers, 14–14).

More importantly, the Badgers made a return trip to the Rose Bowl, in which they had last played in 1963 following that Conference championship season. Powered by Big Ten MVP Brent Moss's 158 rushing yards and two touchdowns as well as a tenacious defense, the UW beat UCLA 21–16, holding the Bruins without a touchdown until the fourth quarter.

More than 70,00 Wisconsin fans cheered the Badgers on. Wisconsin finished the season ranked fifth in the CNN/USA Today poll and sixth in the Associated Press poll, the highest post-season rankings for a Badger team.

WISCONSIN TIMELINE

1994: Comic actor John Candy died at 43 while filming a western comedy in Durango, Mexico.

The first Big Ten women's soccer champion was determined in an eight-team championship tournament at Wisconsin.

Wisconsin claimed its second straight bowl win, a 34–20 victory over Duke in the Hall of Fame Bowl.

WISCONSIN HEADLINER

VALTER KALAUS
SWIMMING

Valter Kalaus, a native of Budapest, Hungary, was one of Wisconsin's top men's swimmers during the early 1990s. Kalaus set school records in the 200-yard freestyle, 500-yard free style and was part of the UW's school record-setting 800-yard freestyle relay team. Named to the all-Big Ten team in 1992, Kalaus earned three all-America selections that season, finishing fifth in the 500 freestyle and 14th in both the 1650 freestyle and 800 freestyle relay. A marketing major, Kalaus was a two-time academic all-Big Ten choice (1993 and 1995). Prior to coming to Wisconsin, Kalaus competed for Hungary at the 1988 Olympics in Seoul, South Korea, finishing 10th in the 400-meter freestyle and 13th in the 1,500-meter freestyle. He was a 15-time Hungarian national champion. He earned three gold and two silver medals at the 1985 and '86 Junior European Championships.

WISCONSIN HEADLINER

BRENT MOSS
FOOTBALL

Wisconsin football returned to prominence in 1993 and one of the primary reasons was the play of tailback Brent Moss. The 5–9, 205-pound native of Racine, Wisconsin, earned the Silver Football, given to the Big Ten MVP, as well as garnering recognition as a second-team all-American and first-team all-Big Ten choice. Moss carried 312 times for a then-UW-record 1,637 yards and 16 touchdowns as a junior in '93, leading the Badgers to a share of the Big Ten title and a berth in the Rose Bowl for the first time since 1963. Moss completed his outstanding campaign by rushing for 158 yards and two touchdowns to help the Badgers defeat UCLA in Pasadena on New Year's Day in 1994. He became the first Badger to lead the Big Ten in rushing since Billy Marek in 1974. Moss finished his career as Wisconsin's second all-time leading rusher with 3,428 yards.

WISCONSIN HEADLINER

AMY WICKUS
TRACK & FIELD

Baraboo native Amy Wickus had a storybook career for Coach Peter Tegen's women's track and field squad from 1992–95. Wickus won eight individual Big Ten titles, ran on three winning relay teams during that span. She won four straight outdoor 800-meter championships and claimed 800-1,500 doubles in both the 1994 and 1995 outdoor meets. Wickus still hold Badger records at 600 meters (1:27.77) and 800 meters (a collegiate record 2:01.65) and is second on the all-time UW list at both 400 meters and 1,500 meters. Wickus was hardly less successful in NCAA competition, winning four NCAA individual titles, including the 1995 outdoor 1,500 and three straight indoor 800 titles from 1993–95. She also anchored Wisconsin's winning 4 × 800 relay quartets in the 1992 and 1993 indoor nationals. She was named the 1994 Big Ten indoor and outdoor athlete of the year and won similar honors for the 1995 indoor season.

WISCONSIN HEADLINER

BEN WALTER
GOLF

When Ben Walter fired his 10-under-par-274 at the Big Ten Championships in Ann Arbor, Michigan, in 1994, he became Wisconsin's first conference medalist in men's golf since 1963. Walter, a native of Menomonie, Wisconsin, led the Badgers to their second consecutive Big Ten title with his record-setting performance. His 274 was just three strokes off the Big Ten record of 271 set by Ohio State's Joey Sindelar in 1981. Walter's 36-hole score of 130 (65–65) and his 54-hole score of 200 (65–65–70) both set Big Ten records. A two-time (1993 and 1994) all-Big Ten selection for Coach Dennis Tiziani's Badgers, Walter advanced to the NCAA Championship as an individual after qualifying with a tie for sixth place at the NCAA Central Regional in Oklahoma City. He missed the cut at the NCAA Championship.

LEADING THE WAY

Barry Alvarez
Football Coach,
Director of Athletics

In 16 years in Madison, former football coach Barry Alvarez rebuilt a program and began a new tradition of high expectations for Wisconsin. The only coach in Wisconsin history to lead the Badgers to consecutive January bowl victories, Alvarez took the 1993 Badgers to a Big Ten co-championship and 21–16 Rose Bowl win over UCLA. His 1994 squad posted an 8–3–1 mark, including a 34–20 win over Duke in the 1995 Hall of Fame Bowl. Alvarez is one of only two coaches in Conference history to turn last-place programs their first year into Big Ten champs. Alvarez came to Madison in 1989 after stops at Notre Dame (as assistant head coach and defensive coordinator, at Iowa and in the high school ranks. He led the Badgers to three Big Ten titles and is the winningest football coach in UW history. In 2005, he retired from coaching in order to focus exclusively on his position as Director of Athletics, which he has held for eight years.

LEADING THE WAY

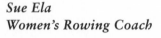

Sue Ela
Women's Rowing Coach

Sue Ela was involved with the UW women's rowing program for 25 years. A 1975 horticulture graduate, Ela was a Wisconsin oarswoman from 1972–75. She served as the assistant rowing coach for three years, prior to her appointment to the women's head coaching position in 1979. Ela was associated with three national championship teams at Wisconsin. As a member of the 1975 national championship rowing team, she brought home the first Wisconsin women's varsity eight trophy. As a coach, she brought the varsity title back to Wisconsin in 1986. Her junior varsity eight boat also won a national title at the 1986 regatta in Cincinnati, In addition to her national championships, Ela's varsity crews have finished in the top four nationally 11 times. In 1989, Ela was recognized by US Rowing as the "Woman of the Year," and in 1990 received a special achievement award from the Madison Pen and Mike Club. She was also recognized as the 1995 EAWRC Coach of the Year.

LEADING THE WAY

Dennis Tiziani
Golf Coach

Dennis Tiziani was head men's golf coach at Wisconsin for 26 years and head women's coach for 14 and, during that time, guided both programs from obscurity to national prominence. He took the men's team to two (1990 and 1992) NCAA Championship tournaments and led the Badger women to their first NCAA Regional appearance in 1994. Tiziani was named men's Big Ten Coach of the Year twice (1989 and 1993) and women's coach of the year once (1994). Wisconsin's men's squad won the Big Ten title in 1993 and then, a year later, Tiziani coached both the men and women to the conference title. Tiziani played three years on the PGA Tour and participated in the U.S. Open four times. Two of his children, Nicki and Mario, were four-year golf letterwinners at Wisconsin. Nicki is married to PGA golfer Steve Stricker.

THE LIST

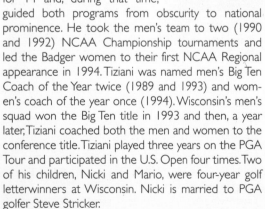

BIGGEST FOOTBALL COMEBACKS

Games (since 1946) in which Wisconsin erased deficits of at least 14 points. These are not necessarily fourth-quarter comebacks, but are games in which the Badgers came back to win or tie after trailing by at least 14 points at some point during a contest.

Date	Opponent	Trailed	Time	Final
Nov. 19, 2011	at Illinois	14-0	8:21 1st	28-17
Sept. 12, 2009	Fresno State	21-7	7:21 2nd	34-31
Nov. 15, 2008	Minnesota	21-7	8:17 2nd	35-32
Sept. 6, 2008	Marshall	14-0	13:34 2nd	51-14
Oct. 28, 2006	Illinois	21-3	5:45 2nd	30-24
Oct. 13, 2001	at Ohio State	17-0	10:27 2nd	20-17
Oct. 2, 1999	at Ohio State	17-0	10:23 2nd	42-17
Sept. 26, 1992	Northern Illinois	17-3	12:41 4th	18-17
Nov. 23, 1991	Northwestern	14-0	14:52 2nd	32-14
Nov. 2, 1985	Indiana	14-0	13:04 2nd	31-20
Sept. 15, 1984	Missouri	28-7	4:42 3rd	35-34
Oct. 2, 1982	Purdue	24-10	9:39 3rd	35-31
Nov. 17, 1979	Minnesota	14-0	8:34 1st	42-37
Nov. 11, 1978	Purdue	24-6	11:42 3rd	24-24 (T)
Nov. 6, 1976	Iowa	14-0	2:46 1st	38-21
Oct. 11, 1975	Purdue	14-0	6:23 2nd	17-14
Nov. 17, 1973	Northwestern	14-0	4:06 1st	36-34
Nov. 14, 1970	Illinois	14-0	4:30 1st	29-17
Oct. 11, 1969	Iowa	17-0	4:11 3rd	23-17

1994-95

BADGER BIG TEN FINISHES...

MEN'S
Football: 3rd
coached by Barry Alvarez
Cross Country: 1st
coached by Martin Smith
Basketball: 9th
coached by Stan Van Gundy
Indoor Track: 1st
coached by Ed Nuttycombe
Swimming: 8th
coached by Nick Hansen
Wrestling: 7th
coached by Barry Davis
Golf: 8th
coached by Dennis Tiziani
Soccer: 1st (tie)
coached by Jim Launder
Tennis: 10th
coached by Pat Klingelhoets
Ice Hockey: 2nd (tie) (WCHA)
coached by Ed Nuttycombe

WOMEN'S
Cross Country: 2nd
coached by Peter tegen
Basketball: 3rd
coached by Jane Albright-Dieterle
Indoor Track: 2nd
coached by Peter Tegen
Swimming: 4th
coached by Nick Hansen
Volleyball: 5th
coached by Dennis Tiziani
Golf: 9th
coached by Dennis Tiziani
Soccer: 2nd
coached by Dean Duerst
Tennis: 3rd
coached by Patti Henderson
Outdoor Track: 2nd
coached by Peter Tegen

The Big Event

Badger men sweep Big Ten cross country and track titles

The 1994–95 Badgers of Ed Nuttycombe and Martin Smith achieved a rarity in Big Ten history, a sweep of the cross country, indoor and outdoor track championships. It marked the second time in a decade that the UW had swept all three Conference titles; the Badgers had also turned the trick in the 1985–86 season.

Smith's cross country team, led by all-Americans Jason Casiano and James Menon, scored a low 42 points at Iowa City in the fall of 1994 to hold off Michigan by 12 points. It also gave the Badgers a measure of revenge against the Wolverines, who had snapped Wisconsin's eight-year Big Ten win streak a year earlier.

In the indoor meet at Champaign, Nuttycombe's trackmen were unfriendly guests, scoring 101 points to hold off Illinois by 1–1/2 points. Four Badgers—hurdler Reggie Torian, middle-distance man Carlton Clark, distance runner Casiano and heptathlete James Dunkleberger–won individual Big Ten crowns and the distance medley relay team also triumphed.

The outdoor Big Ten Championships at Minneapolis gave the Badgers just a bit more breathing room, as the UW tallied 123 points to outlast Michigan (112 1/2) and Illinois (109). Casiano was a double winner, taking the 5,000 and 10,000-meter runs, while steeplechaser Pascal Dobert won his first Big Ten title in his specialty.

WISCONSIN TIMELINE

1995: The federal building in Oklahoma City was bombed, with 267 people dying in the blast.

The Big Ten Conference marked its centennial anniversary.

Michigan and Illinois kicked off the 100th season of Big Ten football competition on September 2.

Wisconsin made its second appearance in the NCAA women's basketball tournament after a third–place Big Ten finish.

MICHAEL FINLEY
BASKETBALL

Thought by many to be one of the greatest players in school history, Michael Finley is Wisconsin's career second-leading scorer with 2,147 points and helped rejuvenate the program during the early 1990s. A three-time honorable mention all-America choice and two-time, first-team, all-Big Ten selection, Finley teamed with Tracy Webster and Rashard Griffith to help guide the Badgers to the second round of the 1994 NCAA Tournament—the school's first appearance in the "Big Dance" in 47 years. Finley scored 500 points in three different seasons and averaged more than 20 points in three separate campaigns, Finley still ranks first or second in several different UW career statistical categories. He was selected in the first round (21st overall) of the 1995 NBA draft by the Phoenix Suns.

CORY RAYMER
FOOTBALL

Cory Raymer in 1994 became Wisconsin's first consensus all-American in 13 years. Raymer, a four-year starting center, earned first-team honors from the Associated Press, United Press International, the American Football Coaches Association, Walter Camp, *The Sporting News, Football News* and *College Sports* magazine. He allowed just one-half of a sack in his last three seasons. Also a two-time all-Big Ten selection, Raymer played a major role in increasing the Badgers' team rushing average from 94 to 244 yards per game during his career. He was a second-round pick of the Washington Redskins in the 1995 National Football League draft.

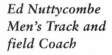

LEADING THE WAY

Ed Nuttycombe
Men's Track and
field Coach

During his 30 years as Wisconsin's head men's track and field coach, Ed Nuttycombe developed one of the most successful programs in the nation. The Richmond, Virginia, native led the program to 26 Big Ten Conference championships. He was selected as Big Ten Coach of the Year 22 times and was named USTFCCCA National Coach of the Year in 2007 when he led the Indoor Track team to the NCAA Championship. He announced his retirement in 2013.

A W FIRST

Griffith debuts with 27 points

Center Rashard Griffith made his first performance at the Wisconsin Fieldhouse, one that Badger fans would long remember. The highly touted freshman showed why he was so heavily recruited, scoring 27 points against Wright State. He also pulled down 12 rebounds and had six assists. Griffith, who lettered at Wisconsin in 1994 and 1995 before leaving school, helped second-year coach Stu Jackson's team to an 18–11 overall mark and 8–10 slate in the tough Big Ten. The NCAA tournament selection committee recognized the strength of the league when it picked the Badgers as an at-large entry in the tournament. It was Wisconsin's first NCAA appearance since 1947. Griffith set a school record for NCAA tournament rebounds with 15 in the Badgers' 80–72 first–round win over Cincinnati.

1995-96

BADGER BIG TEN FINISHES...

MEN'S

Football: 7th (tie)
coached by Barry Alvarez
Cross Country: 1st
coached by Martin Smith
Basketball: 8th
coached by Dick Bennett
Indoor Track: 1st
coached by Ed Nuttycombe
Swimming: 10th
coached by Nick Hansen
Wrestling: 8th
coached by Barry Davis
Golf: 2nd, coached by Dennis Tiziani
Tennis: 10th, coached by Mark Pflughoeft
Ice Hockey: 6th (WCHA)
coached by Jeff Sauer
Outdoor Track: 1st
coached by Ed Nuttycombe,
(6th, NCAA)

WOMEN'S

Cross Country: 1st
coached by Peter Tegen
Basketball: 3rd
coached by Jane Albright-Dieterle
Indoor Track: 2nd
coached by Peter Tegen
Swimming: 2nd
coached by Nick Hanson
Volleyball: 7th
coached by John Cook
Tennis: 1st
coached by Patti Henderson
Outdoor Track: 1st
coached by Peter Tegen

The Big Event

Men's soccer team wins NCAA championship

Coach Jim Launder's UW soccer team to its first NCAA soccer championship in 1995 off the strength of seven consecutive shutouts to close the season. Only the second team in school history to reach the NCAA quarterfinals, the UW swept through tournament play, stopping Duke 2–0 in the championship game at Richmond, Virginia, after edging Portland 1–0 in the national semifinals.

In the championship game, Wisconsin outshot the Blue Devils 15–6 and one-time reserve goalkeeper Jon Belskis saved both Duke shots that reached him. Lars Hansen scored the game-winner 8:12 into the first half; it was his fourth game-winning goal of the season and third in the '95 tournament. The Badgers completed the season with a 20–4–1 mark, setting a school record for victories. They also had 17 shutouts in 25 games, five more than the previous record.

The Badgers started the season 9–2, losing only to Miami of Ohio (1–0) and to 18th-ranked Creighton 2–0 in a game in Wisconsin outplayed the Bluejays. In fact, only Michigan State would score more than one goal on Wisconsin for the rest of the season. The UW dropped Penn State 2–0 to seal the Big Ten regular season title and then avenged a 2–1 overtime loss to MSU with a 2–0 win in the blizzard-shortened Big Ten championship title game.

Pacing Wisconsin in its championship season were co-captains Scott Lamphear, a first-team all-America selection, and Mike Gentile, a third-team pick. Launder was named national coach of the year.

WISCONSIN TIMELINE

1996: Wisconsin won five of its last six football games, including a 38–10 Copper Bowl win over Utah.

Wisconsin had three men's NCAA track and field champions: James Dunkelberger (decathlon), Reggie Torian (110-meter hurdles) and Pascal Dobert (steeplechase).

The Big Ten announced that its first-ever men's post-season basketball tournament would be held after the 1997–98 season at the United Center in Chicago.

President Bill Clinton was re-elected, becoming the first Democrat elected to two terms since Franklin D. Roosevelt.

WISCONSIN HEADLINER

KATHY BUTLER
CROSS COUNTRY,
TRACK & FIELD

In only three years, Kathy Butler became one of the Badgers' most decorated athletes. A transfer from the University of Guelph in Canada, Butler won five NCAA titles, earned 13 all-American honors and won 17 Big Ten titles in only two years of competition in cross country and three years of competition in track. The Waterloo, Ontario, native won three consecutive NCAA Outdoor 3000-meter titles. She also won titles as a member of the distance medley relay at the 1996 NCAA Indoor meet and was the 1995 NCAA cross country champion. Butler was named the 1995–96 Honda Sports Award winner and the U.S. Track Coaches Association Athlete of the Year for cross country. She was also named the USTCA Indoor Track Athlete of the Year in 1997. On the Big Ten level, she was named the 1997 Big Ten/Suzy Favor Female Athlete of the Year. She is a five-time Big Ten Athlete of the Year in track and cross country. A 1996 and 2004 Olympian, Butler is a Canadian national cross country champion and has competed in the four World Cross Country championships.

WISCONSIN HEADLINER

BARB FRANKE
BASKETBALL

The second-leading scorer in UW women's basketball history, Barb Franke concluded her career in 1996 with 1,994 points. She was a two-time honorable mention all-American, two-time All-Big Ten selection, three–time team MVP and 1992 Big Ten Freshman of the Year. A 6–2 forward, Franke led the Badgers to three consecutive 20-win seasons and three NCAA tournament appearances. Franke led the Badgers in scoring, rebounding and blocks for three years in a row even after coming back from knee surgery after her freshman season. She was also a member of the William R. Jones Cup team that won a gold medal in 1994. A former Miss Iowa Basketball from Cedar Falls, Franke continued her playing career after college. She played in France following graduation, but returned to the states after another knee injury. Franke was drafted in 1998 by the Chicago ABL team.

WISCONSIN HEADLINER

JASON CASIANO
CROSS COUNTRY, TRACK

Wisconsin's male athlete of the year in 1994–95, distance runner Jason Casiano was a four-time cross country all-American and a five-time all-American in track and field. A member of three Big Ten cross country championship teams and four (two indoor, two outdoor) conference championship track squads, the Portage, Ind., native won six Big Ten titles (two indoor, four outdoor) and finished second three times and third once in his four appearances at the Big Ten cross country championship. Casiano won the NCAA indoor 5,000-meter title in 1996. He was named Athlete of the Championship at the 1993 Big Ten Indoor Championship and was 1991 Big Ten Cross Country Freshman of the Year.

WISCONSIN HEADLINER

AMY LEE
VOLLEYBALL

Amy Lee goes down in the UW history books as one of its best all-round volleyball players. She ranks among the top 10 in several career categories, including setting UW career records for kills and total attack attempts before both records were broken in 2000. The 6–0 outside hitter finished with 1,661 kills and 4,129 attack attempts in her career. Lee earned all-American and all-region honors as well as unanimous selection as an all-Big Ten pick in 1998. The Badgers won the Big Ten title in 1998 and advanced to the NCAA Central Regional final, the farthest a UW team has advanced. As a senior, the Milwaukee native led the team in kills, ranked second in service aces and third in blocks.

SCOTT LAMPHEAR
SOCCER

Scott Lamphear, a native of Livonia, Michigan, finished in a second-place tie behind Ohio State football player Eddie George in the voting for 1995–96 Big Ten male athlete of the year. Lamphear anchored the defense for Wisconsin's 1995 NCAA champion soccer team and, in the process, earned first-team all-America, all-Midwest and all-Big Ten honors. A four-year starter at sweeper for the Badgers, Lamphear set school records for games played and starts. With Lamphear's help, the 1995 Badgers recorded shutouts in 17 of 25 games, including an unprecedented run of five straight whitewashes in the NCAA Tournament. The '95 Badgers were the only team in NCAA soccer tournament history to shut out all five opponents en route to the title. Lamphear also was a GTE Academic All-America first-team selection in 1995–96.

LEADING THE WAY

John Cook
Women's Volleyball Coach

John Cook posted a 161-73 record as the women's volleyball coach at Wisconsin. In 1997, the Badgers won the Big Ten championship, advanced to the finals of the NCAA Central Regional and ended the season ranked fifth in the nation. Cook, a 1979 graduate of the University of San Diego, was named the 1997 AVCA District 2 Coach of the Year and the Big Ten Conference Co-Coach of the Year. Over the course of seven years at Wisconsin, the Badgers attended six postseason tournaments. He moved on to coach at Nebraska in 1999. Cook came to Wisconsin after serving as an assistant coach with the bronze medal-winning U.S. men's volleyball team at the 1992 Olympics. He also served as an assistant at the University of Nebraska.

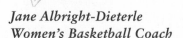

LEADING THE WAY

Jane Albright-Dieterle
Women's Basketball Coach

Jane Albright-Dieterle turned "BadgerBall" into a national phenomenon. After the 2002-2003 season, she left her position as the women's basketball coach after leading the Badgers to four 20-win seasons and five NCAA tournament appearances in nine seasons. Albright-Dieterle was named the 1995 and 1996 WBCA District IV Coach of the Year by her peers, and also the 1995 Big Ten Coach the Year. After four years of coaching in high school, Albright-Dieterle moved to Tennessee as an assistant in 1981, became an assistant at Cincinnati in 1983 and a year later became head coach at Northern Illinois, where she guided the Huskies to four DAA appearances and became NIU's all-time winningest basketball coach. Albright-Dieterle coached the gold medal-winning South team at the 1991 U.S. Olympic Festival. During the summer of 1996, Albright-Dieterle was the head coach of the R. William Jones Cup team that won the gold medal in Taiwan.

THE LIST

WOMEN'S BIG TEN OUTDOOR TRACK CHAMPIONSHIP SEASONS

Wisconsin's women have won Big Ten outdoor track titles at every conference location except Ann Arbor and Iowa City.

Year	Points	Site
1976	194	East Lansing, Michigan
1978	174	Evanston, Illinois
1979	172	Champaign, Illinois
1980	157 2/3	Minneapolis, Minnesota
1981	182	East Lansing, Michigan
1983	94	West Lafayette, Indiana
1984	124	Columbus, Ohio
1985	138	Evanston, Illinois
1986	130	Madison
1990	155	Champaign, Illinois
1991	127	Columbus, Ohio
1996	149	State College, Pennsylvania
1997	121	Champaign, Illinois

1996–97

BADGER BIG TEN FINISHES...

MEN'S
Football: 7th
coached by Barry Alvarez
Cross Country: 1st
coached by Martin Smith
Basketball: 4th (tie)
coached by Dick Bennett
Indoor Track: 1st
coached by Ed Nuttycombe
Swimming: 9th
coached by Nick Hansen
Wrestling: 7th
coached by Barry Davis
Golf: 7th, coached by Dennis Tiziani
Tennis: 9th
coached by Pat Klingelhoets
Ice Hockey: 7th (WCHA)
coached by Jeff Sauer
Outdoor Track: 1st
coached by Ed Nuttycombe
(6th, NCAA)

WOMEN'S
Cross Country: 1st
coached by Peter Tegen
Soccer: 2nd, coached by Dean Duerst
Basketball: 6th (tie)
coached by Jane Albright-Dieterle
Indoor Track: 1st
coached by Peter Tegen
Swimming: 3rd
coached by Nick Hansen
Volleyball: 5th, coached by John Cook
Softball: 6th (tie)
coached by Karen Gallagher
Golf: 9th, coached by Dennis Tiziani
Tennis: 3rd
coached by Patti Henderson
Outdoor Track: 1st
coached by Peter Tegen

The Big Event

Badger men record first cross country and track "triple-triple"

Records, it's said, are made to be broken, but Wisconsin's accomplishments in cross country, indoor and outdoor track over a three-season span culminating with the 1996–97 campaign may be a long time in being equaled, let alone exceeded.

The men's cross country and track teams, coached by Martin Smith and Ed Nuttycombe, respectively, recorded the first "triple-triple" in Big Ten annals, winning championships in each of three consecutive years in the sports. The cross country team, which has advanced to the NCAA meet every year since the start of NCAA district qualifying in 1972, again won the Big Ten crown and finished XX nationally, its XX straight top XX finish. And the 1997 season may have been Wisconsin's best season ever by what is arguably its best team ever.

Indoors, the Badgers had three champions in four events–Reggie Torian in the 55-meter dash and the 55-meter high hurdles; Carlton Clark in the 600; and Matt VanderZanden in the triple jump–as they won their third straight crown. Three UW athletes won outdoor Big Ten titles–hurdler Torian, sprinter Tony Simmons in the 100 and decathlete Greg Gill.

And at the NCAA outdoor championships, Wisconsin finished in a fourth-place tie with 31 points, equal to the Badgers' 1938 finish as the school's best ever and a great follow-up to the sixth place NCAA effort of 1996. The UW's three individual titles–by Torian in the hurdles, James Dunkleberger in the decathlon and Pascal Dobert in the steeplechase–were the most by any school in the meet.

WISCONSIN TIMELINE

1997: Bill Clinton is inaugurated for a second term as president of the United States.

The Big Ten and Nike entered into a five–year agreement to assist women's sports.

The UW and Colorado College played collegiate hockey's longest men's game at 5 hours, 24 minutes. The Tigers scored at the 9:30 mark of the fourth overtime to win 1–0.

REGGIE TORIAN
TRACK AND FIELD

One of the only Badgers ever to earn all-American honors five times in track and field, Reggie Torian put together one of the most impressive seasons in UW history in 1996–97. It culminated with his victory in 110-meter high hurdles in the NCAA outdoor championships that helped the Badgers to a third place finish. The Markham, Illinois, native established himself as one of the world's top hurdlers, setting a new collegiate 60-meter hurdle record indoors with a time of 7.47 which was the 10th-fastest in world history (sixth among Americans) He followed that performance with a win in the 60-meter hurdle at the USATF Indoor Championships in Atlanta, Georgia, over, field that included four Olympians. Torian won the 55-meters and 55-meter hurdles at the '97 Big Ten indoor meet and the 100-meters and 110-meter hurdles at the '97 conference outdoor meet. He was named Big Ten Indoor and Outdoor Athlete of the Year.

RON DAYNE
FOOTBALL

The 5-10, 260-pound running back from Berlin, New Jersey, did not start until his fifth game as a freshman, yet he still became only the 11th player in NCAA history to rush for 2,000 yards in a season. Dayne carried 325 times for 2,109 yards and 21 touchdowns as a rookie, en route to third-team Associated Press all-America honors. He followed up his astounding freshman year with a 1,457-yard, 15-touchdown campign as a sophomore despite missing 12 quarters during the season. Dayne is Wisconsin's rushing leader, with 7,125 rushing yards during his UW career. He also leads UW players in all-purpose yardage in his career, with 7,429. Dayne won the 1999 Heisman Trophy and was the Big Ten Player of the Year.

MELISSA ZIMPFER
TENNIS

Melissa Zimpfer became Wisconsin's first singles all-American in women's tennis in 1996 after advancing to the round of 16. The Dayton, Ohio, native has the distinction of being the highest ranked player in UW history being ranked as high as fifth during the 1996–97 season. During the 1997 NCAA Championship, Zimpfer teamed with Colleen Lucey in 1997 to earn all-American honors in doubles. The duo set the UW season record for most wins in a season with 33 and also hold the UW career record for wins with 57.
Zimpfer was named the Big Ten Conference Player of the Year in 1996 leading the Badgers to their first team title. She set the UW season record for highest winning percentage (.857) in 1996 after finishing with a 36–6 record. Her 36 wins also tied the UW record for most wins in a season. Zimpfer wrapped up her career with the highest winning percentage in singles at .845. Zimpfer is a two-time first-team all-Big Ten selection. She played two years at Wisconsin after transferring from the University of Tennessee.

GINA PANIGHETTI
SWIMMING

Heading into her junior season, Gina Panighetti was one of the most decorated UW women's swimmers. The all-American, Big Ten champion was also the 1998 Big Ten Conference Swimmer of the Year.
The Chico, California, native finished among the top six swimmers in the 100-yard butterfly and 200-yard butterfly at the NCAA Championship as a freshman and as a sophomore. As a freshman, Panighetti was the first UW women's swimmer to earn all-American honors in an individual event and the first to capture all-American honors in two individual events during the same year.
As a sophomore, Panighetti was named the Big Ten Conference Swimmer of the Year after winning the 100 fly and 200 fly at the Big Ten Championships. She also set Conference records in those two events during the season and holds UW records in the 200-yard butterfly.

WISCONSIN HEADLINER

TAREK SALEH
FOOTBALL

Twice an all-Big Ten first-team selection at defensive end, Tarek Saleh earned all-America honors from Football News following his 1996 senior season. The 240-lber. paced the Big Ten in quarterback sacks in both 1995 and 1996. He also led the Conference in tackles for loss as a junior and was third in that category as a senior. For his Wisconsin career, Saleh finished as the school's record-holder in tackles for a loss (58), yardage (283), quarterback sacks (33) and yardage (227). He also set Wisconsin records for tackles (14) and yardage (97) during the 8–5 campaign. Saleh was named most valuable player of the 1996 Copper Bowl, a 38–10 Wisconsin win over Utah.

LEADING THE WAY

Patti Henderson
Women's Tennis Coach

Patti Henderson guided the Wisconsin women's tennis team to its first-ever Big Ten Conference championship and seven NCAA tournament appearances. Wisconsin won the Big Ten title in 1996, earning its first NCAA team berth. The Badgers advanced to the quarterfinals and had their first singles all-American. Henderson led the Badgers to the NCAA Championship again in 1997, this time earning three all-American honors. Henderson, who came to Wisconsin from Northern Illinois, and a 1986 graduate of Florida State, was instrumental in keeping the USTA/ITA Women's National Indoor Team Tennis Championship in Madison for several years. Her last season with the Badgers was 2006-07.

LEADING THE WAY

Dick Bennett Men's
Basketball Coach

The hiring of Dick Bennett as Wisconsin's men's basketball coach in the spring of 1995 raised doubts in the minds of some observers who wondered if the former mentor at UW-Stevens Point and UW-Green Bay could succeed in the rugged and highly competitive Big Ten. It took Bennett less than one year to erase those doubts. In his first season he masterfully guided a team most felt would struggle to win 10 games to a 17–15 overall record and an appearance in the second round of the NIT. Bennett coached his second Wisconsin squad to the school's first 18-win regular season since 1915–16, its first 11-win Conference campaign since 1941 and a spot in the NCAA Tournament for only the fourth time in school history. After losing three starters from the '96–97 squad, the Badgers dipped to 12–19 overall in 1997–98, but Bennett entered his fourth season with more wins-47-than any three-year coach in school annals. In 2000, he led the team to the Final Four before he resigned during the 2000-2001 season.

THE LIST

WISCONSIN'S BIG TEN "ATHLETE OF THE YEAR" AWARD NOMINEES [1990s]

1990: Gary Shuchuk, hockey
*Suzy Favor, track & cross country

1991: Matt Demaray, wrestling; Lisa Boyd, volleyball

1992: Troy Vincent, football; Heather Taggart, socer

1993: Donovan Bergstrom, track & cross country
Claire Eichner, track & cross country

1994: Brent Moss, football
Amy Wickus, track & cross country

1995: Jason Casiano, track & cross country
Amy Wickus, track & cross couotry

1996: Scott Lamphear, soccer
Kathy Butler, track & cross country

1997: Ron Dayne, football
*Kathy Butler, track & cross country

1998: Eric Jetton, wrestling
Angi Kujak, track & cross country

1999: Matt Downin, track & cross country
Jenelle Deatherage, track & cross country

*denotes Big Ten "Athlete of the Year"

1997-98

BADGER BIG TEN FINISHES...

MEN'S
Football: 5th
coached by Barry Alvarez
Cross Country: 2nd
coached by Martin Smith
Soccer: 4th (tie)
coached by Kalekeni Banda
Basketball: 9th (tie)
coached by Dick Bennett
Indoor Track: 2nd
coached by Ed Nuttycombe
Swimming: 8th
coached by Nick Hansen
Wrestling: 5th
coached by Barry Davis
Golf: 8th, coached by Dennis Tiziani
Tennis: 6th coached by Pat Klingelhoets
Ice Hockey: 2nd (WCHA)
coached by Jeff Sauer
Outdoor Track: 2nd
coached by Ed Nuttycombe

WOMEN'S
Cross Country: 1st
coached by Peter Tegen
Soccer: 4th (tie)
coached by Dean Duerst
Basketball: 6th
coached by Jane Albright-Dieterle
Indoor Track: 2nd
coached by Peter Tegen
Swimming: 4th
coached by Nick Hanson
Volleyball: 1st (tie)
coached by John Cook
Golf: 8th, coached by Dennis Tiziani
Softball: 8th (tie)
coached by Karen Gallagher
Tennis: 3rd
coached by Patti Henderson
Outdoor Track: 2nd
coached by Peter Tegen

The Big Event

Kohl Center opens

A six-year plan came to fruition on January 17, 1998, with the opening of the Kohl Center on the Wisconsin campus as the Badgers hosted Northwestern in men's basketball. In 1992–93, athletic department officials had concluded that the venerable Wisconsin Fieldhouse, home to UW basketball, wrestling and myriad other events since 1930, could no longer adequately serve the needs of growing athletic, university and community constituencies.

Named after Sen. Herb Kohl, whose $25 million gift–the largest single donation in the university's history–provided the primary funding for the $76.4 million facility, the Kohl Center seats 17,142 for basketball, more than 15,000 for hockey and from 14,000–17,000 for concerts. It's the second largest arena in the Big Ten. Other major benefactors were Albert (Ab) and Nancy Nicholas, whose $10 million donation was critical, and the Kellner family—Jack F. and sons Ted and Jack W.—which contributed $2.5 million. The Nicholas-Johnson Pavilion and Plaza as well as the Nicholas Suites are named for Ab and Nancy while the Kellner Concourse is named after that family.

The multipurpose facility has been funded entirely through private support from UW alumni and friends as well as through program revenues generated by the Division of Intercollegiate Athletics. The state issue bonding authority for $27 million of the cost, which will be paid off through revenues generated by Kohl Center. The remaining $49.4 million was through private gifts.

WISCONSIN TIMELINE

1998: India and Pakistan tested hydrogen bombs and drew global condemnation led by the United States.

The Big Ten Conference held its first post–season men's basketball tournament to determine the Conference's automatic qualifier to the NCAA tourney. Michigan won.

The Badgers lost 33–6 to Georgia in the Outback Bowl at Tampa, Florida. It was Coach Barry Alvarez's first bowl loss after three victories.

BARBARA URBANSKA
TENNIS

Barbara Urbanska became the first UW women's tennis player to earn all-American honors in singles and doubles in the same year in 1998. Urbanska advanced to the round of 16 at the NCAA Championship and with doubles partner Marjon Copier, advanced to the round of eight to earn all-American honors in both categories. The 1999 Big Ten Player of the Year, Urbanska is a four-time all-Big Ten selection and three-time team Sportsmanship Award winner. She is a three-time Academic all-Big Ten selection and was named to the 1997 Academic all-District team. Urbanska, is one of the top UW singles and doubles players of all time , with 95 career singles victories.

LEADING THE WAY

Pat Klingelhoets
Men's Tennis Coach

Pat Klingelhoets, who played tennis for the Badgers from 1969–72, compiled a 291–286 career mark as coach and led players to first team all-Big Ten status 23 times. The native of Monona, Wisconsin, won the men's title at the 1994 Wisconsin Open. He was ranked No. 1 among state amateurs in 1994. He resigned as coach of the Badgers in April of 2005.

THE LIST

KOHL CENTER
BY THE NUMBERS

460,000	Size in square-feet
17,142	Capacity for basketball
13,344	Capacity for hockey
14,025	Capacity for end-stage concerts
17,300	Maximum capacity for other events
1,827	Capacity of Nicholas-Johnson Pavilion
333	Wheelchair and wheelchair companion locations
6	TDD telephones
26	Public restrooms
7	Family (unisex) restrooms
36	Luxury suites
18	Concession stands
2,400	Square-footage of retail store
14	Ticket sales windows
8	Locker rooms for home and visiting teams, officials and tournament (2)
835	Size of media work room in square-feet

THE LIST

WISCONSIN'S MEN'S BIG
TEN CROSS COUNTRY
CHAMPIONSHIP SEASONS

Through 2011-12, Wisconsin has
won 46 Big Ten team titles

1910	1977	1996
1912	1978	1999
1913	1979	2000
1915	1981	2001
1918	1982	2002
1924	1983	2003
1925	1985	2004
1926	1986	2005
1927	1987	2006
1939	1988	2007
1944	1990	2008
1945	1991	2009
1948	1992	2010
1949	1994	2011
1950	1995	2012

1998-99

BADGER BIG TEN FINISHES...

MEN'S
Footbal: 1st (tie)
coached by Barry Alvarez
Crew, coached by Chris Clark
Cross Country: 3rd
coached by Jerry Schumacher
Soccer: 4th (tie)
coached by Kalekeni Banda
Basketball: 3rd (tie)
coached by Dick Bennett
Ice Hockey: (WCHA) 4th
coached by Jeff Sauer
Indoor Track: 6th
coached by Ed Nuttycombe
Swimming and Diving: 4th
coached by Eric Hansen
Wrestling: 6th, coached by Barry Davis
Golf: 4th, coached by Dennis Tiziani
Tennis: 9th, coached by Pat Klinghoets
Outdoor Track: 3rd
coached by Ed Nuttycombe

WOMEN'S
Cross Country: 1st
coached by Peter Tegen
Soccer 2nd, coached by Dean Duerst
Rowing, coached by Mary Browning
Lightweight Rowing,
coached by Maren Watson
Basketball 4th (TIE)
coached by Jane Albright
Indoor Track: 4th,
coached by Ed Nuttycombe
Swimming and Diving: 4th coached by Eric Hansen
Volleyball 2nd, coached by Peter Waite
Golf: 5th, coached by Dennis Tiziani
Softball: 6th, coached by Karen Gallagher
Tennis: 2nd, coached by Patti Henderson
Outdoor Track: 2nd coached by Peter Tegen

The Big Event

Winningest Badgers claim Rose Bowl, 38–31, over UCLA

Wisconsin's winningest football team ever (11–1 overall) finished its 1998 season in splendid fashion on New Year's Day 1999 with a 38–31 victory over sixth-ranked UCLA in the 85th Rose Bowl game.

It was the Badgers' second Rose Bowl win in six years; that 1994 victory also was over UCLA.

In its regular-season finale, Wisconsin defeated No. 14 Penn State for the first time since 1959 to earn a share of the Big Ten title at 7–1.

Wisconsin finished the year ranked fifth and sixth, respectively, in the ESPN/USA *Today* coaches' poll and the Associated Press media poll. The UW was ranked every week of the season for only the third time in school history.

Pacing Wisconsin's Rose Bowl win was Ron Dayne, who ran for 246 yards, just one shy of Charles White's Rose Bowl record. Dayne's career-high four touchdowns equaled the game's modern-day record. The game winner came early in the fourth quarter when UW freshman Jamar Fletcher intercepted a Cade McNown pass and returned it 46 yards for a TD and a 38–28 Badger lead.

UCLA cut the lead to seven with a field goal and had yet another chance after the Badgers failed to run out the clock. But Wendell Bryant's sack of McNown on a fourth-down effort stopped the Bruins.

WISCONSIN TIMELINE

1999: The UW men's tennis team hosts the Big Ten singles championship at the Nielsen Tennis Center for the first time.

Wisconsin's men's basketball team defeats Minnesota 61–50 before 17,046 spectators at the Kohl Center, the largest home-game crowd in UW history.

The UW softball team sweeps a doubleheader from Loyola to christen the new Robert and Irwin Goodman Softball Complex.

BADGER MOMENT

Badger women win fourth straight conference title

Ho-hum, it was the same old story for Wisconsin's women's cross country team in the fall of 1998.

His Badgers won their fourth straight Big Ten cross country title—and 13th overall—in October at Ann Arbor, upending host Michigan 31–36 in one of the closest meets in conference history. And the Badgers weren't even favored—Michigan came in ranked third nationally, Wisconsin eighth.

But a senior and two freshmen came through for Tegen. Freshman Erica Palmer finished second to eventual NCAA champ Katie McGregor of Michigan in 17:22 and earned Big Ten Freshman of the Year honors. Senior Jenelle Deatherage was the second UW finisher, coming in fourth, while another frosh, Bethany Brewster, was fifth. All three earned All-Big Ten honors.

Junior Stephanie Pesch and senior Jenni Westphal were named All-Big Ten second team with their ninth and 11th place finishes, respectively.

Wisconsin went on to win its third successive NCAA qualifying meet two weeks later in the regional at Terre Haute, Indiana, as the Badgers scored 39 points, 14 better than Michigan.

In the NCAA meet at Lawrence, Kansas, Deatherage and Westphal earned All-America honors-the first for Wisconsin since 1995-piacing 24th and 30th, respectively. Top runner Palmer was unable to finish the national race because of a case of walking pneumonia, but the Badgers nonetheless finished fifth in the meet.

Up to this point, Wisconsin had participated in 22 national championships and was never out of the top 10.

BADGER MOMENT

UW cagers tie for 3rd in Big Ten, advance to NCAA

Wisconsin's winningest basketball season ever was highlighted by a trip to the NCAA Tournament for the third time in six seasons and the second in four years under Coach Dick Bennett. Making the 1998–99 season special:

- The UW's 22–10 mark and .688 winning percentage was the best since the 1961–62 team went 17–7 (.708);
- The 22 victories eclipsed the 20-win seasons posted by the 1915–16 and 1940–41 teams;
- The Badgers' third-place finish in the Big Ten at 9–7 was their highest since the 1962 team finished second with a 10–4 record;
- The UW finished the year ranked 18th in the Associated Press poll and became only the second Wisconsin squad–after the 1949–50 team, ranked 16th–to end the season nationally ranked;
- The Badgers' schedule was rated sixth toughest in the nation by the Sagarin Ratings. Wisconsin entered the NCAA Tournament 8–6 against other teams in the tourney;
- Wisconsin's 10-game reversal of fortune—from 12–19 in 1997–98 to 22–10—made the team one of just five in UW history to win at least 10 games more than it had the previous year;
- The Badgers were hot at the start, getting out of the gate 12–1 for the best start by a UW five since 1929–30, and also hot in starting Big Ten play, posting a 7–2 mark;
- Wisconsin led the Big Ten in scoring defense for the second time in Bennett's four seasons, allowing foes just 56.8 points per game, and ranked second nationally in all games at 55.2 ppg, fourth best in school history;
- Honors came in droves, with Mike Kelley the Big Ten's Defensive Player of the Year; Sean Mason and Ty Calderwood second-and third-team All-Big Ten, respectively; and Kelley, Andy Kowske and Hennssy Auriantal Academic All-Big Ten selections;
- Coach Dick Bennett was one of 15 finalists for the Naismith National Coach of the Year Award, one of 10 nominees for the similar Associated Press award and one of six finalists for the Clair Bee Award.

WISCONSIN HEADLINER

MATT DOWNIN
CROSS COUNTRY

Downin made a big break-through in his junior year to chalk up one of the best cross country seasons ever by a Wisconsin runner. The Hampstead, New Hampshire, native placed fourth in the NCAA cross country championships at Lawrence, Kansas, the best finish for a Badger runner since Tim Hacker won the meet in 1985. Downin also won the Big Ten title and was named Big Ten cross country athlete of the year. He set a course record of 24:06 in the meet at Ann Arbor in becoming the first UW runner to win that race since Donovan Bergstrom in 1992. Downin, who also was second in the 1,500-and 5,000-meter runs at the 1999 outdoor track meet, picked up in the fall of 1999 where he left off in 1998. As a senior, he again won the Big Ten harrier crown—becoming only the third UW harrier to win two or more—and again placed fourth in the NCAA meet, leading the Badgers to a second-place finish.

WISCONSIN HEADLINER

JENELLE DEATHERAGE
CROSS COUNTRY, TRACK

The 1998–99 Wisconsin female athlete of the year, Jenelle Deatherage was also just about "all-everything" during her collegiate career. The East Peoria, Illinois, native was named the 1999 Big Ten outdoor track athlete of the year following an indoor campaign in which she was the conference meet's top performer. A three-event, three-time All-American in track in 1999, Deatherage was also the Big Ten outdoor champ at 3,000 meters. She finished eighth, fifth and fourth in Big Ten cross country in her final three seasons. She also was a 1998 All-American, twice earned All-Big Ten honors in the sport and three times was an all-region pick. Deatherage won three Big Ten track titles during her career and also was a five-time All-Big Ten academic selection in track and cross country.

LEADING THE WAY

Chris Clark
Men's Crew Coach

International experience has proven a strong suit for Wisconsin men's crew coach Chris Clark since his appointment in 1996. Clark was head coach of the U.S. men's pre-elite rowing team during the summers of 1996–98 and was named Developmental Coach of the Year by the U.S. Olympic Committee in 1997. He served as UW assistant men's rowing coach from 1994–96 and guided his Badger freshman crews to an unbeaten record in cup races during his tenure. Clark's rowing experience reads like a map of the world. Prior to his UW appointment, he was an assistant varsity coach for two years at the U.S. Naval Academy and also coached rowing at Drexel University, Oriel College and University College in Oxford, England. A University of California graduate, Clark has rowed and medaled in regattas in the U.S. and nine other countries since 1979. In 2008, he led the varsity eight to the school's first national championship since 1990.

THE LIST

WISCONSIN'S HONORED ATHLETES

Big Ten Medal of Honor

1998-Erik Raygor, Katie Voigt

1999-Brian Doherty, Shannon Brown

2000-Gina Panighetti, Jay Schoenfelder

Jesse Owens Award nominees

1998—Eric Jetton, wrestling

1999—Matt Downin, track & cross country

2000–Ron Dayne, football

Suzy Favor Award nominees

1998–Angi Kujak, track & cross country

1999—Jenelle Deatherage, track & cross country

2000—Erica Palmer, track & cross country

LEADING THE WAY

Frank J. Remington
Big Ten Faculty
Representative

Frank J. Remington served as Wisconsin's faculty representative to the Big Ten and the NCAA from 1959–86. In particular, Remington, a 1947 UW graduate and 1949 Law School graduate, was a strong voice in the NCAA for the development of ice hockey. At the UW, he was an early and strong advocate of a varsity sports program for women. Remington was a member of the Wisconsin Law School faculty for 46 years and was nationally recognized for his pioneering work in criminal law. A continuous member of the UW athletic board, he supported the establishment of the athletic board scholars program in the late 1980s to recognize scholastic achievement by student-athletes. The Frank Remington Scholars Program has been established to honor the graduating male and female student-athlete letter winners with the highest grade-point averages. Remington was inducted into the UW Athletic Hall of Fame in 1999.

WISCONSIN HEADLINER

WALTER LAUTENBACH
BASEBALL, BASKETBALL

Walter Lautenbach starred for Badger basketball and baseball teams from 192–47, with time for military service interrupting his athletic career. The Plymouth, Wisconsin, native earned major "W" awards in baseball and basketball in 1942, 1943 and 1947. He pitched both games of a 1942 doubleheader against Chicago, winning the opener 10–1 and losing the nightcap 10–5. In 1943, as the Badgers' MVP, Lautenbach defeated Minnesota 2–1 in 13 innings and batted in both runs. He captained the 1947 UW Big Ten basketball champions and was third in team scoring as a starting guard. Lautenbach scored two field goals in the final 13 seconds of play that year to lift the Badgers over Northwestern, 45–44. Following his graduation, he signed a contract with the Oshkosh All-Stars of the National Basketball League. He was inducted into the UW Athletic Hall of Fame in 1999.

WISCONSIN HEADLINER

CARL HOLTZ
MEN'S CREW

Carl Holtz starred for Wisconsin crew teams during and after World War II and earned acclaim as the "finest stroke in collegiate rowing" in 1946 and 1947. He captained the 1947 team. The Milwaukee native won major "W" awards in 1942, 1946 and 1947 as the stroke of Wisconsin crews and helped pace Wisconsin to its first national championship in 1946. As a freshman in 1941, Holtz stroked the UW freshman crew to second place at the Poughkeepsie Regatta. He stroked the Badger varsity to second in the 1942 Adams Cup competition before leaving for duty with the U.S. Army Air Corps. Upon his return in 1941 Holtz stroked the crew to the Eastern Sprint Regatta title at Annapolis, Maryland. He was inducted into the UW Athletic Hall of Fame in 1999.

WISCONSIN HEADLINER

SHANNON BROWN
SOCCER

Three-time All-Big Ten selection Shannon Brown, who starred as a defender for the Badgers from 1996–98, had one of the great careers in the annals of Wisconsin women's soccer. Brown, a native of Madison who prepped at Memorial H.S., redshirted her freshman year but then embarked on a stellar career for the UW with the 1996 season. One of the most honored defenders in Wisconsin history, Brown started all 65 games her final three seasons. As a senior in 1998, the tough, speedy and agile Brown became one of the Big Ten's strongest and most feared defenders. She dished out game-winning assists against Michigan State, Iowa and Northern Illinois. Brown was picked as a second-team All-American, a first-team NSCAA Academic All-American and a second-team GTE Academic All-American.

1999—2000

BADGER BIG TEN FINISHES...

MEN'S

Cross Country 1st (2nd, NCAA) coached by
Jerry Schumacher

Football: 1st coached by Barry Alvarez

Soccer: 5th (tie) coached by Kalekeni Banda

Basketball: 6th (final four)
coached by Dick Bennett

Ice Hockey: 1st, WCHA
coached by Jeff Sauer

Swimming: 5th, coached by Eric Hansen

Wrestling: 7th, coached by Barry Davis

Indoor Track: 1st
coached by Ed Nuttycombe

Golf: 6th coached by Dennis Tiziani

Tennis: 8th coached by Pat Klinghoets

Outdoor Track: 1st
coached by Ed Nuttycombe

WOMEN'S

Cross country: 1st (4th, NCAA)
coached by Peter Tegen

Basketball: 6th (1st Women's NIT)
coached by Jane Albright

Soccer: 8th (tie)
coached by Dean Duerst

Swimming: 5th, coached by Eric Hansen

Indoor Track: 2nd
coached by Peter Tegen

Volleyball: 3rd coached by Peter Waite

Golf: 4th, coached by Dennis Tiziani

Softball: 5th, coached by Karen Gallagher

Rowing 4th, coached by Mary Browning

Lightweight Rowing
coached by Maren Waston

Tennis: 9th
coached by Patti Henderson

Outdoor Track: 3rd
coached by Peter Tegen

The Big Event

Big Ten champ Badgers win second consecutive Rose Bowl

Wisconsin's 17–9 Rose Bowl win over Stanford on January 1, 2000, cemented the Badgers' place in history as the first Big Ten team to win the "granddaddy of all bowl games" in back-to-back seasons.

The New Year's Day game was the culmination of a remarkable four-year cycle for the '99 seniors, Wisconsin's all-time winningest group. Its legacy for future Badger squads: a 37–13 record, four bowl berths, two Big Ten championships and three bowl game victories.

Coach Barry Alvarez's 1999 Badgers, who finished fourth in both the coaches' and media polls, won the school's first undisputed Big Ten title in 37 years; recorded 10 wins for the second most victories in UW history; ended the season with eight straight wins; defeated five nationally ranked teams; became just the third team since 1982 to lead the Big Ten in scoring offense and scoring defense; and became the only school to win three Rose Bowls in the 1990s.

The Rose Bowl game itself was somewhat of a surprise in that two high-scoring offenses never really got untracked and battled through a defensive struggle.

After a scoreless first quarter, Stanford scored first on a 28–yard field goal. Vitaly Pisetsky knotted the game at 3–3 on a 31-yard field goal three minutes later. Stanford took the lead at 2:03 of the second quarter on a one-yard run by Kerry Carter.

WISCONSIN TIMELINE

1999: Erica Palmer becomes the third Wisconsin woman to win a national cross country title, taking the NCAA individual championship on her 20th birthday, November 22, 1999.

2000: Wisconsin's men's basketball team is ranked 11th by the Associated Press, the school's highest national ranking since it was rated seventh on December 10, 1962.

Wisconsin romps to an easy victory in the 100th Big Ten men's outdoor track and field championship May 19–21 in Iowa City. UW coach Ed Nuttycombe is named Big Ten Coach of the Year.

DAYNE WINS HEISMAN TROPHY, LEADS BADGERS TO BIG TEN TITLE, ROSE BOWL

The "Great Dayne" was great indeed for Wisconsin in 1999. Running back Ron Dayne became the second Badger to win the Heisman Trophy, symbolic of college football's best player, with first-place votes and 2,042 points in the balloting for the 65th annual award presented by the Downtown Athletic Club in New York. Fullback Alan Ameche won the 1954 Heisman for the UW.

Dayne outdistanced Georgia Tech quarterback Joe Hamilton, who had 994 points in the voting. Dayne was the top vote-getter in all six regions.

Prior to winning the Heisman, Dayne had won nearly every other award he was up for, including the AP College Player of the Year, the Walter Camp, Maxwell and Doak Walker awards. He also named MVP of the Rose Bowl for the second straight year, as he rushed for 200 yards and scored in his final game as a Badger.

In 1999, Dayne became college football's career rushing leader with 6,397 yards when he ran for 31 yards in the second quarter against Iowa on November 13. He's the only

player in the history of college football to rush for more than 7,000 yards (including postseason play). Dayne ended his career with 7,125 yards in 47 games for a 151.6 per game average. He's one of only four players in history to have four seasons of 1,000 rushing yards or more and is the first three-time rushing champion in the annals of the Big Ten.

Dayne personally outrushed the opposition in 29 of his 43 starts and averaged 120.3 yards rushing against nationally ranked opponents during his career. He also tied an NCAA record with 11 career games of 200 yards or more.

DAYNE BY GAME IN 1999

Opponent	Attempts	Yards	Average	TDs
Murray State	20	135	6.8	3
Ball State	31	158	5.1	1
Cincinnati	28	231	8.3	1
Michigan	22	88	4.0	1
Ohio State	32	161	5.0	4
Minnesota	25	80	3.2	1
Indiana	17	167	9.8	2
Michigan State	34	214	6.3	2
Northwestern	35	162	4.6	2
Purdue	32	222	6.9	1
Iowa	27	216	8.0	1
Stanford	34	200	5.9	1
Totals	337	2,034	6.0	20

Dayne's career yardage

Year	YAC*	Yards	Pct.
1996	1,066	2,109	50.5
1997	699	1,457	48.0
1998	704	1,525	46.1
1999	1,098	2,034	50.1
Totals	3,567	7,125	50.1

*It was rare for Dayne to get a carry without contact. His yards after contact (YAC) total alone would be enough to rank him among the top eight in UW history.

The Big Event

Surprising Badgers advance to NCAA Final Four

No one, even the most loyal and optimistic of the Badger faithful, would have predicted the UW men's basketball team would have been playing on April 1.

Or, for that matter, on March 25 or March 18, either.

But play, the Badgers did, and well, through a remarkable run in the NCAA Tournament that culminated in Wisconsin's first appearance in an NCAA Final Four since the magical championship season of 1941.

That Wisconsin's improbable run at the NCAA championship ended with a 53–41 loss to eventual NCAA kingpin Michigan State–which beat the Badgers four times in the UW's final 14 games and was the only team to stop Wisconsin during the span–in no way diminished the season's accomplishments.

And those were legion. The 1999–2000 squad matched the previous year's group for most wins in Wisconsin history with 22.

Wisconsin started the season well enough, beating Missouri 66–55 in its opener and posting a 6–2 mark after eight games. Losses at South Florida and Northern Illinois slowed the Badgers somewhat, but wins over Marquette and Temple set the stage for Big Ten play.

Wisconsin's lone Big Ten win in its first five league games came at home over Illinois, but then Wisconsin surged a bit, taking seven of its final 11 games heading into the Big Ten Tournament, including a 56–53 season-ending win over Indiana at the Kohl Center to perhaps clinch an NCAA Tournament berth. Victories over Northwestern (51–41) and Purdue (78–66) set the stage for the Badgers' semifinal loss to MSU.

In NCAA play, Wisconsin became one of the stories–if not *the* story of the tournament. Oblivious to records or rankings, the Badgers' tenacious defense shredded Fresno State 66–56 in the opening round, followed in the next by a systematic taking-apart of No. 1-seed Arizona, 66–59, and a berth in the Sweet 16. A 61–48 upset win over LSU put the UW into the Elite Eight against Purdue, which Wisconsin had already beaten in two of three games. The 64–60 win in the regional finals sent Wisconsin to Indianapolis.

Defense was again the Badgers' forte, as it has always been with Dick Bennett-coached teams. The Badgers allowed only 55.8 points per game.

Mark Vershaw led the UW in scoring at 11.8 ppg and also had 118 assists to become only the third forward in school history to reach the 100–assist mark.

The Big Event

Wisconsin wins women's NIT

After finishing in a fifth-place tie at 8–8 in the Big Ten standings, Coach Jane Albright's women's basketball squad found the Women's NIT to its liking.

The Badgers culminated their five-game championship run with a 75–74 victory over Florida in the championship game at the Kohl Center. All five Badger wins came on their home court, the last attended by 13,006.

The UW notched its 21st victory with the championship, equaling the school mark achieved three times previously. It was Wisconsin's fourth 20–victory season in the past six years under Albright.

It also marked the Badgers' second successive appearance in the WNIT final. Wisconsin lost to Arkansas 67–64 in Fayetteville in 1999.

Sims averaged a double-double in WNIT play with 17 points and 10.2 rebounds in the five games. She had a season-high 28 points and 16 rebounds in the Badgers' 77–45 quarterfi-

nal win over Michigan State.

Jessie Stomski averaged 13.2 points and 6.8 rebounds per game, while Moore averaged 14 points, 4.8 rebounds, 4.2 assists and 3.2 steals. Kelley Paulus added 9.5 ppg.

Wisconsin tied its own WNIT record for largest margin of victory (37) with its 83–46 opening–round win over Fairfield. As a team, the UW averaged 79 points per game to their opponents' 60 and pulled down an average 44.2 rebounds a game to their foes' 37.6. The Badgers shot at a .472 clip from the field in the tourney and held the opposition to .352 shooting.

Following its opening win over Fairfield, Wisconsin defeated DePaul 82–76 before beating MSU for the second time in their three meetings. A 78–60 win over Colorado State in the semis set the stage for the Badgers' championship heroics.

Wisconsin finished the season 21–12.

STEVE REINPRECHT
HOCKEY

Steve Reinprecht, a first-team All-America selection at forward, was the top scorer for a UW hockey team that posted a 31-9-1 mark and ranked first in the nation through much of the latter part of the season. Reinprecht, a native of Edmonton, Alberta, scored 26 goals and had 40 assists, with his 1.78 points-per-game average helping him to the runner-up spot in balloting for the Hobey Baker Award, collegiate hockey's most prestigious individual honor. The WCHA's Player of the Year, he became the first player in Wisconsin history to lead the Badgers in scoring three straight years. His 15 career game-winning goals tie him for fourth all time at the UW. Reinprecht was named the WCHA Offensive Player of the Week twice in 1999–2000, the sixth and seventh times he was so honored by the league. Following the collegiate season, he played for the Los Angeles Kings of the National Hockey League.

ERICA PALMER
CROSS COUNTRY

Erica Palmer gave herself quite a present for her 20th birthday on November 22, 1999: an NCAA cross country championship. The Wisconsin sophomore out of Gilsum, New Hampshire, became Wisconsin's third NCAA cross country champion by running a personal best 16:39.5 for the 5,000-meter course at Indiana University. She's the youngest NCAA harrier champ in four years. Although some "experts" may not have expected the 5'3" Palmer to win over some better known and more experienced rivals, her seasonal performances clearly set her up as a major contender. Palmer became the UW's 11th Big Ten individual champ October 30 at Penn State, winning in a then personal best 16:46.93, almost 20 seconds ahead of teammate Erin AufderHeide. And two weeks later, Palmer became Wisconsin's seventh regional champ, setting a course record of 16:52.2 as she cruised to a 23-second victory. November 22 offered no real surprise to anyone who had seen Pal run all season.

DON PRITZLAFF
WRESTLING

Junior 155-pounder Don Pritzlaff became the 12th Badger to win a national collegiate wrestling title in March 2000, beating top-ranked Joe Heskett of Iowa State 4–2 in overtime at the NCAA championships in St. Louis. Ironically, it was the second time in the season that Pritzlaff had defeated Heskett by the same score and in overtime. His win was the 16th NCAA wrestling crown for a Wisconsin athlete and helped propel the Badgers into a ninth–place tie, their best finish in eight years. Pritzlaff, a native of Lyndhurst, New Jersey, had won his second consecutive Big Ten title a couple weeks earlier. Pritzlaff earned All-America honors in each of his first three seasons at Wisconsin. He finished his junior year with a 36–2 overall record and an 8–0 Big Ten mark.

ELLEN STONEBRAKER
SWIMMING

Nine-time All-American Ellen Stonebraker won just about every honor that a UW swimmer could garner. The Naperville, Illinois, native earned All-America honors nine times for the Badgers from 1997–2000. Stonebraker holds Big Ten records for the 200-yard freestyle (1:45.78), the 500-yard freestyle (4:41.26), the 1,650-yard freestyle (16:11.42) and as a member of the American record-holding 800-yard free relay (7:09.07). Stonebraker was first in the 500 free and third in 200 free and 1,650 free at the Big Ten championships, earing her Swimmer of the Championship honors. She also won four other Big Ten titles during her career and was a three-time All-Big Ten selection. The 1999 and 2000 UW MVP, Stonebraker also was an Academic All-Big Ten pick for those seasons. She was a member of the 1999 U.S. national team at the Pan-Pacific Games in Australia, where she won a gold in the 800 free relay and bronze medals in the 800 free and 200 free.

WISCONSIN HEADLINER

MIKE KELLEY
MEN'S BASKETBALL

Guard Mike Kelley became the consummate thief during the Badgers' run to the NCAA Final Four in March 2000. His 19 steals in the NCAA Tournament were the most by any player in the tourney and tied for second–most ever in NCAA tourney play. The junior from Menomonee Falls recorded at least five steals in a game 10 times before the March 2000 tournament. At that point, he was the school's career steals leader with 215, and tied for sixth best in Big Ten history with his senior season upcoming. Kelley's 95 steals led the Big Ten and were second-most ever by a conference player. He also led the Big Ten in assist-to-turnover ratio (3.26 to 1). Kelley was the 1998–99 Big Ten Defensive Player of the Year, as selected by the coaches..

LEADING THE WAY

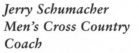

Jerry Schumacher
Men's Cross Country
Coach

In only his first two seasons as Wisconsin's men's cross country coach, former UW standout Jerry Schumacher more than lived up to the expectations for success that his predecessors created among Badger cross country fans. In 1999, his second season at the helm, the Waukesha native– himself a former three-time cross country All-American and track All-American at 1,500 meters–guided the Badgers to second in the NCAA championships, the team's best finish since 1992. Behind two-time All-Americans Matt Downin and Jay Schoenfelder, the Badgers also won the Big Ten title, their first since 1996. For his efforts, Schumacher was named Big Ten and Great Lakes Regional Coach of the Year and was a finalist for national Coach of the Year honors. That followed his rookie season in which the Badgers placed third in the Big Ten and sixth in the NCAA.

A FIRST

Women's ice hockey debuts

It's no surprise that women's ice hockey would be a success at Wisconsin.

The UW completed its first season of the sport (1999-2000) with a 19–14–2 overall mark and a 15–8–1 record in Western Collegiate Hockey Association play.

First–year coach Julie Sasner's Badgers finished third in WCHA regular-season play and fourth in the tournament. Highlights of the season were the Badgers' 4–4 tie with 10th-ranked Princeton and Wisconsin's top-10 rankings in two polls. The UW was rated as high as ninth in the *American Hockey Magazine* poll and 10th in the U.S. College Hockey Online poll.

Six players earned WCHA awards. Defenseman Sis Paulsen and goaltender Jackie MacMillan made the All-WCHA first team, while defenseman Kerry Weiland was a second–team pick. Bridget Buchholz, Michelle Sikich and Leslie Toner made the WCHA All-Academic team.

THE LIST

ROAD TO THE CHAMPIONSHIPS

Badger men's NCAA Tournament games

• First round: #8 UW 66, #9 Fresno State 56

• Second round: #8 UW 66, #1 Arizona 59

• Regional semis: #8 UW 61, #4 LSU 48

• Regional final: #8 UW 64, #6 Purdue 60

• National semis: #1 Michigan State 53, #8 UW 41

Badger women's NIT games

• UW 83, Fairfield 46

• UW 82, DePaul 76

• UW 77, Michigan State 45

• UW 78, Colorado State 60

• Championship: UW 75, Florida 74

BADGER BIG TEN FINISHES...

MEN'S

Cross Country: 1st (5th, NCAA)
coached by Jerry Schumacher
Football: 3rd (tie)
coached by Barry Alvarez
Soccer: 4th, coached by Kalekeni Banda
Basketball: 5th
coached by Dick Bennett & Brad Soderberg
Ice hockey: 5th (WCHA)
coached by Jeff Sauer
Swimming: 4th, coached by Eric Hansen
Indoor Track: 1st
coached by Ed Nuttycombe
Wrestling: 9th, coached by Barry Davis
Golf: 7th (tie), coached by Dennis Tiziani
Rowing: Ten Eyck Trophy winnners
coached by Chris Clark
Tennis: 6th (tie), coached by
Pat Klingelhoets
Outdoor Track: 1st
coached by Ed Nuttycombe

WOMEN'S

Cross Country: 1st (8th, NCAA)
coached by Peter Tegen
Soccer: 2nd, coached by Dean Duerst
Volleyball: 1st (2nd, NCAA)
coached by Peter Waite
Basketball: 2nd, coached by Jane Albright
Ice Hockey: 3rd, WCHA
coached by Julie Sasner
Swimming: 5th, coached by Eric Hansen
Indoor Track: 6th, coached by Peter Tegen
Golf: 8th, coached by Dennis Tiziani
Rowing: 4th, coached by Mary Browning
Lightweight Rowing (2nd, nationals)
coached by Maren Watson
Softball: 5th (tie)
coached by Karen Gallagher
Tennis: 8th, coached by Patti Henderson
Outdoor Track: 6th
coached by Peter Tegen

The Big Event

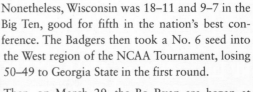

Bennett quits; Soderberg leads UW to NCAA; Ryan named coach

Dick Bennett

Brad Soderberg

Bo Ryan

To say it was a sad year for the Wisconsin men's basketball program would be correct. To call it a winning year would also be correct. And to call it an unusual and memorable year would be an understatement. It was the year of three coaches. It was sad because veteran mentor Dick Bennett, who had led the Badgers to the NCAA Final Four in March 2000, and entertained the notion of calling it a career following that great season, finally said enough was enough when he resigned as head coach November 30, three games into the season and with the Badgers at 2–1.

It was a winning year, too. Assistant Brad Soderberg was immediately elevated to the head job on an acting basis, and the Badgers responded with a season that–in almost any other year at Wisconsin–would have been one for the ages.

Nonetheless, Wisconsin was 18–11 and 9–7 in the Big Ten, good for fifth in the nation's best conference. The Badgers then took a No. 6 seed into the West region of the NCAA Tournament, losing 50–49 to Georgia State in the first round.

Then, on March 29, the Bo Ryan era began at Wisconsin when the former UW assistant returned to Madison after 17 years as head coach at UW-Platteville and UW-Milwaukee. Ryan's Platteville teams won four NCAA Division III titles in the 1990s. Over a 12-year stretch, Ryan's teams were 314–37, won eight conference titles, never won fewer than 23 games in a season and were the winningest NCAA men's team of the decade with a 266–26 record.

WISCONSIN TIMELINE

2000: The fourth-ranked Wisconsin football team opens its season with three straight victories–19–7 over Western Michigan, 27–23 over Oregon and 28–25 (OT) over Cincinnati. The UW defeats UCLA 21–20 in the Sun Bowl.

2001: Wisconsin's men's ice hockey program leads the nation in attendance for the third straight year, with 229,219 fans watching the Badgers at the Kohl Center, an average of 11,461.

Golfer Allie Blomquist and basketball player Mike Kelley are named Wisconsin's 2000–2001 winners of the Big Ten Medal of Honor, presented to a student in the graduating class who has demonstrated proficiency in scholarship and athletics.

A **W** FIRST

UW claims Big Ten all-sports title

Wisconsin won Big Ten championships in men's and women's cross country, men's indoor and outdoor track and women's volleyball to lead the conference's all-sports standings for 2000–01. The UW had finished first three times and second five times since the 1990–91 season and was third in 1999–2000 behind Minnesota and Michigan. The standings are not officially recognized by the Big Ten but offer a good barometer of the success of the league's athletic programs. The Badgers averaged 7.50 points in 21 sports to finish just ahead of Michigan, which averaged 7.48 points for its 25–sport program. Like Wisconsin, Michigan won five championships. The 2000–01 Big Ten all-sports standings follow:

Rank	School	Total Points	Sports	Average
1	Wisconsin	157.5	21	7.50
2	Michigan	187	25	7.48
3	Ohio State	185	25	7.40
4	Minnesota	160.5	23	6.98
5	Penn State	163.5	25	6.54
6	Purdue	129.5	20	6.48
7	Indiana	134	23	5.83
8	Northwestern	98	17	5.76
9	Illinois	120.5	21	5.74
10	Iowa	125	24	5.21
11	Michigan State	128.5	25	5.14

WISCONSIN HEADLINER

ALLIE BLOMQUIST
WOMEN'S GOLF

Wisconsin golfer Allie Blomquist proved in 2001 that she's as far under par on the links as she is above par in the classroom. She was Wisconsin's female winner of the 2000–01 Big Ten Medal of Honor, awarded to the graduating student who has demonstrated proficiency in scholarship and athletics. Blomquist capped her senior season in fine fashion as the most accomplished woman golfer in UW history. She finished tied for sixth in the Big Ten Tournament, carding a 306 off rounds of 72, 75, 82 and 77, and then became Wisconsin's first NCAA qualifier. She tied for 18th in the national tourney. The Afton, Minnesota, native holds every scoring record at Wisconsin, including a 69 for 18 holes, 142 for 36, 216 for 54 and 296 for 72. She broke her own record for lowest scoring average this season with a 76.67 mark, and her career average of 77.48 is first in the UW record book. Blomquist is also a four–time All–Big Ten academic honoree and four–time National Golf Coaches Association Academic All-American. She was a first-team Verizon/ Co-SIDA Academic All-America honoree as both a junior and a senior.

WISCONSIN HEADLINER

LEN HERRING
TRACK & FIELD

With one outdoor season remaining after 2000-2001, Len Herring has already established himself as one of the top horizontal jumpers in Big Ten history. At the 2001 outdoor meet, the Hawthorne, Florida, native won his fourth straight Big Ten long jump title, as the Badgers won their second consecutive conference "triple crown" with cross country, indoor and outdoor track championships. An injury prevented him from going for a title in the triple jump, the event in which he had qualified for the 2000 Olympic Trials. Three times an All-American in the triple jump, Herring has a best in the event of 54'4" and a best in the long jump of 25'9 $\frac{1}{2}$". He ranks second on the UW all-time list in both events.

BADGER MOMENT

UW posts another winning season and bowl victory

The UW's 2000 football season was a roller-coaster one of sorts, with ups like a five-game, season-ending winning streak and downs like two overtime losses. On balance, however, it was another highly successful one for the Badgers, with a 9–4 record highlighted by a 21–20 win over UCLA in the Sun Bowl. Coach Barry Alvarez's team had to overcome more than its share of injuries, the suspensions of 27 players and the country's toughest schedule. It did, becoming the third straight Badger squad to win nine games. Wisconsin also won four road games; claimed the Paul Bunyan Axe for the sixth straight season; equaled the school mark with 10 academic All-Big Ten picks; and had the winners of the Jim Thorpe Award (Jamar Fletcher) and the Ray Guy Award (Kevin Stemke).

WISCONSIN TIME LINE . . . 2001-02 THROUGH 2012-13

2001–2002

- UW men's basketball team wins its first Big Ten title since 1947
- Men's cross country teams wins its third straight Big Ten title in a streak that will reach 14 (through 2012)
- Women's softball team makes its second straight appearance in the NCAA tournament

2002–2003

- Jeff Rohrman debuts as the men's soccer coach
- Men's track wins the Big Ten championship, beginning a six-year win streak
- Women's golf earns its first bid to the NCAA tournament

2003–04

- Lisa Stone becomes the women's basketball coach
- Men's soccer has a double-digit victory campaign
- Women's tennis earns an NCAA tournament bid

2004–05

- Men's soccer gets the 300th victory in U history
- The men's golf team set team and individual records in UW scoring average
- Women's tennis makes a return appearance in the NCAA tournament
- Women's volleyball advances to the Elite Eight in the NCAA tournament
- Softball coach Karen Gallagher—the only coach that team ever had—resigns after leading the Badgers to their third NCAA tournament appearance

2005–06

- Barry Alvarez retires after 16 seasons as head football coach with a record of 118-74-4 and three Big Ten and three Rose Bowl championships
- Simon Bairu repeats as NCAA cross country champion, leading the Badgers to the NCAA championship under coach Jerry Schumacher and giving Wisconsin four individual titles in the history of the meet
- Women's volleyball again makes the NCAA tournament Elite Eight
- The men's and women's hockey teams each win NCAA titles, marking the first time a Division I university had posted the unique double

2006–07

- Bret Bielema becomes the Badgers' head football coach and then wins the Dave McClain Big Ten Coach of the Year award
- Coach Ed Nuttycombe's men's track team wins the NCAA indoor championship to become the only Big Ten team to ever accomplish that feat

- Badger wrestlers get their best NCAA finish in six years, qualifying nine men and placing 13th in the national collegiate tournament as Craig Henning and Tyler Turner earn all-American honors.
- Chris Solinsky takes his second consecutive NCAA win in the outdoor 5,000-meter run and his fifth NCAA title overall, making him the first five-time national collegiate champ in UW track history

2007–08

- Coach Bo Ryan's men's basketball team wins the UW's first Big Ten title since 1947
- Coming off an undefeated season, the men's varsity eight rowing team wins Wisconsin's ninth national championship. The Badgers also took the Rowe Cup at the 2008 Eastern Sprints for the first time since 1946
- Paula Wilkins takes over as head coach of women's soccer

2008–09

- The women's lightweight rowing team wins its third straight Big Ten crown in continuing a streak that will last through 2011
- Mark Johnson's women's hockey team wins the Big Ten tournament

2009–10

- Bret Bielema's football team wins the Badgers' first Big Ten title since 1999
- Both the men's tennis team and the women's soccer team advance to the "Sweet 16" of their respective NCAA tournaments
- Andrew Howe wins the 165-lb. championship in the NCAA wrestling tournament

2010–11

- John Trask becomes men's soccer coach
- Gabe Carimi wins the Outland Trophy as the nation's outstanding interior lineman
- The Badgers' women's hockey team defeats Minnesota 5-4 in overtime to win its fourth NCAA championship

2011–12

- Men's basketball coach Bo Ryan gets his 266th win as UW head coach to become the school's all-time leader in victories
- Monte Ball wins The Silver Football as the Big Ten's most valuable player and also finishes fourth in voting for the Heisman Trophy

2012–13

- The football team defeats Nebraska 70-13 in the Big Ten championship game in Bret Bielema's last game as coach. Athletic director Barry Alvarez coaches the Badgers in the 2013 Rose Bowl

- Men's track and field coach Ed Nuttycombe retires after 30 years as the Badgers' head coach and an astounding 26 Big Ten indoor and outdoor titles and one NCAA championship as well as 22 in Big Ten cross country and two NCAA overland crowns
- The women's golf team competed in the NCAA tournament for the second time in the program's history, finishing 23rd nationally
- Mick Byrne is named director of track and field and cross country
- Swimmer Andrew Teduits wins the 200 backstroke in the NCAA championships
- The women's rowing team advances to the NCAA championships for the sixth straight season
- Wrestler Connor Medbery is named the Big Ten's Freshman of the Year
- The men's swim team wins its 500th dual meet
- Wisconsin posts its seventh straight 20+ win season in men's basketball and advances to the second round of the NCAA tournamentc
- Former Badger running back Ron Dayne is elected to the College Football Hall of Fame

MEN'S SPORTS

BASKETBALL

Season	Big Ten Place	Coach
2001–02	tie-1st	Bo Ryan
2002–03	1st	Bo Ryan
2003–04	T-2nd	Bo Ryan
2004–05	3rd	Bo Ryan
2005–06	4th	Bo Ryan
2006–07	2nd	Bo Ryan
2007–08	1st	Bo Ryan
2008–09	T-4th	Bo Ryan
2009–10	4th	Bo Ryan
2010–11	3rd	Bo Ryan
2011–12	4th	Bo Ryan
2012–13	4th	Bo Ryan

WISCONSIN HEADLINER

DEVIN HARRIS

Broke the UW single-season scoring record with 624 points in 2004 (later topped)...tallied 1,425 career points...consensus 2004 Big Ten Player of the Year and a first team all-Big Ten selection...selected as MVP of the 2004 Big Ten Tournament.

WISCONSIN HEADLINER

ALANDO TUCKER

Finished his career with 2,217 points, the most in UW history...voted the Big Ten Player of the Year as a senior...earned first-team all-America honors in 2007...a two-time all-conference first-team pick in 2006 and 2007.

WISCONSIN HEADLINER

JORDAN TAYLOR

Two-time All-America selection (2011 and 2012)... also named to the Big Ten all-defensive team in 2011... played 1,241 minutes in 2010-11, a single-season school record.

WISCONSIN HEADLINER

MIKE WILKINSON

A four-year mainstay for the Badgers...was an all-Big Ten first-team selection in 2005.

LEADING THE WAY

Coach Bo Ryan

Three-time Big Ten Coach of the Year...Clair Bee National Coach of the Year in 2007...enters his 30th season as Badger coach in 2013-14 with 291 wins, most of any UW basketball coach...his teams have won five Big Ten titles...a member of five halls of fame...won four NCAA-III titles in his previous coaching stint at UW-Platteville.

CROSS COUNTRY

Season	Big Ten Place	Coach
2001	1st	Jerry Schumacher
2002	1st	Jerry Schumacher
2003	1st	Jerry Schumacher
2004	1st	Jerry Schumacher
2005	1st	Jerry Schumacher
2006	1st	Jerry Schumacher
2007	1st	Jerry Schumacher
2008	1st	Mick Byrne
2009	1st	Mick Byrne
2010	1st	Mick Byrne
2011	1st	Mick Byrne
2012	1st	Mick Byrne

WISCONSIN HEADLINER

SIMON BAIRU

Won the NCAA cross country title in 2004 and 2005 to become the UW's first repeat champ…led the Badgers to their fourth NCAA team championship in 2005…won three Big Ten individual titles from 2003-05 to become the second UWV runner to do so…only the seventh man in Big Ten history to win three or more individual crowns…won the Big Ten outdoor 10,000-meter championship in 2004.

WISCONSIN HEADLINER

MOHAMMED AHMED

A 2012 Canadian Olympian at 10,000 meters…led the Badgers to runner-up honors in the NCAA championships in 2012 with an 8th-place finish …placed 5th in the 2011 meet as Wisconsin won its fifth title…a five-time track and three-time cross country all-American…ranks first on the all-time Wisconsin 10K list with a best of 27:34.64 and fourth on the 5K list at 13:34.30…also holds Big Ten record for 10K…won Big Ten outdoor titles in 2010 at 10K and in 2012 at 5K.

LEADING THE WAY

Coach Mick Byrne

Came to Wisconsin in 2008 after 24 years as head track and cross country coach at Iona College…guided harriers to Big Ten and NCAA regional titles in his first season…coached Badgers to their fifth NCAA team title in the sport in 2011…USTFCCCA national coach of the year in 2011…named Wisconsin's first director of men's and women's track and field and cross country in 2013.

FOOTBALL

Season	Big Ten Place	Coach
2001	T-8th	Barry Alvarez
2002	T-8th	Barry Alvarez
2003	T-7th	Barry Alvarez
2004	3rd	Barry Alvarez
2005	T-3rd	Barry Alvarez
2006	T-2nd	Bret Bielema
2007	4th	Bret Bielema
2008	6th	Bret Bielema
2009	T-4th	Bret Bielema
2010	T-1st	Bret Bielema
2011	Big Ten title	Bret Bielema
2012	Big Ten title	Bret Bielema

WISCONSIN HEADLINER

MONTEE BALL

Played from 2009-2012... first team All-Big Ten selection in 2011 and 2012... won the Big Ten Silver Football as conference's top player in 2011...the NCAA's career touchdown leader (83)...first on all-time UW list with 77 career rushing touchdowns...a consensus all-American first-teamer in 2011 and 2012...won Doak Walker Award in 2012 as nation's top running back...fourth in Heisman Trophy voting in 2011.

WISCONSIN HEADLINER

LANCE KENDRICKS

A consensus all-American and Big Ten first-team selection at tight end in 2010...played from 2007-10...finalist for the 2010 John Mackey Award... finished career 18th all-time at UW in receiving yards...played in the 2011 Senior Bowl...team captain as a senior.

WISCONSIN HEADLINER

GABE CARIMI

The tackle won the 2010 Outland Trophy as the nation's outstanding interior lineman...the 2010 Big Ten Offensive Lineman of the Year...all-Big Ten in 2009 and 2010 and a consensus all-American in 2010...started 49 games in his UW career...team captain as a senior...played in the 2011 Senior Bowl.

JOE THOMAS

The 2006 Outland Trophy winner in 2006 as the country's top interior lineman…played from 2003-06…a consensus all-American and all-Big Ten selection…two-time Lombardi Award semifinalist…started 39 games in his UW career…also a National Scholar-Athlete.

ERASMUS JAMES

A mainstay of the Badger defense from 2001-04… earned multiple honors in 2004 as a consensus all-American, a first-team all-Big Ten pick and both the conference's Defensive Player of the Year and Defensive Lineman of the Year…a finalist for the Nagurski, Bednarik, Lombardi and Hendricks awards..

LEADING THE WAY

Coach Bret Bielema

Head coach from 2006-2012…led Badgers to 68 wins in seven seasons, including victories over Michigan State in 2011 and Nebraska in 2012 in the first two Big Ten Championship games…guided UW to three straight conference titles and a record three consecutive Rose Bowl appearances.

 GOLF

Season	Big Ten Place	Coach
2002	11th	Dennis Tiziani
2003	11th	Dennis Tiziani
2004	11th	Jim Schuman
2005	7th	Jim Schuman
2006	8th	Jim Schuman
2007	5th	Jim Schuman
2008	8th	Jim Schuman
2009	10th	Jim Schuman
2010	11th	Jim Schuman
2011	11th	Jim Schuman
2012	11th	Michael Burcin
2013	12th	Michael Burcin

WISCONSIN HEADLINER

DAN WOLTMAN

One of the top golfers in UW history...twice earned second-team all-Big Ten honors (2008 and 2009)...qualified for the NCAA tournament in 2007 and 2008.

 HOCKEY

(Western Collegiate Hockey Association)

Season	Place	Coach
2001–02	5th	Jeff Sauer)
2002–03	8th	Mike Eaves
2003–04	3rd	Mike Eaves
2004–05	T-3rd	Mike Eaves
2005–06	T-2nd	Mike Eaves
2006–07	T-6th	Mike Eaves
2007–08	6th	Mike Eaves
2008–09	T-3rd	Mike Eaves
2009–10	2nd	Mike Eaves
2010–11	7th	Mike Eaves
2011–12	10th	Mike Eaves
2012–13	4th	Mike Eaves

WISCONSIN HEADLINER

JAMIE MCBAIN

A three-veteran defenseman for the Badgers before turning professional...a Hobey Baker Award candidate...ranked second nationally in scoring among defensemen in 2008-09...named WCHA Player of the Year in 2008-09.

WISCONSIN HEADLINER

BLAKE GEOFFRION

A 2010 All-America forward...led the nation with 15 power play goals...won the Hobey Baker Memorial Award, the first UW hockey player to receive the award emblematic of the nation's top player...also named the 2010 USA Hockey College Player of the Year.

WISCONSIN HEADLINER

JUSTIN SCHULTZ

Two-time first-team all-American...twice an all-WCHA defenseman...selected WCHA Defensive Player of the Year in 2010–11 and 2011–12.

LEADING THE WAY

Coach Mike Eaves

Has won more than 200 games in leading the Badgers on the ice...begins his 12th season in 2013–14...guided team to the program's sixth NCAA title in 2006, the first for the UW in 16 years.

ROWING*

Season	Coach
2001–02	Chris Clark
2002–03	Chris Clark
2003–04	Chris Clark
2004–05	Chris Clark
2005–06	Chris Clark
2006–07	Chris Clark
2007–08	Chris Clark
2008–09	Chris Clark
2009–10	Chris Clark
2010–11	Chris Clark
2011–12	Chris Clark
2012–13	Chris Clark

*There is no Big Ten Conference men's rowing competition.

WISCONSIN HEADLINER

BEAU HOOPMAN

Two-time Olympic gold medalist and first Badger to win the Olympic gold in crew...inducted into the National Rowing Hall of Fame in 2010... joined the Badgers' crew team as a walk-on in 1999...a member of the UW team that won the 2002 Eastern Sprints varsity eight title...now an assistant coach of the crew team.

SOCCER

Season	Big Ten Place	Coach
2001	4th	Jeff Rohrman
2002	2nd-T	Jeff Rohrman
2003	6th	Jeff Rohrman
2004	5th	Jeff Rohrman
2005	6th	Jeff Rohrman
2006	3rd	Jeff Rohrman
2007	6th	Jeff Rohrman
2008	7th	Jeff Rohrman
2009	5th	Todd Yeagley
2010	7th	John Trask
2011	3rd	John Trask
2012	6th	John Trask

SWIMMING & DIVING

Season	Big Ten Place	Coach
2001–02	5th	Eric Hansen
2002–03	5th	Eric Hansen
2003–04	5th	Eric Hansen
2004–05	7th	Eric Hansen
2005–06	7th	Eric Hansen
2006–07	8th	Eric Hansen
2007–08	7th	Eric Hansen
2008–09	6th	Eric Hansen
2009–10	8th	Eric Hansen
2010–11	8th	Eric Hansen
2011–12	8th	Whitney Hite
2012–13	8th	Whitney Hite

WISCONSIN HEADLINER

AARON HOHLBEIN

Two-time captain who was the Badgers' top player from 2003–06...earned all-Big Ten honors four times, twice first-team and twice second-team... was a third-team all-America honoree as a senior.

WISCONSIN HEADLINER

DREW TEDUITS

Won the NCAA 200 backstroke in 1:38.27 as a sophomore in 2013...first UW swimmer to win an NCAA title since 1959...earned all-America honors and was a first-team all-Big Ten choice...also won the 200 backstroke in the conference meet.

TENNIS

Season	Big Ten Place	Coach
2001–02	T-8th	Pat Klingelhoets
2002–03	T-10th	Pat Klingelhoets
2003–04	10th	Pat Klingelhoets
2004–05	10th	Pat Klingelhoets
2005–06	T-8th	Greg Van Emburgh
2006–07	4th	Greg Van Emburgh
2007–08	3rd	Greg Van Emburgh
2008–09	7th	Greg Van Emburgh
2009–10	4th	Greg Van Emburgh
2010–11	6th	Greg Van Emburgh
2011–12	8th	Greg Van Emburgh
2012–13	8th	Greg Van Emburgh

WISCONSIN HEADLINER

MORITZ BAUMANN

A four-time All-Big Ten selection from 2006-10…became only the second Wisconsin player to be named to the all-Big Ten team as a freshman.

WISCONSIN HEADLINER

MAREK MICHALICKA

Voted Big Ten Freshman of the Year for 2008…twice captained the Badgers…an all-Big Ten first-team selection…his 7.35 winning percentage in singles is second on the all-time UW list…teamed with Moritz Baumann for two seasons in doubles competition.

 # TRACK AND FIELD

Indoor Track

Season	Big Ten Place	Coach
2002	meet cancelled	Ed Nuttycombe
2003	1st	Ed Nuttycombe
2004	1st	Ed Nuttycombe
2005	1st	Ed Nuttycombe
2006	1st	Ed Nuttycombe
2007	1st	Ed Nuttycombe
2008	1st	Ed Nuttycombe
2009	5th	Ed Nuttycombe
2010	3rd	Ed Nuttycombe
2011	3rd	Ed Nuttycombe
2012	5th	Ed Nuttycombe
2013	1st	Ed Nuttycombe

Outdoor Track

Season	Big Ten Place	Coach
2002	1st	Ed Nuttycombe
2003	6th	Ed Nuttycombe
2004	1st	Ed Nuttycombe
2005	1st	Ed Nuttycombe
2006	1st	Ed Nuttycombe
2007	1st	Ed Nuttycombe
2008	2nd	Ed Nuttycombe
2009	6th	Ed Nuttycombe
2010	2nd	Ed Nuttycombe
2011	5th	Ed Nuttycombe
2012	1st	Ed Nuttycombe
2013	3rd	Ed Nuttycombe

WISCONSIN HEADLINERS

Demi Omole: UW 100-meter record-holder at 10.11...four-time Big Ten outdoor champ at 100 meters....200-meter conference winner in 2007...the Big Ten's athlete of the year and athlete of the championships for the 2007 outdoor season...a five-time all-American and a four-time all-Big Ten selection from 2004-07

Japheth Cato: NCAA heptathlon runner-up in 2012 and 2013...first-team all-American in 2012 and 2013...Big Ten athlete of the year and athlete of the championships for 2012 indoor season...indoor conference freshman of the year in 2011...won Big Ten heptathlon title in 2011, 2012 and 2013...set conference meet record of 6,090 points in 2013...three-time all-Big Ten choice...first collegian to top 6,000 points in heptathlon four times in a career...seventh collegian to score more than 6,000 points in heptathlon

WISCONSIN HEADLINERS

Chris Solinsky: The most decorated distance runner in Wisconsin history... won a UW track record five NCAA titles (two in the outdoor 5K, two in the indoor 3K and one in the indoor 5K)...third in the NCAA cross country championships in 2005 as Badgers won their fourth title... former U.S. record-holder at 10K.

Matt Tegenkamp: A Big Ten champ in cross country and track...ranks second on UW all-time 5K list (13:25.36)...8th in NCAA cross country in 2001, 12th in 2002 and 11th in 2004..he has made two U.S. Olympic teams (5K in 2008, 10K in 2012)...fourth in the 5K in the 2011 IAAF World Championships.

WRESTLING

Season	Big Ten Place	Coach
2002	9th	Barry Davis
2003	9th	Barry Davis
2004	7th	Barry Davis
2005	T-5th	Barry Davis
2006	7th	Barry Davis
2007	2nd	Barry Davis
2008	6th	Barry Davis
2009	4th	Barry Davis
2010	3rd	Barry Davis
2011	4th	Barry Davis
2012	12th	Barry Davis
2013	10th	Barry Davis

WISCONSIN HEADLINERS

ANDREW HOWE

Won the 2010 NCAA title at 165 lbs. to become the first UW wrestling champ in nine years...a three-time NCAA all-America selection...won three Big Ten championships... selected as 2009 Big Ten Freshman of the Year, the first Badger so honored since 1992.

WISCONSIN HEADLINERS

KYLE RUSCHELL

A two-time all-America selection in 2009 and 2010...placed third at the third in the NCAA tournament in 2009 and fourth in 2010 at 149 lbs.

WISCONSIN HEADLINERS

TREVOR BRANDVOLD

Two-time all-America selection...won Big Ten titles at 197 lbs. in 2010 and 2011.

WISCONSIN HEADLINER

TOM CLUM

Finished third in the NCAA tournament at 133 lbs. as a junior and fifth as a senior... won the 2006 Big Ten 133-lb. title and the 2004 conference 125-lb. crown...twice named all-America...a three-time all-Big Ten honoree...named Big Ten Wrestler of the Championships in 2006.

BASKETBALL

Season	Big Ten Place	Coach
2001–02	5th-T	Jane Albright
2002–03	8th-T	Jane Albright
2003–04	8th-T	Lisa Stone
2004–05	8th-T	Lisa Stone
2005–06	9th	Lisa Stone
2006–07	5th-T	Lisa Stone
2007–08	7th-T	Lisa Stone
2008–09	7th-T	Lisa Stone
2009–10	3rd-T	Lisa Stone
2010–11	3rd-T	Lisa Stone
2011–12	9th-T	Bobbie Kelsey
2012–13	11th	Bobbie Kelsey

WISCONSIN HEADLINER

JOLENE ANDERSON

A 5-8 guard who was a scoring machine...the Big Ten Player of the Year in 2008 and the conference's Freshman of the Year in 2005...a four-time all-Big Ten pick from 2005-08...remains the only UW basketball player—man or woman—to score more than 2,000 career points...her UW record stands at 2,132 points.

CROSS COUNTRY

Season	Big Ten Place	Coach
2001	3rd	Peter Tegen
2002	5th	Peter Tegen
2003	5th	Peter Tegen
2004	8th	Jim Stintzi
2005	6th	Jim Stintzi
2006	2nd	Jim Stintzi
2007	6th	Jim Stintzi
2008	2nd	Jim Stintzi
2009	10th	Jim Stintzi
2010	7th	Jim Stintzi
2011	4th	Jim Stintzi
2012	5th	Jim Stintzi

WISCONSIN HEADLINER

BETHANY BREWSTER

An all-American in 2000 off her ninth place NCAA finish...won the Big Ten title in 2001 in 17:02.7....a four-time all-Big Ten selection from 1998-2001...won Big Ten "Athlete of the Week" honors for October 2, 2001...placed 54th in the 1999 NCAA meet as a sophomore and 62nd as a freshman.

GOLF

Season	Big Ten Place	Coach
2001–2002	10th	Dennis Tiziani
2002–2003	2nd	Dennis Tiziani
2003–2004	5th-T	Todd Oehrlein
2004–2005	8th	Todd Oehrlein
2005–2006	9th	Todd Oehrlein
2006–2007	9th	Todd Oehrlein
2007–2008	6th	Todd Oehrlein
2008–2009	8th	Todd Oehrlein
2009–2010	4th	Todd Oehrlein
2010–2011	4th	Todd Oehrlein
2011–2012	9th	Todd Oehrlein
2012–2013	6th	Todd Oehrlein

WISCONSIN HEADLINER

KRIS YOO

led the women's golf team in six tournaments in 2013... earned second-team all-Big Ten honors...shot a 65 to set school and course records at the NCAA Regional tournament...an Academic All-Big Ten selection... as a freshman in 2011, tied the record in the 72-hole Big Ten individual Championship... her season average of 74.97 ranks second in UW history.

ICE HOCKEY

Season	Big Ten Place	Coach
2001–02	2nd	Trina Bourget
2002–03	3rd	Mark Johnson
2003–04	2nd	Mark Johnson
2004–05	3rd	Mark Johnson
2005–06	1st	Mark Johnson
2006–07	1st	Mark Johnson
2007–08	3rd	Mark Johnson
2008–09	2nd	Mark Johnson
2009–10	N/A	Mark Johnson
2010–11	1st	Mark Johnson
2011–12	1st	Mark Johnson
2012–13	2nd	Mark Johnson

WISCONSIN HEADLINER

SARA BAUER

Won the Patty Kazmaier Award in 2006, the first Wisconsin player to be so honored...Western Collegiate Hockey Association Player of the Year for 2006 and 2007....

WISCONSIN HEADLINER

JESSIE VETTER

Record-breaking goaltender won the 2009 Patty Kazmaier Memorial Award as a senior...a first team all-WCHA selection...made the Big Ten's all-tournament team...2009 Sportswoman of the Year.

WISCONSIN HEADLINER

MEGHAN DUGGAN

Patty Kazmaier Memorial Award winner in 2010-11...an RBK Hockey/AHCA Division I first-team All-American for 2011...also named WCHA Player of the Year that same year...made the 2010-11 WCHA all-tournament team...earned all-WCHA first-teams honors for the second time...all-time UW leader in career points at 238 and in power play goals with 31.

WISCONSIN HEADLINER

BRIANNA DECKER

The 2012 Patty Kazmaier Memorial Award winner...a three-time AHCA Division I All-America selection...the 2011-12 WCHA Player of the Year...three-times an all-WCHA first-team choice...ranks first on the UW all-time list in career plus/minus (+175).

LEADING THE WAY

Coach Mark Johnson

Former Badger star...winningest coach in program history...has guided the Badgers to four NCAA titles, four WCHA tournament championships and four WCHA regular season titles.

ROWING

Season	Big Ten Place	Coach
2001–2002	4th	Mary Browning
2002–2003	5th	Maren LaLiberty
2003–2004	2nd	Maren LaLiberty/ Sue Ela
2004–2005	3rd	Bebe Bryans
2005–2006	5th	Bebe Bryans
2006–2007	5th	Bebe Bryans
2007–2008	2nd	Bebe Bryans
2008–2009	4th	Bebe Bryans
2009–2010	1st	Bebe Bryans
2010–2011	3rd	Bebe Bryans
2011–2012	3rd	Bebe Bryans
2012–2013	3rd	Bebe Bryans

KRISTEN HEDSTROM

A lightweight rower...was a key part of the 2005-06 national championship crew, the team's third straight... first-team all-America selection in 2007 and 2008... competed in the 2012 London Olympics.

LEADING THE WAY

Coach Bebe Bryans:

Now in her 10th season as head coach of the UW openweight and lightweight teams...has guided the lightweight teams to five national titles...her openweights placed seventh in the NCAA in 2010, best ever by a UW openweights team...her 2006 team was 8th in the NCAA.

SOCCER

Season	Big Ten Place	Coach
2001	11th	Dean Duerst
2002	5th-T	Dean Duerst
2003	7th-T	Dean Duerst
2004	5th-T	Dean Duerst
2005	6th-T	Dean Duerst
2006	7th-T	Dean Duerst
2007	10th	Paula Wilkins
2008	10th	Paula Wilkins
2009	3rd	Paula Wilkins
2010	3rd	Paula Wilkins
2011	4th	Paula Wilkins
2012	6th	Paula Wilkins

WISCONSIN HEADLINER

LAURIE NOSBUSCH

Starter since her freshman season in 2008... Big Ten Medal of Honor winner... All-Big Ten selection in 2010... member of the Big Ten All-Freshman team... led the Badgers in scoring from 2008 to 2010, the only member of the women's soccer team to do so for three consecutive years.

SOFTBALL

Season	Big Ten Place	Coach
2001	5th-T	Karen Gallagher
2002	4th	Karen Gallagher
2003	8th	Karen Gallagher
2004	10th	Karen Gallagher
2005	5th	Karen Gallagher
2006	10th	Chandelle Schulte
2007	9th	Chandelle Schulte
2008	11th	Chandelle Schulte
2009	11th	Chandelle Schulte
2010	8th	Chandelle Schulte
2011	6th-T	Yvette Healy
2012	6th-T	Yvette Healy
2013	4th	Yvette Healy

WISCONSIN HEADLINER

CASSANDRA DARRAH

The pitcher ranks second all-time at Wisconsin with a 2.17 career ERA...her .684 winning percentage (65-30) is first on the all-time list...made the NCAA all-region team in 2013...was the 2013 Big Ten Tournament MVP and also a first-team all-conference selection.

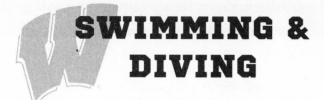

SWIMMING & DIVING

Season	Big Ten Place	Coach
2001-02	5th	Eric Hansen
2002-03	5th	Eric Hansen
2003-04	5th	Eric Hansen
2004-05	7th	Eric Hansen
2005-06	7th	Eric Hansen
2006-07	8th	Eric Hansen
2007-08	7th	Eric Hansen
2008-09	6th	Eric Hansen
2009-10	8th	Eric Hansen
2010-11	8th	Eric Hansen
2011-12	8th	Whitney Hite
2012-13	6th	Whitney Hite

WISCONSIN HEADLINERS

BETHANY PENDLETON

Earned National Swimmer of the Week accolades multiple times in 2003-04, her senior season…broke the Big Ten record in the 400-yard IM…named Big Ten Swimmer of the Year and Big Ten Swimmer of the Championships in 2004.

WISCONSIN HEADLINER

CARLY PIPER

The sole Olympic gold medalist in Wisconsin swimming history…member of the 800-meter freestyle relay that set a world record at the 2004 Olympics…a 17-time all-American with 11 first-team AA honors…a four-time NCAA champion in the 500 and 1650 freestyles…the 2005 Big Ten Swimmer of the Year.

 # TENNIS

Season	Big Ten Place	Coach
2001-02	2nd	Patti Henderson
2002-03	6th	Patti Henderson
2003-04	4th-T	Patti Henderson
2004-05	5th-T	Patti Henderson
2005-06	8th-T	Patti Henderson
2006-07	11th	Patti Henderson
2007-08	9th	Brian Fleishman
2008-09	7th	Brian Fleishman
2009-10	8th	Brian Fleishman
2010-11	5th	Brian Fleishman
2011-12	10th	Brian Fleishman
2012-13	8th-T	Brian Fleishman

WISCONSIN HEADLINER

CAITLIN BURKE

A three-time all-Big Ten first-team selection...competed in the NCAA tournament in each of her four years at UW... ranked as high as No. 14 during her senior year... compiled a record of 65-27 at Wisconsin... won the women's singles title at the Intercollegiate Tennis Association (ITA) national summer championships in 2005.

 # TRACK AND FIELD

Indoor Track

Season	Big Ten Place	Coach
2002	6th	Peter Tegen
2003	5th	Peter Tegen
2004	7th	Peter Tegen
2005	8th	Jim Stintzi
2006	5th	Jim Stintzi
2007	6th	Jim Stintzi
2008	4th	Jim Stintzi
2009	7th	Jim Stintzi
2010	5th	Jim Stintzi
2011	10th	Jim Stintzi
2012	6th	Jim Stintzi
2013	8th	Jim Stintzi

Outdoor Track

Season	Big Ten Place	Coach
2002	5th	Peter Tegen
2003	9th	Peter Tegen
2004	9th	Peter Tegen
2005	6th	Jim Stintzi
2006	8th	Jim Stintzi
2007	8th	Jim Stintzi
2008	6th	Jim Stintzi
2009	9th	Jim Stintzi
2010	3rd	Jim Stintzi
2011	6th	Jim Stintzi
2012	5th	Jim Stintzi
2013	7th	Jim Stintzi

WISCONSIN HEADLINER

DEANNA LATHAM

A USTFCCCA second-team all-America pick for the pentathlon...also a 2012 second-team choice outdoors for the heptathlon... qualified for the 2012 NCAA outdoor championships in the heptathlon...a Big Ten all-academic selection.

VOLLEYBALL

Season	Big Ten Place	Coach
2001	1st	Pete Waite
2002	2nd-T	Pete Waite
2003	4th	Pete Waite
2004	4th	Pete Waite
2005	2nd	Pete Waite
2006	3rd	Pete Waite
2007	2nd	Pete Waite
2008	7th-T	Pete Waite
2009	7th-T	Pete Waite
2010	10th	Pete Waite
2011	8th-T	Pete Waite
2012	9th-T	Pete Waite

WISCONSIN HEADLINER

ERIN BYRD

A second-team All-America choice in 2002...captained the Badgers...one of the all-time UW leaders in both kills and digs.

THE LIST

UW Hall of Famers

1991

Alan Ameche, Football

George "Buck" Backus, Administration

Rolland Barnum, Football, Basketball & Baseball

Cindy Bremser, Track

Milt Bruhn, Football

Howard Buck, Football

Omar Crocker, Boxing

Gene Englund, Basketball

Chuck Fenske, Track

Harold Foster, Basketball

Don Gehrmann, Track

Carie Graves, Rowing

Pat Harder, Football

Elroy "Crazylegs" Hirsch, Football & Administration

Mark Johnson, Hockey

Tom Jones, Track & Cross Country

Lee Kemp, Wrestling

John Kotz, Basketball

Harvey Kuenn, Baseball

George Levis, Basketball

Pat Matzdorf, Track

Walter Meanwell, Basketball

Arlie Mucks Sr., Track & Football

Pat O'Dea, Football

Don Rehfeldt, Basketball

Pat Richter, Football, Basketball, Baseball & Administration

Harlan Roger, Football, Basketball & Baseball

Dave Schreiner, Football

Chris Steinmetz Sr., Basketball

John Walsh, Boxing

Howard Weiss, Football

Fred Westphal, Swimming

Rollie Williams, Football, Basketball & Baseball

Ivan Williamson, Football

Robert "Red" Wilson, Football & Baseball

1992

Marty Below, Football

Robert Butler, Football

Robert Cook, Basketball & Baseball

D'Lynn Damron, Swimming

Mike Eaves, Hockey

Walter Mehl, Cross Country & Track

Eddie Jankowski, Football

"Badger Bob" Johnson, Hockey

Arthur Nielsen Sr., Tennis

Gene Rankin, Boxing

Woodie Swancutt, Boxing

Ed Withers, Football

1993

Ray Arrington, Track & Cross Country

Cathy Branta, Track & Cross Country

Rufus Ferguson, Football

Lloyd Larson, Football & Basketball

Cliff Lutz, Boxing

Arthur Mansfield, Football & Baseball

Charles McGinnis, Track

John Messmer, Football, Track & Baseball

Pat O'Donahue, Football

George Paskvan, Football & Track

Rolf 'Chub' Poser, Basketball & Baseball

Guy Sundt, Football, Track, Cross Country & Administration

Charles Walter, Cross Country & Track

1994

Eddie Cochems, Football

John Gerlach, Baseball

Billy Marek, Football

Albert "Ab" Nicholas, Basketball

John Roberts, Football & Wrestling

Harry Stuhldreher, Football

Rose Thomson, Cross Country & Track

Frank Weston, Football & Basketball

1995

Russ Hellickson, Wrestling

Greg Kabat, Football

Jim Mott, Administration

Ted Shaw, Track

Otto Stangel, Basketball

Ed Templin, Wrestling

Al Toon, Football & Track

Mike Webster, Football

1996

Dale Hackbart, Football, Basketball & Baseball

Bobby Poser, Basketball & Baseball

Oscar Damman, Administration

Suzy Favor Hamilton, Cross Country & Track

Mickey McGuire, Football

1997

John Hickman, Swimming

Pat Johnson, Track

Jack Kellner, Track

Don Kindt, Football & Track

Bob Ranck, Boxing

Joe Franklin, Basketball

Ron Vander Kelen, Football

1998

Tom Bennett, Track, Football & Golf

Dick Cable, Basketball

Theresa Huff, Basketball

Gene Jaroch, Baseball

Fred Negus, Football & Baseball

Kit Saunders-Nordeen, Administration

1999

William Aspinwall, Administration

Ann French, Badminton

Carl Holtz, Rowing

Tim Krumrie, Football

Walter Lautenbach, Baseball & Basketball

Frank J. Remington, Administration

2000

Lisa Boyd, Volleyball

Tony Granato, Hockey

Ken Huxhold, Football & Track

Russ Rebholz, Football & Basketball

Rick Reichardt, Football & Baseball

Stu Voigt, Football, Baseball & Track

Fred Wegner, Baseball & Basketball

2001

Jim Bakken, Football & Baseball

John Jamieson, Golf

Dick Murphy, Boxing

Ray A. Patterson, Basketball & Track

Dave Suminski, Football

Heather Taggart, Soccer

2002

Hal Faverty, Football

Tim Hacker, Track & Cross Country

Stephanie Herbst, Track & Cross Country

John Powless, Tennis & Basketball

Andy Rein, Wrestling

Clarence Sherrod, Basketball

2003

Peggy Anderson, Diving

Robert Espeseth, Men's Rowing

Danny Jones, Basketball

Dan McClimon, Track & Cross Country

Arlie Mucks Jr., Special Service

George Poage, Track

Amy Wickus, Track & Cross Country

2004

Kathy Butler, Track and Cross Country

Michael Finley, Basketball

Randy "Jabo" Jablonic, Men's Rowing, Men's Rowing Coach

Steve Lacy, Cross Country & Track

Dennis Lick, Football

Oscar Osthoff, Football, Track, Swimming & Gymnastics

Bob Rennebohm, Special Service

2005

Jefferson Burrus, Football and Crew

Barb Franke, Basketball

Jim Jordan, Wrestling

George Martin, Wrestling Coach

Mike Richter, Hockey

Glen Selbo, Basketball & Baseball

Mark Winzenried, Track

2006

Marc Behrend, Hockey

Paul Gruber, Football (84 - 87)

Duane Kleven, Wrestling Coach

Pam Moore, Track & Basketball

Ken Siebel, Basketball

Don Voss, Football & Track

2007

Burt DeHate, Men's Hockey

Matt Demaray, Wrestling

Earl Girard, Football

Bill Gregory, Football

Sherisa Livingston, Volleyball

Jim Temp, Baseball & Football

Vern Woodward, Boxing, Boxing Coach

2008

Otto Breitenbach, Football, Administration

Milo Lubratovich, Football

Craig Norwich, Men's Hockey

Rick Olson, Basketball

Megan Scott, Women's Basketball, Track, Volleyball

Palmer 'Butch' Strickler, Special Service

Troy Vincent, Football

Tom Wiesner, Special Service

Sidney Williams Jr., Football

2009

Ron Dayne, Football

Claire Eichner, Track and Field, Cross Country

Wayne Esser, Mendota Gridiron

Thornton Kipper, Baseball

Joe Panos, Football

Bill Reddan, Men's Soccer Coach

Robin Threatt, Basketball

2010

Don Davey, Football

Dick Houden, Track & Field

Dan Lanphear, Football & Track

Donny Pritzlaff, Wrestling

Ellen Stonebraker, Swimming & Diving

Theran Welsh, Hockey

2011

Chris Chelios, Hockey

Sue Ela, Women's Rowing

Lou Holland, Football & Track

Scott Lamphear, Soccer

Dave McClain, Football Coach

Carly Piper, Swimming

Judith Sweet, Special Service

2012

Dick Bennett, Basketball

Jim Haines, Wrestling

James Haluska, Football

Lawrence Johnson, Football, Track & Field

Karen Lunda, Soccer, Field Hockey

Cory Raymer, Football

2013

Jamar Fletcher, Football

David Greenwood, Football & Track

Claude Gregory, Basketball

Andrea Kirchberg, Softball

Chuck LaBahn, Special Service

Jack Reinwand, Wrestling

Dean Talafous, Hockey

Peter Tegen, Women's Track and Cross Country Coach

THE LIST

WISCONSIN'S BIG TEN SPORTSMANSHIP AWARD WINNERS

(awards first presented for the 2002–03 season)

2003
Kirk Penney, basketball
Tara Clack, track & field
2004
Eric Hanson, soccer
Kaitlin Reiss, softball
2005
Joe Ebinger, swimming & diving
Boo Gillette, softball
2006
Tyler Turner, wrestling
Lindsay McMillan, golf
2007
Joe Detmer, track & field
Sara Bauer, ice hockey
2008
Luke Swan, football
Audra Jeffers, volleyball
2009
Nate Larkin, track & field
Audra Jeffers, volleyball
2010
Chris Maragos, football
Vicky Opitz, rowing
2011
Scott Tolzien, football
Meghan Duggan, ice hockey
2012
Kyle Jefferson, track & field
Anya Covington, basketball
2013
Jared Berggren, basketball
Lindsay Danielson, golf

THE LIST

UW Olympians

1904

Emil Breitkreutz, Men's Track and Field

George Poage, Men's Track and Field

Frank Waller, Men's Track and Field

1912

Arlie Mucks, Sr., Men's Track and Field

1920

Arlie Schardt, Men's Track and Field

1925

Charles McGinnis, Men's Track and Field

1948

Don Gehrmann, Men's Track and Field

Tom Jones, Men's Track and Field

Lloyd LaBeach, Men's Track and Field

1964

Charles Walter, Men's Track and Field

1968

Stewart MacDonald, Men's Rowing

1971

David Bush, Men's Diving

1972

Paul Jarvey, Men's Swimming

Mike Manley, Men's Track and Field

Tim Mickelson, Men's Rowing

Neil Rogers, Men's Swimming

1976

Steve Alley, Men's Ice Hockey

Bob Espeseth, Men's Rowing

Carie Graves, Women's Rowing

Jim Haines, Wrestling

Neil Halleen, Men's Rowing

Russ Hellickson, Wrestling

Bob Johnson, Men's Ice Hockey

Bob Lundeen, Men's Ice Hockey

Peggy McCarthy, Women's Rowing

Alte Melberg, Men's Swimming

John Taft, Men's Ice Hockey

Fritz Warncke, Men's Swimming

Jackie Zoch, Women's Rowing

1980

Chris Cruz, Women's Rowing

Gunnar Gunderson, Men's Swimming

Mark Johnson, Men's Ice Hockey

Lee Kemp, Wrestling

Steve Lacy, Men's Track and Field

Bob Suter, Men's Ice Hockey

1984

Marc Behrend, Men's Ice Hockey

Cindy Bremser, Women's Track and Field

Chris Chelios, Men's Ice Hockey

Bruce Driver, Men's Ice Hockey

Patrick Flatley, Men's Ice Hockey

Ed Lebler, Men's Ice Hockey

Stewart McDonald, Men's Rowing

Andy Rein, Wrestling

Bruce Roberts, Men's Track and Field

Kris Thorsness, Women's Rowing

Chari Towne, Women's Rowing

Harry Wozniak, Men's Swimming

1988

Erika Brown, Curling

Cindy Eckert, Women's Rowing

Sarah Gengler, Women's Rowing

Tony Granato, Men's Ice Hockey

Jim Johannson, Men's Ice Hockey

Valter Kalaus, Men's Swimming

Mara Keggi, Women's Rowing

Dave Krmpotich, Men's Rowing

Mike Richter, Men's Ice Hockey

Kim Santiago, Women's Rowing

1992

Mark Berkner, Women's Rowing

Yasmin Farooq, Women's Rowing

Suzy Favor Hamilton, Women's Track and Field

Carol Feeney, Women's Rowing

Sean Hill, Men's Ice Hockey

Robert Pinter, Men's Swimming

1994

Barry Richter, Men's Ice Hockey

1996

Kathy Butler, Women's Track and Field

Melissa Iverson, Women's Rowing

Eric Mueller, Men's Rowing

Maxwell Seales, Men's Track and Field

1998

Gary Suter, Men's Ice Hockey

2000

Pascal Dobert, Men's Track and Field

Torrey Folk, Women's Rowing

Kirk Penney, Men's Basketball

2002

Curtis Joseph, Men's Ice Hockey

Brian Rafalski, Men's Ice Hockey

2004

Carly Piper, Women's Swimming

Adam Mania, Men's Swimming

Beau Hoopman, Men's Rowing

Matt Imes, Men's Rowing

Matt Smith, Men's Rowing

2006

Dany Heatley, Men's Ice Hockey

Carla MacLeod, Women's Ice Hockey

Molly Engstrom, Women's Ice Hockey

2008

Micah Boyd, Men's Rowing

Matt Tegenkamp, Men's Track and Field

Amy Vermuelen, Women's Soccer

2010

Meaghan Mikkelson, Women's Ice Hockey

Meghan Duggan, Women's Ice Hockey

Hilary Knight, Women's Ice Hockey

Erika Lawler, Women's Ice Hockey

Joe Pavelski, Men's Ice Hockey

Ryan Suter, Men's Rowing

Jessie Vetter, Women's Ice Hockey

Kerry Weiland, Women's Ice Hockey

Jinelle Zaugg, Women's Ice Hockey

2012

Mohammed Ahmed, Men's Track/Cross Country

Hilary Edmonson, Women's Track

Kristen Hedstrom, Women's Rowing

Evan Jager, Men's Track

Grant James, Men's Rowing

Ross James, Men's Rowing

Gwen Jorgensen, Women's Track, Cross Country, Swimming

Egle Staisiunaite, Women's Track

WISCONSIN'S ATHLETES OF THE YEAR & NOMINEES FOR BIG TEN ATHLETE OF THE YEAR HONORS

2002
Lee Evans, football
Lizzy Fitzgerald, volleyball

2003
Matt Tegenkamp, track & field/cross country
Carly Piper, swimming

2004
Devin Harris, basketball
Bethany Pendleton, swimming & diving

2005
Simon Bairu, cross country/track
Carly Piper, swimming

2006
Simon Bairu, cross country/track
Sara Bauer, ice hockey

2007
Alando Tucker, basketball
Sara Bauer, ice hockey

2008
Travis Beckum, football
Jolene Anderson, basketball

2009
Jamie McBain, ice hockey
Jessie Vetter, ice hockey

2010
Blake Geoffrion, ice hockey
Maggie Meyer, swimming

2011
Jordan Taylor, basketball
Meghan Duggan, ice hockey

2012
Montee Ball, football
Brianna Decker, ice hockey

2013
Montee Ball, football
Cassandra Darrah, softball

WISCONSIN'S BIG TEN MEDAL OF HONOR WINNERS (2002–13)

2002
Danny Westerman, tennis
Andrea Wanezek, swimming & diving

2003
Kirk Penney, basketball
Erin Byrd, volleyball

2004
Ryan Tremelling, track & field
Morgan Shields, volleyball

2005
Jim Leonhard, football
Carla MacLeod, ice hockey

2006
Nathan Brown, track & field
Jessica Ring, soccer

2007
Joe Thomas, football
Sara Bauer, ice hockey

2008
Adam Barhamand, rowing
Katrina Rundhaug, track & field & cross country

2009
Joe Krabbenhoft, basketball
Gwen Jorgensen, track & field

2010
Jack Bolas, track & field
Chavon Robinson, track & field

2011
Gabe Carimi, football
Maggie Meyer, swimming & diving

2012
Peter Konz, football
Laurie Nosbusch, soccer

2013
Elliot Krause, cross country & track & field
Kendall Schmidt, rowing

APPENDICES

UNIVERSITY OF WISCONSIN
ATHLETICS ADMINISTRATORS AND COACHES

Faculty Representatives

1896	C.R. Barnes
1896–1899	E.A. Birge
1899–1905	C.S. Slichter
1905–1906	T.S. Adams
1906–1909	C.P. Hutchins
1910–1912	G.W. Ehler
1912–1931	J.F.A. Pyre
1932–1935	A.T. Weaver
1936–1947	William F. Lorenz
1947–1951	Kenneth Little
1951–1954	Kurt F. Wendt
1954–1959	George Young
1959–1970	Frank Remington
1970–1971	George Young
1971–1986	Frank Remington
1981–1987	Diane Lindstrom
986–1987	David Tarr
1987–1989	Jane Voichick
1987–1991	Ted Finman
1989–1992	Cyrena Pondrom
1991–Present	James Hoyt
1992–1994	Jane Robbins
1994–1996	Barbara L. Wolfe
1996–1999	Robin Douthitt
1999–2003	Gloria Ladson-Billings
2000–2003	Robert Haveman
2003–2007	Bruce Jones
2007–2011	Walter Dickey
2009–Present	Sheila McGuirk
2011–Present	Dale Bjorling

Athletic Directors

1920–1924	Tom E. Jones (acting)
1925–1932	George Little
1933–1935	Walter Meanwell
1936–1950	Harry Stuhldreher
1950–1955	Guy Sundt
1955–1969	Ivan Williamson
1969–1987	Elroy L. Hirsch
1987–1989	Ade Sponberg
1989–2004	Pat Richter
2005–Present	Barry Alvarez

Women's Athletics Administrators

1974–83	Kit Saunders–Nordeen women's athletic director
1983–89	Paula Bonner associate athletic director
1986–89	Kit Saunders–Nordeen primary women's administrator
1990–2005	Cheryl Marra associate athletic director and senior women's administrator
2005–Present	Terry Gawlik associate athletic director and senior women's administrator

Sports Information Directors

1923–1929	Les Gage
1929–1941	George Downer
1941–1946	Bob Foss
1946–1956	Arthur G. Lentz
1956–1957	James A. Mott (acting)
1957–1966	George L. Lanphear
1966–1990	James A. Mott (men's)
1975–1977	Phyllis Krutsch (women's)
1977–Present	Tamara Flarup (women's)
1990–2001	Steve Malchow (men's)
2001–2009	Justin Doherty
2009–Present	Brian Lucas

Baseball Coaches

1900–1901	Phil King
1902–1903	Oscar Bandelin
1904–1905	Bemis Pierce
1907	C.P. Hutchins
1908–1911	Tom Barry
1912	Gordon (Slim) Lewis
1913	William Juneau
1914–1917	Gordon (Slim) Lewis
1918	Guy Lowman
1919–1920	Maurice A.. Kent
1921–1932	Guy Lowman

1933–1934	Irvin Uteritz
1935–1936	Robert Poser
1937–1939	Lowell Douglas
1940–1970	Arthur Mansfield
1971–1984	Tom Meyer
1984–1991	Steve Land

Men's Basketball Coaches

1899–1905	James Elsom
1905–1908	Emmett Angeli
1909–1911	Haskell Noyes
1912–1917	Dr. Walter Meanwell
1918–1920	Guy Lowman
1921–1934	Dr. Walter Meanwell
1935–1959	Harold Foster
1960–1968	John E. Erlckson
1969–1976	John Powless
1977–1982	Bill Cofield
1983–1992	Steve Yoder
1993–1994	Stu Jackson
1994–1995	Stan Van Gundy
1995–2000	Dick Bennett
2001	Brad Soderberg
2002–Present	Bo Ryan

Women's Basketball Coaches

1974–1976	Marilyn Harris
1976–1986	Edwina Quails
1986–1994	Mary Murphy
1994–2003	Jane Albright-Dieterle
2003–2011	Lisa Stone
2011–Present	Bobbie Kelsey

Men's Cross Country Coaches

1909	J.C. Elsom
1910–1911	Charles Wilson
1912	Clarence Cleveland
1913–1914	Thomas E. Jones
1915	Fred G. Lee
1916	Irvin A. White
1917	Thomas E. Jones
1918–1920	George T. Bresnahan
1921–1925	Meade Burke
1926–1947	Thomas E. Jones
1948–1949	Guy Sundt
1950–1959	J. Riley Best
1960	Tom Bennett
1961–1963	Charles Walter
1964	Tom Bennett
1965–1967	Charles Walter
1968–1970	Robert Brennan
1971–1982	Dan McClimon
1983–1997	Martin Smith

1998–2007	Jerry Schumacher
2008–Present	Mick Byrne

Women's Cross Country Coach

1974–2003	Peter Tegen
2004–Present	Jim Stintzi

Diving Coach

1951–1964	Art Krueger (men's)
1964–1994	Jerry Darda
1994–1999	Jim Fischer
1999–2003	Lee-Jay Strifler
2003–2006	Josh Seykora
2006–2011	Tom Michaël
2011–Present	Anton Slobounov

Fencing Coaches

1911	Walter Meanwell
1912–1914	H.D. MacChesney
1915	George Breen
1916–1917	H.D. MacChesney
1918–1919	No Team
1920–1926	Fred Schlatter
1927–1951	Arpad L. Masley
1952–1972	Archie Simonson
1972–1990	Tony Gillham
1990–1991	Jerzy Radz

Football Coaches

1889	Alvin Kletsch
1890	Ted Mestre
1891	Herb Alward
1892	Frank Crawford
1893	Parke Davis
1894–1895	H.O. Stockney
1896–1902	Phil King
1903–1904	Art Curtis
1905	Phil King
1906–1907	C.P. Hutchins
1908–1910	J.A. Barry
1911	J.R. Richards
1912–1915	W.J. Juneau
1916	Paul Withington
1917	J.R. Richards
1918	Guy Lowman
1919–1922	J.R. Richards
1923–1924	Jack Ryan
1925–1926	George Little
1927–1931	Glenn Thistlewaite
1932–1935	Dr. C.W. Spears
1936–1948	Harry Stuhldreher
1949–1955	Ivan B. Williamson
1956–1966	Milt Bruhn
1967–1969	John Coatta

1970–1977	John Jardine	1924	Robert Blodgett
1978–1985	Dave McClain	1925–1926	Kay Iverson
1986	Jim Hides	1927	W.R. Brandow
1987–1989	Don Morton	1928–1930	John Farquhar
1990–2005	Barry Alvarez	1931	Spike Carlson
2006–2012	Bret Bielema	1932–1935	Art Thomsen
2013–Present	Gary Anderson	1936–1963	No Team
		1963–1964	Art Thomsen
			John Riley

Men's Golf Coaches

1926	Joe Steinauer	1965–1966	John Riley
1927–1931	George Levis	1967–1975	Bob Johnson
1932–1951	Joe Steinauer	1975–1976	Bill Rothwell
1952–1969	John Jamieson		(acting)
1970–1977	Tom Bennett	1977–1982	Bob Johnson
1977–2003	Dennis Tiziani	1983–2002	Jeff Sauer
2003–2011	Jim Schuman	2002–Present	Mike Eaves
2011–Present	Michael Burcin		

Men's Rowing Coaches

Women's Golf Coaches

		1894	Andrew W. Marston
1975–1976	Jane Eastham	1895–98	Andrew W. O'Dea
1976–1984	Jackie Hayes	1899	C.C. McConville
1985–1989	Chris Regenberg	1900–1906	Andrew W. O'Dea
1989–2003	Dennis Tiziani	1907–1910	Edward Ten Eyck
2003–Present	Todd Oehrlein	1911–1928	Harry "Dad" Vail
		1929–1934	George "Mike" Vail
		1935–1940	Ralph Hunn

Men's Gymnastics Coaches

		1941–1942	Allen Walz
1902–1905	J.C. Elsom	1943	George Rea
1906–1907	Emmett Angeli	1944–1945	none
1908–1909	J.C. Elsom	1946	Allen Walz
1910	Felix Zeidelhack	1947–1968	Norm Sonju
1911–1917	H.D. MacChesney	1969–Present	Randy Jablonic
1918	Joe Steinauer	1996–Present	Chris Clark
1919–1922	Fred Schlatter		
1923	Frank Leitz		

Women's Rowing Coaches

1924–1926	Fred Schlatter		
1927–1935	Arpad L. Masley	1974–1979	Jay Mimier
1936–1947	No Team	1979–1997	Sue Ela
1948–1959	Dean Mory	1997–2002	Mary Browning
1960–1961	George Bauer	2002–2003	Maren LaLiberty
	Gordon Johnson	2003–2004	Maren LaLiberty/Sue Ela
1962–1971	George Bauer	2004–2013	Bebe Bryans
1972–1978	Raymond Bauer		
1978–1991	Mark Pflughoeft		

Men's Soccer Coaches

		1977–1981	Bill Reddan
		1982–1996	Jim Launder

Women's Gymnastics Coaches

		1997–2001	Kalekeni Banda
1974–1978	Marian Snowdon	2002–2008	Jeff Rohrman
1978–1984	Jenny Hoffman–Convisor	2009	Todd Yeagley
1984–1991	Terry Bryson	2010–2012	John Trask

Ice Hockey Coaches

Women's Soccer Coaches

		1981–1986	Craig Webb
1916–1919	Joe Steinauer	1986–1994	Greg Ryan
1922–1923	Dr. A.K. Viner	1994–2006	Dean Duerst

2007–Present	Paula Wilkins

Softball Coaches

1996–2005	Karen Gallagher
2006–2010	Chandelle Schulte
2011–Present	Yvette Healy

Men's Swimming Coaches

1912–1913	Chauncey Hyatt
1914–1919	Harry H. Hindman
1932–1951	Joe Steinauer
1951–1969	John Hickman
1970–1994	Jack Pettinger
1994	John Davey
	(acting)
1994–2000	Nick Hansen
2001–2011	Eric Hansen
2011–Present	Whitney Hite

Women's Swimming Coaches

1973–1974	Jack Pettinger
1974–1977	Roger Ridenour
1977–1992	Carl Johansson
1992–2001	Nick Hansen
2001–2011	Eric Hansen
2011–Present	Whitney Hite

Men's Tennis Coaches

1919–1922	George E. Linden
1923–1925	Arpad Masley
1926–1930	William Winterble
1931	Loren Cockrell
1932–1935	Arpad Masley
1936–1937	William Kaeser
1938–1939	Roy Black
1941–1943	Carl Sanger
1944–1945	Harold A. Taylor
1946–1947	Carl Sanger
1947–1951	Al Hildebrandt
1952–1962	Carl Sanger
1963	David G. Clark
1964–1968	John Powless
1969–1972	John Desmond
1973–1981	Denny Lee Schackter
1982–1983	Dave Pelisek
1983–2005	Pat Klingelhoets
2006–Present	Greg Van Emburgh

Women's Tennis Coaches

1974–1976	Pam McKinney
1976–1977	Laurel Holgerson
1977–1978	Katie Munns
	(acting)
1978–1981	Laurel Holgerson
1981–1994	Kelly Ferguson

1994–2007	Patti Henderson
2007–Present	Brian Fleishman

Men's Track and Field Coaches

1893	R.G. Booth
1894	M.J. Gillen
1895	W.B. Overson
1896	Charles Craigie
1897	E.W. Moulton
1898	James Temple
	Charles Craigie
1899	John T. Moakley
1900–1904	C.H. Kilpatrick
1905	James Temple
1906	George Downer
	Emmett Angell
1907–1908	Emmett Angell
1909	E.W. Moulton
1910	Charles Hutchins
	James Lathrop
1911–1912	Charles Wilson
1913–1948	Thomas E. Jones
1949–1950	Guy Sundt
1951–1960	Riley Best
1961–1969	Charles Walter
1970–1971	Robert Brennan
1972–1977	Bill Perrin
1978–1983	Dan McClimon
1983–2013	Ed Nuttycombe
2013–Present	Mick Byrne

Women's Track and Field Coaches

1974–2004	Peter Tegen
2004–Present	Jim Stintzi

Volleyball Coaches

1973–1975	Kay Von Guten
1975–1978	Pat Hielscher
1978–1981	Kristi Conklin
1981–1982	Niels Pedersen
1982–1985	Russ Carney
1986–1991	Steve Lowe
1991	Margie Fitzpatrick
1992–1998	John Cook
1999–2012	Pete Waite
2013–Present	Kelly Sheffield

Wrestling Coaches

1914–1916	Fred Schlatter
1917–1918	Arthur Knott
1919–1920	Joe Steinauer
1921–1933	George Hitchcock
1934–1935	Paul Gerlin
1936–1942	George Martin

1943	John Roberts	1971–1982	Duane Kleven
1944	Jim Dailey	1983–1986	Russ Hellickson
	Frank Jordan	1987–1993	Andy Rein
1945	Frank Jordan	1994–Present	Barry Davis
1946–1970	George Martin		

UNIVERSITY OF WISCONSIN NCAA CHAMPIONS

Men's Basketball
Team (1)
1941: UW 39, Washington State 34 (Coach Bud Foster)

Boxing
discontinued as NCAA championship sport after 1960
Team (8)
1939: UW, 25 points (Coach John J. Walsh)
1942: UW, 23 points (Coach John J. Walsh)
1943: UW, 32 points (Coach John J. Walsh)
1947: UW, 24 points (Coach John J. Walsh)
1948: UW, 45 points (Coach John J. Walsh)
1952: UW, 27 points (Coach John J. Walsh)
1954: UW, 19 points (Coach John J. Walsh)
1956: UW, 47 points (Coach John J. Walsh)

Individuals (38)
1936: Robert Fadner, 125 lbs.
1939: Gene Rankin, 135 lbs.
1939: Omar Crocker, 145 lbs.
1939: Woodrow Swancutt, 155 lbs.
1939: Truman Torgerson, 175 lbs.
1940: Woodrow Swancutt, 155 lbs.
1940: Nick Lee, Hwt.
1941: Gene Rankin, 135 lbs.
1942: Gene Rankin, 135 lbs.
1942: Warren Jollymore, 145 lbs.
1942: Cliff Lutz, 155 lbs.
1942: George Makris, 175 lbs.
1943: Cliff Lutz, 145 lbs.
1943: Don Miller, 155 lbs.
1943: Myron Miller, 165 lbs.
1943: George Makris, 175 lbs.
1943: Verdayne John, Hwt.
1947: Cliff Lutz, 145 lbs.
1947: John Lendenski, 165 lbs.
1948: Donald Dickinson, 148 lbs.
1948: Steve Gremban, 148 lbs.
1948: Calvin Vernon, 176 lbs.
1948: Vito Parisi, Hwt.
1951: Dick Murphy, 155 lbs.
1951: Bob Ranck, Hwt.
1952: Bob Morgan, 147 lbs.

1952: Bob Ranck, Hwt.
1953: Pat Sreenan, 147 lbs.
1953: Ray Zale, 178 lbs.
1954: Bob Meath, 156 lbs.
1956: Dean Plemmons, 112 lbs.
1956: Dick Bartman, 139 lbs.
1956: Vince Ferguson, 156 lbs.
1956: Orville Pitts, 178 lbs.
1956: Truman Sturdevant, Hwt.
1959: Charles Mohr, 165 lbs.
1960: Brown McGhee, 132 lbs.
1960: Jerry Turner, 156 lbs.

Cross Country
Team (5)
1982: UW, 59 points (Coach Dan McClimon)
1985: UW, 67 points (Coach Martin Smith)
1988: UW, 105 points (Coach Martin Smith)
2005: UW, 37 points (Coach Jerry Schumacher)
2011: UW, 97 points (Coach Mick Byrne)

Individual (5)
1939: Walter Mehl, 20:30.9 (4 miles)
1985: Tim Hacker, 29:17.88 (10,000 meters)
2004: Simon Bairu, 30:37.7 (10,000 meters)
2005: Simon Bairu , 29:15.9 (10,000 meters)

Ice Hockey
Team (6)
1973: UW 4, Denver 2 (Coach Bob Johnson)
1977: UW 6, Michigan 5 (OT) (Coach Bob Johnson)
1981: UW 6, Minnesota 3 (Coach Bob Johnson)
1983: UW 6, Harvard 2 (Coach Jeff Sauer)
1990: UW 7, Colgate 3 (Coach Jeff Sauer)
2006: UW 2, Boston College 1 (Coach Mike Eaves)

Rowing
Varsity 8 National Championships Team (10)
1951: 2 miles, 7:50.5,
1959: 3 miles, 18:01.7
1966: 3 miles, 16:03.5
1973: 2000 meters, 6:21.0
1974: 2000 meters, 6:33.0

1975: 2000 meters, 6:08.2
1986: 2000 meters, 5:57.8
1990: 2000 meters, 5:52.5
1990: 2000 meters, 5:55.5
2008: 2000 meters, 5:31.173

Soccer
Team (1)
1995: UW 2, Duke 0 (Coach Jim Launder)

Swimming
Individuals (3)
1927: Winston Kratz, 200-yard breaststroke, 2:46.3
1959: Fred Westphal, 50-yard freestyle, 22.3
2013: Andrew Teduits, 200-yard backstroke, 1:39.98

Indoor Track and Field
Team (1)
2007: UW, 40 points (Coach Ed Nuttycombe)

Individual (10)
1967: Ray Arrington, 1,000-yard run, 2:07.8
1968: Ray Arrington, 1,000-yard run, 2:09.3
1969: Ray Arrington, 1,000-yard run, 2:08.0
1970: Mark Winzenreid, 880-yard run, 1:51.7
1971: Mark Winzenreid, 880-yard run, 1:50.9
1971: Pat Matzdorf, high jump, 7'2"
1996: Jason Casiano, 5,000-meter run, 13:50.08
2005: Chris Solinsky, 3,000-meter run, 7:53.59
2006: Chris Solinsky, 3,000-meter run, 7:59.68
2007: Chris Solinsky, 5,000-meter run, 13:38.61

Relays (2)
1976: Two-mile relay (Mark Randall, Steve Lacy, Mark Sang, Dick Moss), 7:26.79
1985: Distance Medley Relay (Pat Ames, Robert Hackett, John Easker, Tim Hacker), 9:39.40

Outdoor Track and Field
Individuals (18)
1921: Lloyd Wilder, pole vault, 12í0î
1937: Chuck Fenske, mile run, 4:13.9
1938: Walter Mehl, 2 mile run, 9:11.1
1944: Bob Ray, javelin throw, 174í 5/8î
1948: Don Gehrmann, 1,500–meter run, 3:54.3
1949: Don Gehrmann, mile run, 4:09.6
1950: Don Gehrmann, mile run, 4:12.4
1952: Walter Deike, 10,000-meter run, 32:25.1
1970: Pat Matzdorf, high jump, 7íIî
1971: Mark Winzenreid, 880–yard run, 1:48.8
1973: Skip Kent, 880-yard run, 1:47.2
1980: Randy Jackson, 3,000-meter steeplechase, 8:22.81
1993: Donovan Bergstrom, 3,000-meter steeplechase, 8:29.08
1997: Pascal Dobert, 3,000-meter steeplechase, 8:31.68

1997: James Dunkleberger, decathlon, 7,924 points
1997: Reggie Torian, 110-meter hurdles, 13.39
2006: Chris Solinsky, 5,000-meter run, 14:11.71
2007: Chris Solinsky, 5,000-meter run, 13:35.12

Wrestling
Individual (18)
1974: Rick Lawinger, 142 lbs.
1976: Jack Reinwand, 126 lbs.
1976: Lee Kemp, 158 lbs.
1976: Pat Christenson, 167 lbs.
1977: Lee Kemp, 158 lbs.
1978: Lee Kemp, 158 lbs.
1978: Ron Jeidy, 190 lbs.
1977: Jim Haines, 118 lbs.
1980: Andy Rein, 150 lbs.
1985: Jim Jordan, 134 lbs.
1986: Jim Jordan, 134 lbs.
1989: Dave Lee, 167 lbs.
1991: Matt Demaray, 150 lbs.
1992: Matt Demaray, 150 lbs.
1996: Jeff Waiter, Hwt.
2000: Donny Pritzlaff, 165 lbs.
2001: Donny Pritzlaff, 165 lbs.
2010: Andrew Howe, 165 lbs.

Women's Sports
*NCAA women's competition began in 1981-82
*Other organizations' championships so indicated:

Badminton
Team (1)
1983: National Intercollegiate Badminton Championship

Individuals (4)
1981: Ann French/Claire Allison, AIAW Doubles Champions
1982: Ann French/Claire Allison, AIAW Doubles Champions
1983: Claire Allison, NIBC Singles Champion
1983: Claire Allison/Sandy Colby, NIBC Doubles Champions
*Association of Intercollegiate Athletics for Women (AIAW)

Cross Country
Team (2)
1984: UW, 63 points (Coach Peter Tegen)
1985: UW, 58 points (Coach Peter Tegen)

Individual (2)
1984: Cathy Branta, 16:15.6 (5,000 meters)
1995: Kathy Butler, 16:51 (5,000 meters)
1999: Erica Palmer, 16:39.5 (5,000 meters)

Ice Hockey
Team (4)
2006: UW 3, Minnesota 0 (Coach Mark Johnson)
2007: UW 4, Minnesota Duluth 1 (Coach Mark Johnson)
2009: UW 5, Mercyhurst 0 (Coach Mark Johnson)
2011: UW 4, Boston University 1 (Coach Mark Johnson)

Varsity 8 Openweight Rowing*
Team (2)
1975: 1000 meters, 3:07.3
1986: 2000 meters, 6:53.28

*National Collegiate Rowing Championships

Varsity 8 Lightweight Rowing*
Team (5)
2004: 2000 meters, 7:06.36
2005: 2000 meters, 6:40.47
2006: 2000 meters, 6:46.51
2008: 2000 meters, 6:35.117
2009: 2000 meters, 6:56.26

*International Rowing Association National Championship

Swimming & Diving
Individual (4)
1970: #D'Lynn Damron, 1-meter diving
1970: #D'Lynn Damron, 3-meter diving
1973: *D'Lynn Damron, 1-meter diving
1976: *Peggy Anderson, 3-meter diving

#National Association of Girls' and Women's Sports
*Association of Intercollegiate Athletics for Women (AIAW)

Indoor Track and Field
Individual (14)
1980: *Pat Johnson, long jump, 21'4 1/2"
1981: *Pam Moore, 400-meter dash, 53.88
1981: *Pat Johnson, long jump, 20'10"
1984: Cathy Branta, 3,000-meter run, 9:04.81
1986: Stephanie Herbst, 3,000-meter run, 8:58.68
1987: Suzy Favor, mile run, 4:41.69
1989: Suzy Favor, mile run, 4:30.63
1990: Suzy Favor, mile run, 4:38.19
1990: Suzy Favor, 3,000-meter run, 9:02.30
1993: Amy Wickus, 800-meter run, 2:04.80
1993: Claire Eichner, mile run, 4:38.64
1993: Claire Eichner, 3,000-meter run, 9:09.66
1994: Amy Wickus, 800-meter run, 2:02.05

1995: Amy Wickus, 800-meter run, 2:04.86

Relays (5)
1981: *4x800-meter relay (Sue Beischel, Maryann Brunner, Ellen Brewster, Sue Spaltholz), 8:44.26
1983: Two-mile relay (Ellen Olson, Mary Anne Brunner, Sue Spaltholz, Rose Thomson), 8:53.5
1992: 3,200-meter relay (Sarah Renk, Julie Cote, Sue Gentes, Amy Wickus), 8:28.41
1993: 3,200-meter relay (Julie Cote, Sarah Renk, Kim Sherman, Amy Wickus), 8:26.77
1996: Distance Medley (Markesha McWilliams, Jenni Westphal, Janet Westphal, Kathy Butler), 11:08.91

*Association of Intercollegiate Athletics for Women (AIAW)

Outdoor Track and Field
Individuals (19)
1982: *Pat Johnson, long jump, 2114 æî
1984: Cathy Branta, 3,000-meter run, 8:59.57
1985: Cathy Branta, 1,500-meter run, 4:12.64
1985: Cathy Branta, 3,000-meter run, 9:08.32
1986: Stephanie Herbst, 5,000-meter run, 15:42.36
1986: Stephanie Herbst, 10,000-meter run, 32:32.75
1987: Suzy Favor, 1,500-meter run, 4:09.85
1988: Suzy Favor, 1,500-meter run, 4:13.91
1989: Suzy Favor, 1,500-meter run, 4:15.83
1990: Suzy Favor, 800-meter run, 1:59.11
1990: Suzy Favor, 1,500-meter run, 4:08.26
1992: Sue Gentes, 1,500-meter run, 4:16.38
1993: Kim Sherman, 800-meter run, 2:02.99
1993: Clare Eichner, 1,500-meter run, 4:20.12
1993: Clare Eichner, 3,000-meter run, 9:03.06
1995: Amy Wickus, 1,500-meter run, 4:14.53
1995: Kathy Butler, 3,000-meter run, 9:09.02
1996: Kathy Butler, 3,000-meter run, 9:16.19
1997: Kathy Butler, 3,000-meter run, 9:01.23

Relays (1)
1981: *4×800-meter relay (Sue Beischel, Maryann Brunner, Ellen Brewster, Sue Spaltholz), 8:53.44

*Association of Intercollegiate Athletics for Women (AIAW)

UNIVERSITY OF WISCONSIN
BIG 10 TEAM CHAMPIONS

Men
includes co-championships

Baseball
1902, 1912, 1930, 1946, 1950, 2008

Basketball
1907, 1912, 1913, 1914, 1916, 1918, 1921, 1923, 1924, 1929, 1935, 1941, 1947

Cross Country
1910, 1912, 1913, 1915, 1924, 1925, 1926, 1927, 1939, 1944, 1945, 1948, 1949, 1950, 1977, 1978, 1979, 1981, 1982, 1983, 1985, 1986, 1987, 1988, 1989, 1990, 1991, 1992, 1994, 1995, 1996, 1999, 2000, 2001, 2002, 2003, 2004, 2005, 2006, 2007, 2008, 2009, 2010, 2011, 2012

Fencing
1955, 1957, 1959, 1967, 1976, 1978, 1979, 1982, 1984, 1985

Football
1896, 1897, 1901, 1906, 1912, 1952, 1959, 1962, 1993, 1998, 1999, 2010, 2011, 2012

Golf
1957, 1993, 1994

Gymnastics
1902, 1905, 1908, 1913, 1915, 1916, 1923

Ice Hockey
1972, 1973, 1974, 1977, 1978, 2000

Indoor Track
1927, 1930, 1949, 1962, 1965, 1967, 1968, 1969, 1970, 1971, 1986, 1995, 1996, 1997, 2000, 2001, 2003, 2004, 2005, 2006, 2007, 2008, 2013

Outdoor Track
1915, 1916, 1931, 1964, 1969, 1984, 1986, 1995, 1996, 1997, 2000, 2001, 2002, 2004, 2005, 2006, 2007, 2012

Women
includes co-championships

Cross Country
1983, 1984, 1985, 1986, 1987, 1988, 1991, 1995, 1996, 1997, 1998, 1999, 2000

Fencing
1986, 1987

Golf
1994

Ice Hockey
2006, 2007, 2009, 2011, 2012

Rowing
2010

Lightweight Rowing
2005, 2006, 2007, 2008, 2009, 2010, 2011

Tennis
1996

Indoor Track
1982, 1984, 1985, 1986, 1987, 1990, 1996

Outdoor Track
1983, 1984, 1985, 1986, 1990, 1991, 1996

Volleyball
1991, 1997, 2000, 2001

ABOUT THE AUTHORS

DON KOPRIVA has spent almost 50 years writing and editing in a career that has included stops as SID at UW-Parkside and Southern Illinois University, as manager of the press center at the 1984 Olympic Games, and as an editor at the *Chicago Sun-Times* and at a regional business paper. He continues writing books and articles, speaking on sports and media issues, mentoring young writers, and advocating an eagerness to read and ability to write as fundamental to life success. He is also the author of *Coming Back Strong*, which profiles top U.S. distance runners and their rehabilitation efforts following injuries. He lives in Lisle, Illinois, and regularly covers Big Ten and national cross country and track meets.

JIM MOTT spent a lifetime in Madison. The former Wisconsin sports information director (1966–90), who was knowledgeable on all things Wisconsin, used his remarkable recall of Badger athletic events and athletes to help him with this book. A 1954 graduate of Wisconsin, Mott was assistant sports information director for 12 years before becoming SID. Well respected by his peers, Mott was named to the College Sports Information Directors Hall of Fame in 1979. No less respected and revered in Madison, Mott was inducted into the UW Athletic Hall of Fame in 1990. Jim passed away in 2009.

H. 1/15